Table of Contents

One Loud Voice

Introduction

With one loud voice, I want to shout out, "NO MORE!" The complexity of life, the daily stress we all endure; we must ask ourselves what brought us to this point? How can we possibly desire to live this life that has been molded for ourselves or our children? Are we living the American dream? The life that has been molded for us was not done by our hands or the deeds of past generations. For well over a century there has been a brutal attack on our moral fabric through political corruption and secret organizations. We were once a nation of the people by the people, where the people truly had a voice to ensure accurate representation. Today our politicians are nothing more than glorified mediators for giant corporations. The elite has become the grand puppet master over governments around the world and as they tightened their grip to assert dominant control has left billions in despair. Today our Constitution is considered outdated or as our president has indicated, "An impractical document." This impractical document, our Constitution, is what our forefathers fought and died for. They fought for freedom, representation, and fair taxes which later led to their independence. Today we are burdened with over taxation. Be honest, do you honestly feel like you're being represented in Washington? Our Constitution is no outdated document; it is our Bill of Rights. These indelible rights are what it means to be an American.

Today our rights are under siege from both major parties: Republican and Democrat. Our politicians have neglected their responsibility to represent the people, as they grasp for power they anoint themselves as our leaders! I want to know when we started having leaders instead of representatives. This is no more than a course for socialism! The first and second amendment, the right of freedom of speech or to bear arms is being restricted more and more through each administration. The privacy act is also no more; our government can listen to our phone conversations and even invade our computers. The fourth amendment is no longer enforced due to unconstitutional bills being passed such as the Patriot Act passed by Pres. George Bush Jr. or the NDAA bill passed by Pres. Barack Obama. The fourth amendment protects our rights not to be harassed or treated as a criminal without due process. This amendment was written by our forefathers to prevent harassment from governmental officials or law enforcement officers, which clearly states it is illegal to search your property or papers without a search warrant signed by a Judge. This would also make it illegal for law enforcement officers to randomly ask for your ID if you committed no wrong. Today law enforcement officers are taught how to use racial profiling and can search your property or papers under reasonable suspicion. This would also include your cell phone, computer, and any other materials they desire to search. The media has coined the term "big brother watching", but I tell you America this is no big brother. Their grasp for world dominance has unfolded before us all as they strive for a one world government. For well over a century they have swung their hammers demolishing our foundation, as they step on to our freedom to replace our once great government with socialism. The super elite is a grand architect of our corrupted society as they have manipulated the world into a New World Order. They have strategically positioned their selves as our masters and socialism will be the law of the land. America, we must wake up, for it is all our responsibility to protect our freedom and our Constitution!

We are losing the American dream while our freedom fades into the night. Our government is bent on passing more bills for control and restrictions without having the competence to balance our budget. Our national debt has irresponsibly increased to $20 trillion. This monstrous debt will not only fall upon our shoulders; our children will be burdened with this horrendous debt. Even our gold reserves are being depleted, since the 1950s our gold reserves were at 20 metric tons while today we are at 8 metric tons. The fact our deficit has increased to 20 trillion along with losing 12 metric tons of gold in little over a half a century is a tremendous loss to America's wealth. Tell me the truth, is our nation better today with all the radical changes that have occurred over the last half-century? American this is an indication that we are on the wrong path, and if we do not alter our course we will be shackled into enslavement. Our forefathers warned us of the dangers of allowing too much governmental control, and with their self- anointing authority has given them the power to control almost every aspect of our lives.

America if we are not careful, we will be enslaved to this political monster and our national debt! We must mandate our government to control their spending and follow a budget. We must shrink the size of our government, because of their immense size has come with a hefty price tag for all taxpayers. Too many of our politicians forge their careers with corporate elites for power and wealth. America, it is time to shatter this union of crooked politicians and the powerful elites. We must mandate our government to establish term limits for Senate and Congress to destroy this unfavorable bond. Services in such high office come with a large responsibility to the people, and we can no longer allow our politicians to be corrupted by those lobbyists, who carry out the evil plots of the elite. By establishing term limits will shatter these corrupted bonds that have been forged over the years and would allow new and genuine representation.

For decades, our politicians have forged their careers with corporate giants, creating tremendous wealth for a very small class of people. Less than 1% of the world's population controls over 50% of the world's wealth. This grab for power has corrupted all branches of our government and has brought a tremendous debt upon us all. Even the average personal debt has increased to 500% from the 1950's to today. Our grandparents, as well as past generations, believe in saving money and they kept their debt minimum, while today we are encouraged to have a high revolving debt. These massive changes have had a dramatic impact on our society today. Homeownership, a big part of the American dream has plunged since the 1950s. The average cost for a house during the 50s was less than $8,000 while today the average price for a home is around $180,000. Inflation has increased to over 2000% since the 1950s, which has had a massive impact on how we purchase goods today. In the 1950s it only to one provider to support a family, while today it takes two incomes. We have gone from a nation of prosperity and wealth to a country of neglect and a tremendous debt. We have become a nation that once produced most of the goods sold around the world to a country who gives their technology and wealth away. To have politicians freely give away our wealth and knowledge is ludicrous and has created a dark pathway for our own destruction. Is this the life our forefathers intended for us? How did we go from a nation of creativity and excellent engineering to a country of neglect and disarray? We are so far behind in repairing our infrastructures, that there are bridges and dams far past their life expectancy. There are towns in America literally falling apart due to factories and industries moving overseas. How can we possibly think we have a bright future on the road we are traveling? Our government has surrendered the will of the people for the wealth of the corporate elite.

The people no longer have a voice in Washington, for they have turned a deaf ear and has left our society in fear of their own government. America the path we are taking is submission, for we no longer know our politicians and our government only knows us by a number. Our government has brought disparity upon us through immense regulations and over taxation's that has wrecked our economy. This is nothing more than a path for political dominance at taxpayer's expense. Through their dominance, they have destroyed our economy and polluted our educational system with their socialist ideology. They have destroyed the sanctuary of our educational system with the teachings of sex education to our young and since the removal of prayer crime has intensified in our schools. They have corrupted the moral fabric of our society, and family unity is no longer a priority for so many.

Today our family bond has disintegrated with broken families across our nation. Many issues have contributed to the collapse of so many families, but I think the most destructive force was poverty. Through over taxation to support our over bloated government, along with their severely abused welfare system has destroyed the middle class. Through corruption in our government, along with corporate greed has left so many families broken and abandon to life in poverty. Through impoverishment, a criminal society has emerged filled with sinfulness and hate. We have become a nation without faith and honor. Our grandparents and past generations lived with faith in God and believed in the Commandments as a standard for good morals. Through their belief in God and there believe in the family helped establish a great society. These generations worked extremely hard because they did not have all the technological advancements we have today. Yet their era was known as the Golden years, where children were safe to play outside, and people felt secure enough to leave their doors unlocked. In those years, they truly had a strong family bond and a chance to make it in life. They lived in a time when America was truly free, and a market system was honest. The Golden years our grandparents had once lived is no more. Life was simpler in those days and family had more time to spend together. Today in modern society there are very few people that have the opportunity to see their family. I hear many of them complain they just don't have the time. I have to ask myself, what happened to our family bond? How could we have allowed the family unity to simply fade away? Family unity is essential to establish a foundation for any civilization. Through the destruction of faith and family has severely weakened the moral fabric of our society. I also blame corporate greed with the expansion of the workweek. Our politicians tell us that we are lazy, and yet we work more hours than any other nation. We once had a day that we could count on for family unity, it was not just a day for worship it was a day to strengthen the family bond.

In the past decades, our government has misled or deceived the American people through many programs or departments. The IRS is one of those departments that is nothing more than a tool for redistribution of wealth, which is socialism. Today the IRS has been given the power to police every American to ensure that we all have insurance and penalize those who do not. The IRS is not even a governmental department and is a separate international entity. The truth is America our government has never voted into law for a federal income tax. The IRS has the power to seize your property or garnish your wages without due process, which according to our Constitution should be illegal. How can we possibly think our politicians are truly representing the people if bills are written and signed behind closed doors? The number of politicians that have become wealthy by supporting laws that would only benefit the super elite is inconceivable. Even the Federal Reserve was brought in under false pretenses, and our forefathers strongly oppose the central bank concept. The Federal Reserve Act was established a little over a century ago, and the fact that this bill was written by the elite bankers is unconstitutional. This bill allowed the elite bankers to have control over the economy and the financial structure of America. One of the strongest reasons the colonists supported the revolutionary war was because they oppose the central bank concept. They believed this concept was a money manipulating machine that would only increase our deficit through a never-ending debt cycle. Most people in our nation would never know this history because this knowledge has been purposely removed from most history books.

Our government has failed miserably in the way our politicians has handle foreign affairs, and we look more like oppressors than bringers of democracy. In the last half-century, we have been involved in many conflicts and wars around the world with little resolve. Nation's like Iraq or Afghanistan are still extremely volatile and lack a strong political structure. Our relationship is still very volatile with the Vietnamese, and the Vietnam War was over a half a century ago. North Korea poses a severe threat to South Korea and after half a century of sanctions we still do not have relations with Cuba. America's also facing a huge trade deficit with nations around the world. There's not a day that goes by that we do not hear something horrific on the news. The stress in our lives is magnified with the news that we see every day. With battles raging around the world, terrorist attacks, threats of a world war, and the fear of an oil shortage has left so many without hope. The continuous price rise of the necessities that we need in our everyday lives has left so many in poverty. Most of the conflicts fault around the world was either for governmental dominance or for those in the elite circle to profit. Let me ask you America, what life are we leaving for our children? What is the future of our grandchildren and future generations? How can they possibly pay off the deficit we have so recklessly left for their generation? I blame our government for devaluing the dollar by recklessly printing money and by allowing the elite to manipulate the world's economy for their own profitability. What troubles me the most is the irresponsible spending we see in Washington through their multiple departments and a corrupted welfare system. Our Federal and state Government receives well over six trillion in revenue from taxes or other regulation fees. America, I ask you to do the math, divide the population of our nation into this tremendous revenue our government receives every year. What baffles me is the fact we continue to borrow from other nations allowing our deficit to continually increase. America, our politicians, are out of line and we are losing control of what goes on in Washington. Can we correct our mistakes or do we simply give up and not try at all?

We must wake up! There are people in America without jobs and children going to bed hungry, due to so many factories closing their doors and relocating overseas. It's not just the jobs we have lost; our markets are being flooded with cheap, quality goods. I would like to know whatever happened to "Made in America." What truly devastated America was the NAFTA treaty that was signed in by Pres. Bill Clinton. The quality of the goods that were manufactured in our country was greater than any quality produced around the world. Due to so many factories moving overseas has crippled America's workforce and today more people work for minimum wage than ever before. America this path is reckless and will lead to the destruction of America. We cannot have free trade with nations that does not have an equivalent minimum wage or no employee rights. This foolish political decision that was signed in by Pres. Clinton has left more people in poverty and chained to a welfare system. We have to make amendments to the NAFTA treaty to reestablish fair trade for the world. It must be a requirement for nations to have an equivalent minimum wage, employee rights, and must never violate human rights. The NAFTA treaty should've been used as a tool to raise the standard of living worldwide. Instead, it was used as a tool for redistribution of wealth on a global scale at the destruction of America's economy.

We are one of the richest countries in minerals, natural gasses, and even large deposits of oil. Yet, we allow the EPA and many other organizations to put a tremendous burden on our fossil fuel industries. It is imperative that we learn to utilize our resources and stop leaning on other countries for their resources. America, it is time for us to start drilling our own oil, which would help stimulate our economy. This would also create a tremendous revenue in oil taxes for our government, and we must mandate our government to utilize the extra revenue for research in finding an alternative fuel source that is dependable. I would like to know what has happened to our pride. Do we no longer have dignity? We attempt to bribe the world with programs like foreign aid or the promise to secure borders, yet many of the same nations continue to spread hateful propaganda about us. Our brave men and women have sacrificed their lives to bring forth democracy, while these nations have allowed safe refuge for Islamic terrorists. We have built schools, power plants, and water treatment facilities for these rogue nations at taxpayer's expense. We've spent well over 700 million in building or repairing Islamic Mosques, while millions of Americans were left in poverty. We give these rogue nations technology and wealth, and in return, they threaten our brave soldiers with terroristic threats as they burn our flag. How can our government honestly say they are representing the people while they give away our technology and pass intense regulations giving our industries no alternative but to move overseas? If we continue to give away our jobs and technology overseas, where will this leave us and our children in their future? Properly utilizing our resources could create a tremendous amount of jobs in our nation which would help stimulate our economy. I am not just referring to the fossil fuels or natural gasses; I am also referring to the most precious resource we have on earth. Fresh water is the cradle of life, and that is one resource we are rich in. America with our ingenuity we could bring water to drought-stricken areas in our country. Farmers out west were not able to grow their crops due to their water being shut off by the EPA. This left many farmers out of work, enabling them to take care of their families. America, are we even coming close to utilizing our resources? We have billions of gallons of fresh water draining into our oceans every day. Tell me, is there not a solution to these problems we are facing? Can our great engineers not create extraordinary feats once again? We have to ask ourselves, when did we change from a "can-do nation," to a "can't do nation." Why can't we find a solution? We can harvest this water through a pipeline system that would create an abundance amount of fresh water and aid in flood control. This plan can be paid for by mandating our government to sell the one-third of the real estate they own in our nation. America this project could create thousands of jobs and many opportunities for new farming or livestock ranches. When the world told us it was impossible to build the Panama Canal, it did not deter us, but in fact, we strived and built the Panama Canal. When the world did not believe we could put a man on the moon, we believed and proved it could be done. Since when have our problems become so complicated that we cannot fix them? Farmers are now paid not to grow a variety of certain crops so that the value of the food stock commodity does not drop, while billions of people are starving. What I find more alarming is the fact that we, the taxpayers are the ones flipping the bill so those in the elite circle may profit immensely. Yet, we live our lives with blinders trying not to see the problems around us.

The problems in our society are too big for you or I to fix alone, but all of us working together, solving the problems, we can fix this; but we must bury our differences. This great divide in our government is destroying America. We must restore common sense in Washington for there is only one right path. Today we've been divided by age, religion, gender, and even race. We must learn to forgive one another for what has happened in the past and stand shoulder to shoulder. Before we can solve our problems, we must figure out how we got to this point. We must analyze our problems and break them down one by one. We must find a solution. We can no longer allow the government to divide us. I find that our own politicians in Washington are continuously dividing the people. They falsely accuse other parties of being racist or accuse each other of being socialist every time they meet opposition. How can we ever stand shoulder to shoulder? Is it their plan to divide us? A divided people can be conquered. A divided people can be molded into whatever a political leader wants to shape them into. I have often heard most elections are won by the media, which I find disturbing because the people have been influenced to give away their vote. America why you slept, the elite class have asserted their dominance through the purchasing of most media networks to ensure their influence over the people. I find the media extremely bias and getting the truth from the media seems almost impossible. I find this very frustrating because how can the people make an intelligent choice, if the news they are receiving is bias? Do you honestly believe our political leaders are there for us? No. We elect them, put these politicians in office and who do they serve? Is it the people or the lobbyist that lines their pockets with wealth? How many times have you heard a politician proclaim they are working on their agenda? Whatever happened to the needs of the people who they should be serving? If our voice has been silenced, then have we not already lost our rights?

We were once a proud nation with a strong faith in God, and many of our morals or laws were based on the Ten Commandments. Today with the teachings of evolution and the Big Bang theory has shattered faith in God for so many. The truth is we have been lied to; evolution is nothing but a theory that has never been proven, nor is there evidence to support the Big Bang theory. Paleontologists and other archaeologists have falsified records and have even presented fake fossils to fraudulently prove their theory. Why has there been such a strong movement to destroy our faith in God? America there is a true evil, and their wicked assaults on our moral fabric have spawned a corrupted and sinful nation. The aftermath is a society who believes there are no consequences for their actions, which led us to a society without a conscience. The truth, there is a God! Our faith in God has been ruthlessly attacked by a government as well as other organizations in our society. They have removed prayer from schools and ripped the Ten Commandments from our courthouses. There has been an intensive movement to remove in God we trust. We have to stand together to undo this madness that has spread like a disease across our country. Let us strive to reestablish the Commandments as a standard for good morals and once again have faith "In God We Trust." If we could only learn to come together, I truly believe we can solve these problems we are facing. We need to become a society that utilizes our intelligence and not allow those in the elite circle to control our destiny. America if we do not learn to come together peacefully to save our nation or then we will be forcefully bonded into enslavement together. We must rise against this evil elite who have stolen the wealth from the world and reestablish our true foundation. For if we do not rise now, then when shall we rise, when it's too late? When our children go to bed hungry or when we lose our homes or even worse our freedom? America, we must wake up, for our destiny is no longer in our hands. Let our faith in God strengthen our cause and let us have faith in one another so we shall come together to face this evil. Let our forefather's wisdom illuminate our path so we may reestablish our true foundation. The fight is within us to save our nation! Let us take our place at the watch tower so we may stand against tyranny, fight persecution and vanquish oppression. I say it's time to wake up now! It's time for us to come together. No longer shall we be divided. No longer shall our resolve be weakened. We must come together in one loud voice and say, "No more!"

Voices from the Past

•The means of defense against foreign danger historically have become the instruments of tyranny at home. -James Madison

•Fear is the foundation of most governments. -John Adams

•Does the government fear us? Or do we fear the government? When the people fear the   government, tyranny has found victory. The federal government is our servant, not our master! -Thomas Jefferson

•   I consider trial by jury as the only anchor ever yet imagined by man, by which a government can be held to the principles of its constitution. -Thomas Jefferson

•   They that can give up essential liberty to obtain a little temporary safety deserve neither liberty nor safety. -Benjamin Franklin

•   Once a republic is corrupted, there is no possibility of remedying any of the growing evils but by removing the corruption and restoring its lost principles; every other correction is either useless or a new evil. -Thomas Jefferson

•   Without morals, a republic cannot subsist any length of time; they therefore who are decrying the Christian religion, whose morality is so sublime and pure (and) which insures to the good eternal happiness, are undermining the solid foundation of morals, the best security for the duration of free governments. -Charles Carroll, signer of the Declaration of Independence

- Every step we take towards making the State our Caretaker of our lives, by that much we move toward making the State our Master. -Dwight D. Eisenhower

- Democracy is two wolves and a lamb voting on what to have for lunch. Liberty is a well-armed lamb contesting the vote! -Benjamin Franklin

- Freedom is not a gift bestowed upon us by other men, but a right that belongs to us by the laws of God and nature. -Benjamin Franklin

- Man will ultimately be governed by God or by tyrants. -Benjamin Franklin

- Now more than ever before, the people are responsible for the character of their Congress. If that body be ignorant, reckless and corrupt, it is because the people tolerate ignorance, recklessness and corruption. If it be intelligent, brave and pure, it is because the people demand these high qualities to represent them in the national legislature.... If the next centennial does not find us a great nation ... it will be because those who represent the enterprise, the culture, and the morality of the nation do not aid in controlling the political forces. -James Garfield

- It is when people forget God that tyrants forge their chains. -Patrick Henry

- America will never be destroyed from the outside. If we falter and lose our freedoms, it will be because we destroyed ourselves. -Abraham Lincoln

Through Treachery and Fire, Gave Birth to Greatness

I look upon our great nation and see so many people in despair. A feeling of hopelessness has fallen upon our land. Today numerous people claim they are powerless; unable to make a change.   They live with hunger and desperately seek employment in vain. I sound the alarm for our government has become the very tyranny we fought against centuries ago. Their desire is to destroy the Constitution and the very foundation our forefathers set for us all. They spread their lies and claim the Constitution is outdated and no longer relevant. We must understand their true desire is power and domination. Our government would be more than happy to write another Constitution, leaving the people with fewer rights and our leaders with more power. America, we must realize a larger government will always have a grander thirst for power. Through each administration our government has created more departments at taxpayers' expense for almost a century. Socialism has infiltrated our government for almost half a century. It is apparent our nation is under siege from socialism.

Socialism is about control, and today in America government controls housing, business, auto industry, manufacturing, transportation, education, banking and much more. Our government is also continuously regulating fossil fuel companies, which increases our cost for utilities. Through all of this control, our government is bankrupting America. Another tentacle of socialism is the redistribution of wealth which has brought America to her knees. Today our president has enacted plans for worldwide redistribution which will break our nation's back. Taking money from the working class in this manner is stealing and it destroys drive. Socialism is like a sweet venom, the idea that everyone is getting an equal share of the wealth along with a home is beautiful. Though, this simply will not work and if you look around you will see it for yourself. Today more people depend on welfare or some other form of governmental assistance than ever before. The sad truth is a good percentage of people would rather not work and depend on government assistance. America, we must wake up for we cannot sustain this course for much longer. I ask you America, what results are you seeing in Washington? The answer is an out-of-control government that cannot control their spending. Our deficit is an indication that we are on the wrong path and yet most of America is silent.

Over the decades our government has allowed big businesses to become monopolies and today our government has control or strong influence over the monopolies. Big businesses and their lobbyists have stolen our voice in Washington. Lobbyists are one of the reasons we have been dependent on oil for so long. America, lobbyists need to be booted out of Washington for we have allowed them to control our fate for far too long. There is a grand puppet master pulling the strings to control the world. The corporate elite sends out their Army of deceivers to bribe politicians to do there evil bidding. They lobby our politicians with wealth and the promise of a future career as a payment for their submission. The elite as well as other secret organizations has polluted our government with socialist ideology and the plan for a New World Order. We must realize that many of our politicians have fallen to the ideas of socialism with the laws they have passed such as the NDAA, which gives law enforcement officers the power to arrest you and imprison you without trial and jury.

These laws have stepped all over our constitutional rights and is smothering capitalism. America, we must reset our roots and restore America to her true foundation. Our forefathers understood the importance of America's Constitution with the amendments of freedom of speech and other amendments like the fourth amendment. They believed in free enterprise and had a stronger economy. Our forefathers understood free will, which gave us the freedom to worship freely in the way you believe. This is the reason why they had a separation between church and state, they did not want church controlling government nor did they want a national religion. Today you can see a small comparison on what our forefathers had to contend with over taxation, no voice in parliament and they were not free. Today we are overtaxed and have lost our voice in Washington. I pray we do not lose our freedom. Let us unite with the patriots of our past so we may reestablish our true foundation. If we do not act quickly our children will have no future.

While our government pretends to be blind, corporations continue to leave our lands. They recklessly sell away our technology with little care of where it leaves our future generations. Have we forgotten what it was like to live in tyranny? It is as if tyranny has gripped our land once again. So many feel clueless for they cannot grip the vast changes that is happening to our country today. We all realize that our government is out of control, but how is it possible for us to regain control when we ourselves are being kept silent?

America, we must wake up. We must once again learn what it is to be an American. We must reverse some of the idiotic policies our government has burden us with for so many decades. We must research our past and understand what true Democracy is so we can restore freedom and liberty. We must bring back prosperity for we all deserve the opportunity for a brighter future. We must realize the sacrifices that were made by our forefathers that brought this new idea to our land; the very idea of establishing a government for the people by the people. To truly understand why our forefathers constructed the Constitution in the manner they did, you must first understand what it was like living in the dark ages. For us to seek the right path, we must first understand the true path to Democracy, liberty, and freedom because we have lost our way for far too long. Today we are a people that have lost the true meaning of what it is to be an American. We must research our past and find a true understanding of what our forefathers intended for our great nation.

Ages before America, humankind had lived in darkness. In these dark times the world was ruled through monarchs. Mankind was nothing but a slave, for they were considered just simple subjects to their kings. To know that their flesh and blood, their very being was controlled by the king was horrific. Their wages were meager, barely enough to feed their families. Most were ordered to work the fields from sunup to sundown. In these dark ages, kingdoms demanded their subjects to worship their Gods and crucify men who refused to worship them. Even Christians met the same fate in Rome when they were fed to the lions. The brutal attacks that many Christians suffered because of their strong faith was horrific. Many were crucified or considered an outcast in ancient Roman society. Without the freedom to think independently, be themselves, or worship freely how could they possibly be free?

During this time science was forbidden; people were forced to believe the Universe revolved around the Earth and that the Earth was flat. Those who believed different or dared to teach new ideas stood a chance of being executed. Even the practice of medicine was forbidden in many kingdoms. During this time, there was a thirst for knowledge. People not only wanted to worship freely, they wanted to think freely. They wanted to challenge old ideas with new ideas, but for a long time it was just a simple dream. Through the ages many scientists such as Sir Isaac Newton came forth with evidence that proved the old beliefs were wrong, but later he was put on trial by the Catholic Church for heresy. Even Christopher Columbus wanted to prove the world was not flat. As a boy, he sat and observed the ocean and studied the curvature of the Earth. Christopher Columbus spent many years debating his theory with little acceptance. People claimed that he was mad and if he was to take a vessel and sail into the uncharted oceans he would fall off the Earth. He later gained support through Queen Isabella from Spain to prove his theory.

Christopher Columbus believed that if he continued to sail across the ocean he would eventually reach China or India. He never imagined the ocean being so vast or the Earth so large. His voyage continued for months, while many of his crew grew weary and urged him to go back. This did not deter him. He continued his voyage and proved the Earth was around, and the land he sought was still half way across the world. Instead he came upon a new land with a warm climate and beautiful beaches. The land was rich in timber and filled with animals he had never seen before. Christopher Columbus made many more voyages and claimed he had found paradise. Tales of the beautiful land and exotic people reached Europe. Dreams of opportunity spread through Europe like wild fire, from England to France and other kingdoms throughout the region. So many people still felt oppressed but a new idea had emerged. In their hearts their true desire was to govern themselves, as well as to have the freedom to practice their religion without persecution. The laws were handed down from the monarchs, for they were ruled by kings and queens. They continuously tightened their iron grip over the lands. Nine out ten people worked in the country where they had little choice but to farm the lands. Some had special skills such as blacksmithing. Many people found it hard during this time, due to high taxes they could not afford to buy their own land, so they would have to lease the lands from lords to simply grow their own food. Not only did they have to rent the land, they would have to pay taxes and even share their bountiful harvests with the lords.

During the 15th century England had broken away from the Roman Catholic Church. They created their own church called the Church of England. Many people disagreed with such a dramatic change and did not want to be told how to worship. With the invention of the printing press in this century it gave many people the opportunity to have their own bible. During this time the bible was translated from its original text which gave people the ability to self-interpret how they should worship. With little regard for the people's wishes, England expected their subjects to worship in the Church of England, while other kingdoms in Europe declared their subjects should worship as Roman Catholics. A group of people called the separatists wanted to leave England so they could create their own church. They saw America as a great opportunity to worship freely and even those in Europe desired the same freedom. They understood God gave man free will but how could they have free will if they were being controlled?

For the Europeans, I imagine the opportunity of owning a piece of land in America sparked an interest among many. They had heard stories of an unexplored world, the wild animals that inhabited it and the people who lived on the land. They knew many of the natives were friendly and eager to trade with explorers. Merchants saw the opportunity to move to this great land. It wasn't just the dream of owning their own land it was the opportunity to be free. The very opportunity which lay before them offered freedom and the ability to govern themselves. Many came to the new world to create a living and a better life for their families. The puritans and pilgrims were so invested in this dream that they came from faraway lands, through mountains and valleys. Many sold their possessions and livestock to pay for the trip. They left their homes in search for a new start in the New World; setting sail on a voyage into the unknown to have the opportunity to worship freely or a chance to own their own land.

It took them over two months to arrive in the new world. Fear had run deep for many of the Europeans, for the ocean was uncharted and this strange new world was unmapped and unexplored. I see the courage for those who took such a voyage into the unknown. They sacrificed their way of life in hope for a new, better life. Many of these people were simple farmers that found the land was beautiful and prepared to farm the land. The work was tedious as they clear land to create settlements and worked hard to bring irrigation to farm the land.

As time passed England, France, and Spain realized the new world was rich with natural resources. The land was rich with timbers which were shipped back to their kingdoms to be used as building materials. England and France used the timbers to build merchant ships and their naval fleet. Eventually, Britain and France went to war over the new world. Many of the colonists were massacred during this time. After the War, Britain expanded their land over the thirteen colonies, where King George continued to tighten his grip. Britain drastically raised taxes on essential items the colonists could not produce such as sugar, paper goods and other vital materials. These taxes were used by King George to repay the debt he had incurred during the French and Indian war. King George also demanded the colonists to stop printing their own currency and to receive their currency from the Central Bank of England. Our forefathers strongly opposed this concept and was one of the contributing factors for the Revolutionary War.

The thirteen colonies were forbidden to sell or trade with any other country other than England after the war. They were without representation; it was as if they were subjects to the king of England without moral rights. Without representation, they had no voice and their very will to speak out had been stricken from them. Their words were without power, for they fell on deaf ears. Each of the thirteen colonies had different laws that governed them. They had no voice in parliament while laws continued to be written to govern them.

Throughout the decades, the colonists grew tired of over taxation. More people became poor while others already lived in poverty. The people grew tired of being oppressed by King George of England. Many great leaders such as George Washington, Benjamin Franklin, and John Adams began to emerge in the late 18th Century. During this time, many people had become passionate about the thirteen colonies and the idea of creating their own nation. With roads connecting all colonies the idea traveled fast. A revolt started in the streets in Boston as well as several other cities throughout the colonies. England answered the revolt by militarizing the colonies. One day the people gathered in the streets of Boston to protest about the taxes and the unfair treatment colonists were receiving. English soldiers then answered the protest by firing their guns into the crowd killing one man by the name of Crispus Attucks. As the crowd started to scatter, the soldiers fired into the fleeing crowd once more, killing 4 more men. Paul Revere wrote about this gruesome action in a famous writing called the Boston Massacre that spread throughout the colonies. This horrific action angered the people and caused them to take up arms against the crown. Pockets of resistance had united through the colonies and colonist leaders began discussing their options. In 1773 Benjamin Franklin proposed a colonial meeting but failed to gain support. During this time, only one third of the colonists supported the idea of becoming an independent nation. Many of the colonists feared the immense power of England while many rich colonists dreaded losing their wealth. Shortly after, the people of Boston continued to revolt by dumping tea and other cargo into the Boston Harbor. This motivated the colonists to boycott trade with England and inspired the Virginia House of Burgesses to propose the Continental Congress.

In August 1, 1774, they held a meeting to vote for delegates for better representation. Later that year the very first Colonial Congress met at Carpenter's Hall in Philadelphia. Only twelve out of thirteen colonies sent delegates. While the colonist cried out for freedom and independence, congress did not advocate an independent nation. Instead they felt it was their duty to right the wrongs that the colonists endured. The Continental Congress believed that unifying their voice would allow them representation in the Courts of England. Yet, England continued to deny their request. The fifty-five delegates met on several occasions unifying their bonds and friendships. This very bond was tested on many occasions because many of the delegates had different ideas and solutions to the problems faced by the colonists. The congress composed a list of grievances and they argued for life, liberty, and property to King George.

King George dismissed the letters of grievances against the colonists as if the people had no rights. Instead King George responded by sending the mighty British Navy and its massive army. The Colonial Congress quickly met once again which was a pivotal point in our nation's history. The only course of action was to declare war on England. They appointed George Washington commander and chief of the Continental Army in 1775. Thomas Paine invoked the spirit for independence by writing Common Sense. Many great speakers spoke out passionately for an independent America. The most powerful and passionate speech given during our country's finest hour was, "Give me liberty or give me death," by Patrick Henry.

St. John's Church, Richmond, Virginia March 23, 1775

"Mr. PRESIDENT: No man thinks more highly than I do of the patriotism, as well as abilities, of the very worthy gentlemen who have just addressed the House. But different men often see the same subject in different lights; and, therefore, I hope it will not be thought disrespectful to those gentlemen if, entertaining as I do, opinions of a character very opposite to theirs, I shall speak forth my sentiments freely, and without reserve. This is no time for ceremony. The question before the House is one of awful moment to this country. For my own part, I consider it as nothing less than a question of freedom or slavery; and in proportion to the magnitude of the subject ought to be the freedom of the debate. It is only in this way that we can hope to arrive at truth, and fulfill the great responsibility which we hold to God and our country. Should I keep back my opinions at such a time, through fear of giving offence, I should consider myself as guilty of treason towards my country and of an act of disloyalty toward the majesty of heaven, which I revere above all earthly kings.

Mr. President, it is natural to man to indulge in the illusions of hope. We are apt to shut our eyes against a painful truth, and listen to the song of that siren till she transforms us into beasts. Is this the part of wise men, engaged in a great and arduous struggle for liberty? Are we disposed to be of the number of those who, having eyes, see not, and, having ears, hear not, the things which so nearly concern their temporal salvation? For my part, whatever anguish of spirit it may cost, I am willing to know the whole truth; to know the worst, and to provide for it.

I have but one lamp by which my feet are guided; and that is the lamp of experience. I know of no way of judging of the future but by the past. And judging by the past, I wish to know what there has been in the conduct of the British ministry for the last ten years, to justify those hopes with which gentlemen have been pleased to solace themselves, and the House? Is it that insidious smile with which our petition has been lately received? Trust it not, it will prove a snare to your feet. Suffer not yourselves to be betrayed with a kiss. Ask yourselves how this gracious reception of our petition comports with these war-like preparations which cover our waters and darken our land. Are fleets and armies necessary to a work of love and reconciliation? Have we shown ourselves so unwilling to be reconciled, that force must be called in to win back our love? Let us not deceive ourselves, these are the implements of war and subjugation; the last arguments too which kings resort. I ask, gentlemen, what means this martial array, if its purpose be not to force us to submission? Can gentlemen assign any other possible motive for it? Has Great Britain any enemy, in this quarter of the world, to call for all this accumulation of navies and armies? No, sir, she has none. They are meant for us; they can be meant for no other. They are sent over to bind and rivet upon us those chains which the British ministry have been so long forging. And what have we to oppose to them? Shall we try argument? Sir, we have been trying that for the last ten years. Have we anything new to offer upon the subject? Nothing. We have held the subject up in every light of which it is capable; but it has been all in vain. Shall we resort to entreaty and humble supplication? What terms shall we find which have not been already exhausted? Let us not, I beseech you, sir, deceive ourselves. Sir, we have done everything that could be done, to avert the storm which is now coming on. We have petitioned; we have remonstrated; we have supplicated; we have prostrated ourselves before the throne, and have implored its interposition to arrest the tyrannical hands of the ministry and Parliament. Our petitions have been slighted; our remonstrance's have produced additional violence and insult; our supplications have been disregarded; and we have been spurned, with contempt, from the foot of the throne. In vain, after these things, may we indulge the fond hope of peace and reconciliation. There is no longer any room for hope. If we wish to be free if we mean to preserve inviolate those inestimable privileges for which we have been so long contending if we mean not basely to abandon the noble struggle in which we have been so long engaged, and which we have pledged ourselves never to abandon until the glorious object of our contest shall be obtained, we must fight! I repeat it, we must fight! An appeal to arms and to the God of Hosts is all that is left us!

They tell us, that we are weak; unable to cope with so formidable an adversary. But when shall we be stronger? Will it be the next week, or the next year? Will it be when we are totally disarmed, and when a British guard shall be stationed in every house? Shall we gather strength by irresolution and inaction? Shall we acquire the means of effectual resistance, by lying supinely on our backs, and hugging the delusive phantom of hope, until our enemies shall have bound us hand and foot?

Sir, we are not weak if we make a proper use of those means which the God of nature hath placed in our power. Three millions of people, armed in the holy cause of liberty, and in such a country as that which we possess, are invincible by any force which our enemy can send against us. Besides, sir, we shall not fight our battles alone. There is a just God who presides over the destinies of nations; and who will raise up friends to fight our battles for us. The battle, sir, is not to the strong alone; it is to the vigilant, the active, the brave. Besides, sir, we have no election. If we were base enough to desire it, it is now too late to retire from the contest. There is no retreat but in submission and slavery! Our chains are forged! Their clanking may be heard on the plains of Boston! The war is inevitable and let it come! I repeat it, sir, let it come.

It is in vain, sir, to extenuate the matter. Gentlemen may cry, Peace, Peace but there is no peace. The war is actually begun! The next gale that sweeps from the north will bring to our ears the clash of resounding arms! Our brethren are already in the field! Why stand we here idle? What is it that gentlemen wish? What would they have? Is life so dear, or peace so sweet, as to be purchased at the price of chains and slavery? Forbid it, Almighty God! I know not what course others may take; but as for me, give me liberty or give me death!"

What an inspiration! The call to arms was heard throughout the colonies. People of all nationalities joined the Continental Army. Even women enlisted to fight for the cause of freedom. People truly understood the importance of coming together to break the chains of tyranny. The colonists understood their only course of action was to fight for their independence. With their iron clad will, they prepared their militia groups for they knew the British were coming. One group of the militias was known as the minutemen who were mostly made of farmers and shop owners. The minutemen got their nickname because they had to be ready with a minute's notice.

In April 1775, the British had advanced toward Lexington in the early hours of morning. They had a regiment of eight hundred soldiers. While the British advanced, Paul Revere had ridden ahead warning the colonists the redcoats were coming which gave them time to prepare.

In Lexington, there were 77 minutemen that bravely faced off an advance guard of 250 British soldiers. Captain John Parker told his militia, "Stand your ground and do not fire unless fired upon, but if they want a war, let it begin here." Major John Pittman, in charge of the British attachment, upon his arrival ordered the minuteman, "Disperse you scoundrels and throw down your arms! Disperse you rebels!" The minuteman bravely stood their grounds then suddenly the British ranks opened fired upon the minutemen. Without hesitation, the minutemen returned fire. Eight men had bravely given their lives as the minutemen found cover behind rock walls and continued to fire back at the British. At the close of the skirmish eight patriots laid dead on the field. I admire the courage of these men that bravely stood against such great odds. We must realize the sacrifice these men and so many others made in the name of freedom.

The British then advanced towards Concord, where Reverend William Abrasion, with rifle in hand was the first to meet the British in the field. Accompanying him was over four hundred members of the militia. When the British closed ranks the militia opened fire. They bravely stood their ground, found fortification and continued to fire back. The British were overwhelmed and started to retreat from the battle ground. With much determination, the militia continued to advance while firing into the British ranks. When the smoke cleared, the militia had won the battle. The British were beaten back, with several wounded and well over two hundred dead. This was such a massive victory for the colonists the news traveled quickly throughout the colonies. The people then started to truly believe they could overcome tyranny.

The British they were demoralized. They were known as the most advanced army in the world and were defeated by a ragtag group of simple farmers. The news of the British defeat traveled quickly back to England and the rest of Europe. It was later known as, "The Shot Heard Around the World." While many towns throughout the colony were finding victory, Boston did not fare so well. The English Navy had created a blockade in the Boston Harbor. The people of Boston found themselves without work and with very little food to feed their families. These times were very trying for the people of Boston. What made matters worse was later the British Army had invaded Boston and demanded the people of Boston to give their soldiers refuge and food.

From 1775 to 1776, many battles were fought on different fronts and at times seemed colonists were losing their war. However, their dreams did not fade away nor would they submit their will to the iron fist of Britain. The Continental Congress assigned five great men to draft the Declaration of Independence. This was such an important time for our country and the fact that we were blessed with such great men to shoulder this heavy burden was astronomical. These men included Thomas Jefferson, John Adams, Benjamin Franklin, Roger Sherman, and Robert R. Livingston. These five men met to discuss the outline of the draft. Our delegates truly understood that mankind was entering a new era as they birthed our great nation. John Adams assigned Thomas Jefferson to write the Declaration of Independence in June of 1776 and was approved on July the Fourth.

It was not just elegantly written; it was a true masterpiece. It established that all men were created equal and that a government should be formed by the people to represent the people. The people cried out for an independent nation. Americans stood in wait for the opportunity to read the Declaration of Independence. Many stood in the streets as the document was read to the crowds. It filled American hearts with pride and gave them the courage to keep on fighting. The very birth of greatness was born. Americans were determined to never give up their sovereignty to England. Even though the war was not over, many people's hearts cried out in joy as the people shouted, "We are free and independent!" When the news that America had declared their independence reached European nations, many of them thought the colonists were arrogant. Most of the Europeans thoughts America was ill prepared, uneducated, and lacked a professional army to stand up to the mighty British. King George claimed they could smite this rebellion and put the colonists back in their place. King George even declared his desire to hang the delegates who signed the Declaration of Independence for treason.

For the next several years, the Revolutionary War continued to ravage the land. The death toll continued to climb as the patriots so bravely gave their lives, but it had only strengthened their cause. The land was plagued with diseased and wounded men but America did not lose hope as they opened their hearts and gave care to those in need. As the British decimated the land by burning homes and businesses to the ground Americans did not give in to despair; they stood shoulder to shoulder and rebuilt our nation. The British underestimated the Continental Army and thought we would crumble under their might, but we proved them wrong. Even though the British had defeated us in numerous battles throughout the beginning of the war we continued to bravely stand our ground. Our resolve would not be shaken for we fought for freedom while they fought for a king.

During the Revolutionary war the illuminati was formed and one of the primary goals was to destroy the church's influence over kingdoms in Europe. The illuminati members were primarily made up of Freemasons and they strongly supported the naturalist movement. Within the first couple of years the ranks were filled with those in the elite circles. This secret organization was founded in Germany by; Adam Weishaupt who defected from the Catholic Church. Eventually their true agenda was revealed, which led to Adam being exiled from Germany. Their goal was to infiltrate governments through secret organizations to fulfill their agenda. Their goal was to create a one world order, and they chose the Unfinished Pyramid with the All-Seeing Eye as their symbol. Their goal was to infiltrate and break the will of all governments around the world to establish a one world government. They supported the evolutionist movement and even sent out false propaganda to destroy Christian faith. I can understand why so many people felt oppressed by the church during this time, but there is no excuse for such malevolent behavior.

Humankind during this time did not have free will as the people were ordered how to worship. Science was forbidden in many kingdoms, and the advancements of medicine was prohibited. For centuries, a small proportion of humankind controlled Christian faith through the church and has use this power to manipulate Nations to their will. For those who would not accept Catholicism was executed, such as the Celtic's, Vikings, Mayans, and the American Indians. The illuminati gave the appearance they had disband, but that was a deception. This organization had gone underground and continued to infiltrate other organizations and governments. Even America was conflicted with their ideology with symbols as the unfinished pyramid was placed on the reverse side of the America's Seal and eventually on the back of the US Dollar. The Washington Monument is an Egyptian obelisk with Egyptian symbols and the illuminati as well as Freemasons are both known for using the symbols. Washington was laid out to create patterns from the sky, such as the unfinished pyramid, the inverted pentagram, and the Freemasons symbol. The illuminati's secret dark agenda was kept hidden from the public, as Adam Weishaupt had instructed. He stated "conceal the very fact of our existence, our real objectives by profession of benevolence. If our real objective is perceived, for 10 to disband, and relinquish the whole thing, assume another name and put forward new agents." This proves for centuries there has been an attempt to control humankind destiny and how far these secret groups will go to hide their evil agenda.

Through the very beginning stages of the War General George Washington did not fare so well. Through many battles his army had been pushed back. Many soldiers were overwhelmed by the elements. Due to the lack of revenue in Congress, the soldiers did not have appropriate clothing for winter. Many of the soldiers had to cut strips from blankets to wrap around their torn shoes or even their bare feet. Numerous soldiers died due to frostbite and starvation. Even General Washington and his staff ate poorly. You must admire their strength and will to overcome such great obstacles. You obligated to ask what was their passion and motivation which helped them endure such hellacious trauma? For their spirit never dragged the ground even in the face of defeat.

The fall of Boston, New York, and New Jersey to British forces and the defeat in so many battles many of the delegates thought George Washington was too incompetent to command the Continental Army. Yet, the majority of the delegates and soldiers had absolute confidence in General Washington. General Washington was ill equipped to take on the most powerful military on Earth. Not only did General Washington have to train his men he had to utilize his surroundings as resources. His tactical plans were brilliant and his ability to out maneuver the British Army displayed a tremendous amount of cunning. General Washington understood he was facing overwhelming odds and had to avoid falling into British traps. He skillfully planned his attacks with hit and run tactics to wear down the British army. He understood the need for a victory in order to boost the morale of his men.

In late December of 1776, General Washington realized the British had left Trenton in the hands of 1,500 Hessians who were well trained German mercenaries. His army was camped across the Delaware River. He brilliantly strategized a plan to retake Trenton from British control. His plan was to attack Trenton on Christmas Day. This would catch the Hessians off guard. On the afternoon of Christmas Eve, General Washington gathered his 2,400 men to navigate row boats through the icy waters of the Delaware.

Then they had to march nine miles through the snow to reach Trenton. General Washington had planned a three-prong attack on the unsuspecting Hessians. His plan had succeeded and the victory came swiftly. The Hessians attempted to flee but were outflanked and were forced to surrender. This victory was a major turning point for America. It boosted the morale of the army as well as the thirteen colonies. General Washington commandeered all Hessian supplies and weapons which included cannons.

Days later, General Washington marched into Princeton and won another decisive victory. He ordered his armies to set up defensive positions around Philadelphia. General Sir William Howe outmaneuvered General Washington's army and gave him no option but to retreat. On September 11, 1777, the British moved in and occupied Philadelphia. The British had control of all coastal cities but had difficulty capturing cities further in land. However, General Washington had a massive victory at Saratoga.

A few weeks later, General Washington won another battle at Bemis Heights where six thousand British soldiers surrendered. The war was far from being over but Americans began to see that victory was within their grasp. Benjamin Franklin petitioned France for an alliance to assist with the war for quite some time. When France received the news of so many victories, they too started realizing that America could win the war. Benjamin Franklin's petitions to France finally succeeded on February 6, 1778 and an alliance treaty was signed.

For the next couple years, George Washington continued to out maneuver the British army. The British commanders concocted a plan to bring southern British forces north in order to trap General George Washington's army. The British controlled most of the Southern Theater. They had won decisive victories, capturing one regiment and slaughtering another. Even those who surrendered and unarmed were slaughtered.

The only thing that prevented the British forces from moving North was the constant harassment they received from the militia. Daniel Morgan was one of the leaders of a militia group in South Carolina. To the British, he was nicknamed "patriot" and specialized in hit and run tactics. Another great militiaman was Francis Marion or better known as the "Swamp Fox" for his ability to disappear. General George Washington realized he could not allow the British to pull their forces from the South. General George Washington then ordered Nathaniel Greene and 2,300 men to South Carolina to meet up with Daniel Morgan. Daniel Morgan was later given command of over 500 riflemen.

This prevented the British from pulling their forces from the Southern Theater. This led to a key defeat at the battle of King's Mountain.

When the French fleet finally arrived in 1781 General George Washington had already pushed the main British force back to Yorktown. General Washington asked the French commander to create a blockade around Yorktown to prevent General Cornwallis from escaping.

When General Washington arrived with 7,000 troops the British were trapped by both land and sea. There were 9,000 British troops stationed in Yorktown. Protecting Yorktown were separate defensive positions called canon forts. The French Navy heavily bombarded the defensive positions which led to the destruction of 8 of the 10 cannon forts. It is hard to imagine the excitement General Washington and the Continental Army felt when they were so close to victory. The war had raged for six long years and many patriotic Americans had given their lives in the name of victory. The British must have known defeat was at hand because they saw General Washington's troops marching in and a fleet of French ships blocking their retreat. The British were demoralized. The war was to have never escalated so far and so many British lives were not to have been lost. General Washington strategically positioned his troops to attack Yorktown. He understood that he had to capture the two remaining defensive positions so he could seize their canons.

His plan was to turn the cannons toward Yorktown and fire upon the British within. When George Washington ordered the attack on the canon forts the Patriots charged through the battlefield through a hail of bullets and canon fire. A force of 400 broke through British lines and stormed the cannon forts. They charged with their bayonets fixed and pushed the Redcoats onto their heels. Once General Washington seized the cannon forts he ordered them to be turned on Yorktown.   The bombardment of Yorktown lasted for two days until General Cornwallis realized he had no choice but to surrender. Cornwallis was so ashamed he refused to attend the ceremony of surrender. Instead he gave his sword to his second in command and ordered him to present the sword to General George Washington at the ceremony. When Cornwallis' second in command attempted to present the sword to General George Washington, he then ordered the British officer to give the sword to his second in command. The Americans were exuberant in their celebration. The people cheered in the streets as they shouted out, "We won the war! We are an independent and free people!"

They fired the cannons 13 times in salute to the thirteen colonies. It is hard to imagine the exhilaration many Americans felt as they finally realized they were free. It was estimated that 50,000 Patriots had given their lives for this dream. We must never forget that these men gave their lives for the freedom and liberty we enjoy today. Their new country had been ravaged and many families lost loved ones. However, Americans still came together because they knew they could create a great nation.

In 1783, the Paris Peace Treaty was officially signed ending the Revolutionary War. Benjamin Franklin was the true architect of the Peace Treaty. George Washington returned to Mount Vernon, while many of the delegates remained in office. The very foundation of our nation was created and indelible rights were put into law for all Americans. To ensure true representation they needed a government for the people by the people. In 1787, our delegates wrote the Constitution. The first Amendment made was to ensure freedom of speech and religion.

"Congress shall make no law respecting an establishment of religion, or prohibiting the free exercise thereof; or abridging the freedom of speech, or of the press; or the right of the people peaceably to assemble, and to petition the government for a redress of grievances."

No other nation on Earth had bestowed such rights for their people. We are truly blessed. A government was established that truly understood the tyranny and horrors of dictatorship. Our government understood the meaning of free enterprise without governmental interference. They also understood that over taxation weakened the people and the economy.

In 1789, George Washington was elected as our first President. It wasn't enough that he bravely led our country into victory in the Revolutionary War, but his heroic wisdom as a President brought prosperity. Throughout the years, America grew not only through commerce but in size as well.

In 1803, America purchased the Louisiana territory for $15 million. We paid 3 cents per acre for this rich fertile land. Even though the Revolutionary War was over England continued to harass American merchant ships which later led to the War of 1812.

The United States understood their small naval fleet had no chance against the mighty British naval fleet. Britain had the strongest naval fleet in the world. Their ships were extremely large and carried many cannons. America created a new navy from the ground up. They understood that the British Navy had slow and heavy ships, so they had to create smaller and faster vessels. They created a vessel called the Clipper, which was later known as the speedy Clipper. Their strategy was hit and run tactics or out maneuver the British ships. It paid off significantly. America won many naval battles against the British during this war. Due to the lack of success in the water, the Britain invaded the United States and burnt Washington D.C to the ground. Their forces were turned back at Fort Sumter through ferocious fighting, which was a huge victory for America. The Star Spangle Banner was written at this battle which would later be America's national anthem.

The Battle of New Orleans ended the War of 1812. There Andrew Jackson and his 4000 soldiers demolished the British force of 11,000 troops. This was a massive turning point for America. It was our first stepping stone on the way to becoming a world superpower. We proved ourselves by beating back the British, the world's most powerful nation, twice. We must never forget the spirit shared by our forefathers. The call for freedom and independence did not come without sacrifice. We must never take for granted the very essence our great nation was founded upon. Let us not be the generation that slips into the darkness. It is our duty to ensure that freedom and independence, a true people's government will endure for generations to come.

From Industrial Revolution and Ingenuity, We Became a Superpower

The birth of our nation was based upon brilliant ideas that were established by our forefathers. They sacrificed their lives and well-being to establish a government for the people by the people. They believed in free trade and less interference through government, which is a Republic. These sacrifices were made by all races, and even women who wanted to ensure freedom for all. When Thomas Jefferson was appointed to write the constitution his idea that all men were created equal was brilliant. Many of our forefathers did not believe in slavery however a majority of others did. This corruption of slavery began at the birth of our nation. Even later the Irish and the Chinese felt the sting of racial discrimination which had burdened our great nation. Even women felt this pain. They were denied the right to vote and were rarely considered for work positions held by men. Unfortunately, it would take almost two centuries to right the wrongs of our past. The treatment of Native Americans is another stain of shame on our nation's great history. To make matters worse it is often downplayed as our history is taught to our children. This horrific attack on Native American culture began long before our nation's birth. The onslaught of violence and land grabbing began when England, France, and Spain began colonizing America. America was also guilty of this same criminal act. There were whole Native American nations that were completely destroyed. However, a few tribes such as the Cherokee were forced to relocate to Oklahoma in a grueling march west known as The Trail of Tears.

America was such a young country that desired to establish a government by the people, unfortunately all of the peoples' voices could not be heard. If you have read the constitution you realize many of the ideas of our forefathers were beautiful until the seed of corruption rooted itself in law. This corruption eventually led to civil unrest in the form of racial tensions and women fighting for their rights.

I am proud of our forefathers, but I am not proud of the path America has taken. I believe it is important to understand our nation's history.

The very foundation of our government may not have been laid perfectly, but with time we would become the freest society on Earth. The right to freedom of speech gave people the right to be heard. This allowed people to speak out against racial prejudices, unfair work conditions and even cry out for the right to vote. The civil unrest which sprang up from workers' rights led to an outbreak of violence. America was not a perfect nation but as we grew we gained wisdom. What is remarkable about our great nation is not just the freedom that we have been blessed with but our ingenuity to overcome any challenge. It did not matter if the world viewed us as an uneducated nation. Throughout the decades America witnessed an economic boom. The nation was growing stronger and larger. Many states joined the United States and when Texas won its independence they joined as well.

In 1848, America purchased the South-Western territory from Mexico for $10 million. With the purchase of this vast territory, America stretched from the Atlantic Ocean to the Pacific Ocean. Later many other North Western states joined the United States, including Oregon in 1859. During this time America witnessed a massive growth in land and a huge economic boom. This had increase prosperity for many Americans, while many others were left shackled into enslavement. Our nation was divided with the Northern States that was predominately Republican opposing slavery and the Southern Democratic States supported this horrific crime against humanity. The Northern Republicans states set in motion to prohibit slavery in the new Western States. Violence had spread throughout our nation to end slavery before the war had even started. Our nation was about to be ripped apart, for a great man had set in motion to undo a terrible wrong. Abraham Lincoln did not believe in slavery and he set out to abolish this horror. The nation would divide on the issue in 1861 with the outbreak of the Civil War. Pres. Lincoln was a strong supporter of the Constitution and believed by those indelible rights no man had a right to own another. I admire him for not only his principles but strength in character. After the Civil War Pres. Lincoln brought forth a federal income tax to help rebuild the country after the horrible war. The federal income tax was removed ten years later as unconstitutional.

Over six hundred thousand soldiers died to correct this horrendous mistake. Abraham Lincoln was assassinated for his belief and his role in ending slavery. In my heart, I truly believe that Abraham Lincoln belongs in the same class as our great forefathers from the Revolutionary War. He truly understood the Declaration of Independence and that all men were created equal. Abraham Lincoln's dream that all Americans should be free was accomplished. I only wish our forefathers could have corrected this heinous form of labor. The fact slavery had continued well into our nation's first century was a true injustice for many people and families.

Throughout the next decade, America faced many hardships, especially in the Southern States. The land was ravaged from warfare and massive reconstruction was ongoing. Even though slavery was abolished, black Americans were still not treated as equals nor where they allowed to vote. They received constant harassment and were even murdered by racially motivated groups such as the Ku Klux Klan. During this time, many great people came forth to fight for equality for all races. What I find shocking is how our nation had continued to stay divided even after the Civil War with Republican Party in control of the North and the Democrat Party in control of the South. Soldiers had to be sent from the North to ensure that blacks had the right to vote and attempted to end racial equality. These truly were trying times for America but change was on the horizon.

Great feats of engineering occurred during this time. The railroad was completed and connected the Atlantic to the Pacific. In the same decade America purchased Alaska for a little over 7.2 million dollars. Many Americans were skeptical of this purchase and believed that we had bought a block of ice. From 1850 to 1870 many Americans moved out west in search for gold. With the completion of the railroad, many more Americans had moved westward in search for a better life. In the 1870's silver was discovered in the South-Western territory and gold was discovered in Alaska. This created a massive building boom across America. Cities were springing up throughout the Midwest to the western shores.

With the invention of electricity and its many different applications, it revolutionized America's industrial power. For the very first time America's homes and streets were lit with light, even shop owners would light up their signs which encouraged more Americans to stay out later. In 1889 Washington became part of the United States. I don't believe our forefathers could have ever imagined America could have grown to such a size in a little over hundred years. The stage was set for America to become the most powerful nation in the world. America was rich with many minerals and other resources. We had an abundance of fresh water and had the ability to grow massive quantities of food.

In the 1900's, America challenged colonialism by liberating Cuba and other islands from Spain in the Spanish American War. During this time oil was discovered in the Southwestern territories. In 1908 Henry Ford mass produced the first personal motor vehicle with the introduction of the assembly line. America had truly shown their industrial might. The explosion of factories producing goods, and American steel industry going global is a good indication of what a free market can do without governmental restrictions. The Wright Brothers took to the air which was the precursor to commercial flight. Even though America was becoming an industrial power it had no desire become a military might.

At this time, America was still a very young country. There were many issues with workers' rights. This led to strikes which turned violent and the government had to step in to dissolve this serious issue. Many of the working class employed were forced to work grueling hours six days a week. The government had no alternative but to establish rights for these workers. Even with the issues of employment rights America was beginning to become an industrial might. Powerful men such as

Rockefeller cornered the oil market. Carnegie established a huge steel company that would go international while Vanderbilt made his millions in the railroad industry. These three men played an important part in America's industrial might. Unfortunately, many of the corporate elites' thirst for wealth was unquenchable, as they would even commit violence against competing companies.

In the early 1900s the banking system were controlled by four prominent families: JD Rockefeller, J.P. Morgan, Paul Warburg, and Baron Rothschild. These four men were ruthless in attempting to control the market and the banking Institute. The prominent banking leaders realized the only way to establish a central bank for America was to create a panic in the financial system. Later J.P. Morgan created a panic in New York by spreading false rumors that a bank in New York was about to go bankrupt. This created the panic of 1907 where New Yorkers lined up outside the banks to collect their savings. An article was written in Life Magazine, by Frederick Allen who accused Mortgage Interest of taking advantage and precipitating the panic of 1907. Shortly after this Panic Sen. Nelson Aldrich recommended that a central bank should be established so we may prevent another panic in our financial system. Sen. Aldrich had close ties to the banking Institute and later married into the Rockefeller family. In 1910 a secret meeting was held on J.P. Morgan's estate at Jackal Island off the coast of Georgia. This meeting of the elite was to establish a central bank in America by writing the Federal Reserve Act.

The fact that this bill was written by the elite class of bankers is atrocious. This bill was then giving to Sen. Aldrich where he pushed it through Congress. In 1913 Woodrow Wilson, would become president through tremendous sponsoring from corporations and the banking industry. Pres. Woodrow Wilson pledged on his campaign trail that he would sign in the Federal Reserve Act for campaign support. Congressman Lewis McFarland stated it was a carefully contrived occurrence, international bankers sought to bring about a condition of despair so that they might emerge the rulers of us all. This was a tremendous amount of power that was given to the Federal Reserve. The Federal Reserve have the power to control interest rates and inflation, by controlling the production of money. The Federal Reserve works on a debt system where every dollar that is created is loaned to the government with interest. If the Federal Reserve created the dollar and loan it to our government, then how can the government pay back the interest? The federal government has no alternative but to borrow more money from the Federal Reserve to pay back the interest on the previous loan. This will only create a debt cycle that will continue to increase our debt. Pres. Woodrow Wilson regretted supporting the Federal Reserve act and later he stated, "I am a most unhappy man. I have unwittingly ruined my country. A great industrial nation is controlled by its system of credit. Our system of credit is concentrated. The growth of the nation, therefore, and all our activities are in the hands of a few men. We have come to be one of the worst ruled, one of the most completely controlled and dominated Governments in the civilized world — no longer a Government by free opinion, no longer a Government by conviction and the vote of the majority, but a Government by the opinion and duress of a small group of dominant men".

Another major issue that had a huge effect on America's economy was the Federal Income Tax. The terminology our government likes to use is withheld, but I call it stealing. To take personal income from the working people stifles the economy because people have less money to spend. In 1909 the 16th amendment was signed in and ratified in 1913. According to the 16th Amendment, Americans are required to pay all lawful taxes, and these lawful taxes are oil, tobacco, firearms and sales tax. There is no law in the 16th amendment that requires Americans to pay a Federal Income Tax and we were deceived by our own government a century ago. Is it not ironic in the same year the elite successfully pushed in the Federal Reserve Act our government would establish a Federal Income Tax? The reason this deception played out in Washington was because our politicians would have never voted in Fort income tax or central bank concept unless they were deceived. America it is time to wake up for it was us that build our great nation and the elite profited from our labor.

The fight for equality still continued, as black Americans desperately needed a voice to carry their message to Washington. In 1909, the NAACP was founded. This established a strong voice that could be heard by the politicians in Washington DC as well as the American populous. This encouraged more people of different races to speak out for racial equality and women's rights. Employee rights was another major issue during this time, with extreme low wages and cruel treatment of workers. Employees were forced to work grueling shifts from sunup to sundown and for a good percentage of the workforce had to work six days a week. Dew of low wages and no employee rights had increase the profitability allowing business owners to become extremely wealthy. This was a time when the elite of the world began to emerge for world dominance. The greed of Carnegie, Rockefeller, Morgan, Warburg, and the Rothschild's family had run deep as they had already begun taking the wealth from the world. These great monopolies will set in stone who will be the elite of the world. Their low wages and horrendous working conditions was just another form of enslaved workforce for so many.

Due to the thirst for world dominance and their greed to control the world's wealth has left millions of families impoverished. They infiltrated our government through lobbying and bribing our politicians. They have even bypass the legislative branch by writing their own laws, such as the Federal Reserve Act. The issue I find shocking is how these families of the elite have maintained their status in wealth and power through several past generations. Some of these family's power goes back to the early ages of Europe and how long shall we allow them to continue their dominant reign, is to be seen. The people did rise against the powers of greed by protesting in even rioting in the streets of cities across America. Many of these protests turned violent such as the Homestead Massacre because of men like Fritz who was a manager at Carnegie Steel. Fritz paid well over 300 armed Pinkerton detectives to break up a protest for better wages. Even with the violence the people continue to stand and fight for fair wages. Through all the turmoil America continued to grow through the decades and the elite became wealthier. While Europe was deadlocked in World War I Americans enjoyed a time of peace and economic growth. Eventually, America entered WW I to prevent Germany from destroying the rest of Europe. This war created industrial boom for the United States and corporations profited immensely. Multitudes of factories and industries sprung up across our nation with fair wages and even employee benefits. The increase income and employment opportunities helped so many families pull out of poverty.

The massive increase in income for many families allow them to purchase new homes and even send their kids to college. The introduction of the affordable automobile dramatically changed our country. Many families could now afford an automobile and suddenly Americans were traveling farther and more frequently than before. With vacation spots exploding across the country we transitioned into a new life style. Roads and highways were paved across America and interstates connected our nation from east to west and north and south. Industries moved their products much faster and people could easily travel from state to state. With cities growing and new homes being built everywhere, America was in a true building revolution. Many American workers were taking on the monstrous task of building interstates over the mountains and even through them and some continued to build the railroad network.

America was truly a nation of creative engineers, they harvested water from rivers like the Colorado and channeled this precious resource to the southwestern states. Later agriculture farms including poultry and livestock ranches exploded across this region. Inventions centered on the agricultural industry such as the tractor shifted work from the beasts of burden and suddenly farmers were able to yield larger crops. America suddenly had an abundance of food and even a surplus of food. In Alaska, the fishing industry exploded. American towns began forming throughout Alaska especially when oil was discovered there. America accomplished another momentous task in building the Alaskan Pipeline. Many Americans thought it was foolish to purchase the southwestern and Alaskan territories. They did not consider America's ingenuity and creative spirit. Not only did we move oil through a pipeline, we channeled water to the South West. America built skyscrapers and even the world's tallest buildings. America was creating a reputation for great engineering and the entire world began taking notice. Not only were they envious of the beautiful construction but of enormous projects like the Panama Canal. Some of the great minds behind these life changing inventions were Alexander Graham Bell of the telephone and Thomas Edison of the light bulb. America was also on the cutting edge of medical advances creating vaccines and cures for many of the aliments of earlier centuries. America would soon have a reputation of having one of the best health care systems in the world.

America enjoyed a time of prosperity after World War I, while Europe was rebuilding our nation came to their aid by sending supplies in first aid and tons of food to aid in a reconstruction. Americans were shocked when the economy collapsed a decade later in the 1930s. The hatchet job that was reconstruction in Europe eventually led to the collapse of the European markets and crippled the American market as well. Another important factor is how banks were accepting uninsured loans, and deposits were uninsured as well. In the early 1930s, over 9000 banks close their doors. When those elite bankers wrote the Federal Reserve Bill had ensured all Americans that a recession or depression would never happen again, this was another lie from the elite as well as our government to ensure their control over the economy. The Federal Reserve as well as the Federal Income Tax helped contributed to the depression. The corporate elite has bribed, manipulated governments around the world to obtain their wealth and power. Our forefathers fought and died for a new idea, for a people's government with liberty, true freedom, and a free market. Those in the elite circle have bribed our government and restricted liberty and freedom. They have asserted their control over the economy and control the banking industry destroying the free market. There were other contributing factors that crippled our nation such as a great drought that led to the horrific dustbowl. This horrific dust storm destroyed many farms across our nation and limiting food supplies. America's spirit was truly tried during this time. With the fall of Wall Street and banks closing their doors, many small businesses had no alternative but to close their doors.

Parents were not able to feed their own children and so many had lost their homes. During this time, many Americans were angry with the government and had even lost hope for their nation. Many Americans were out of work, out of food, and had little faith. During this time of universal suffering other countries were sending propagandas to deceive the American public by establishing many reformist parties. This included Communists, Nazi's Socialists, and other Socialists Parties. They attempted to gain power by brainwashing Americans into believing their government had failed them.

They spread their ideology by creating a false image of a utopian society where everyone would earn the same wage and how governmental control with solve our problems. The propaganda that would spill from their lips like poison betrayed a capitalist society as a government for the rich. They villainize corporations and even CEOs for stealing the people's wealth, yet America had one of the largest middle class in the world. This betrayal was rejected by most but they were those who were sickened by this illusion. If those who fell for this ideology had simply looked abroad to those nations with Communists or Socialist style dictatorships would have realized the majority of the population in these countries lived in poverty. They were even propagandists from the socialist parties that blame the Jewish people for the problems we were facing our nation.

Most Americans were too wise to fall for such ideology or be deceived by their propagandists. They understood people's true desire was freedom and democracy. America's problems began when those in wealthy circles began to corrupt our government to ensure their control over the economy. Europe economy crashing was another cause for the Depression, with risky investments and inflation from increased printing money. Another major factor was the fact that more Americans were dealing with small wages which contributed to a smaller middle class. Many Americans lost their riches from investing in European banks. Americans also understood the utopian society was unrealistic.

You have to realize a capitalist society creates ambition. It motivates the young to do well in school so they may reap the rewards when their education is finished. It inspires creativity and breathes confidence into people to start their own businesses. Pres. Roosevelt took steps in 1933 by establishing laws for employee rights, and a required minimum wage to aid in raising the living standards for all Americans. Soon America's industrial might started to crawl out of the Depression. Most Americans never lost confidence. They believed by working together and solving the problems, America's economy would recover. When America's economy pulled out of the Depression these cancerous groups that attempted to spread their venom had fallen to a whisper. During this time, most Americans were very patriotic and understood you cannot have a free society under a communist or socialist regime. Unfortunately, they were many people in our nation and politicians who began to adopt some forms of socialist ideology.

In 1935, Pres. Franklin D. Roosevelt signed in the Social Security Act. This bill would also include unemployment compensation, and would establish a federally funded social welfare program. Pres. Roosevelt's new deal has been compared to socialism since the day it was signed in. The German Nazi newspaper Volkischer Beobachter had claimed Pres. Roosevelt has adopted the national Socialist ideology in economics and social policies. Even to this day I have heard many people claim that our welfare system should never been established. I have also heard many argue this bill should have never been passed into law, I could not disagree more. You cannot declare yourself a civilized society while turning a blind eye to those in need. I have also heard those indicate that our welfare system is corrupt, I could not agree more. In future decades to come, people would take advantage of these programs. I only wish that FDR would have signed stricter guidelines and would have developed programs that would have encouraged Americans to stay off the welfare system.

In 1938, Europe was at war once again and America chose to stay neutral. Pres. Roosevelt extended the neutrality act which prevented the sale of ammunition, weapons, or raw metals to any nation that was at war. There were multiple reasons why Americans did not want to be involve in this war, especially after witnessing the carnage of World War I. Another fact that cannot be ignored is how $25 billion in loans from World War I was never paid and how so many investors and bankers profited from this war. Over 21,000 U. S. Investors became millionaires during World War I and the Rockefeller family had profited over 200 million. In the early 1930s America was not prepared for war but that would quickly change as we began to industrialize our nation. Amendments were made to the neutrality act which allowed the sale of guns, ammunition, tanks and even warplanes to England, China, and the Soviet Union on a cash and carry policy. We were also supplying many of our allies with the shipment of food and medical supplies.

America entered a new era as an industrial giant in world trade which created an economic boom of new growth in our nation. Our industrial productivity had increased to almost 100% which created over 17 million civilian jobs. Factories exploded across our nation which not only stabilized our economy, but also created higher-paying jobs. Even the housing market exploded with new homes being built across our nation. Research facilities in medicine, chemistry, and also, mechanical development had advanced during this time. I do find it disturbing that war had stimulated our economy and wonder what it would be like to live in a society where peace and goodwill was all that was needed. The strength of our will, with our industrial might was needed during this time to stop the spread of Nazi Germany and Imperial Japan. Americans felt a sense of financial security which led to another boom in entertainment as movie theaters were full, and people filled the dance halls. America had a reason for celebrating and family unity had never been stronger. Americans were traveling to their favorite tourist locations to relax or to find new excitement. The people were truly enjoying their time for stability and peace. Unfortunately, America's dream to live in peace would unravel. During this time, Americans felt the false sense of security. They believed the war was in faraway lands and they felt safe being nestled between the mighty Atlantic and Pacific Ocean. Most Americans were still unaware of the bombing attacks from the Nazi terrorists or even later the Japanese strategy of sending balloons over the Pacific Ocean caring incendiary bombs. The media was either unaware of these attacks or was ordered not to report them to the public. The Socialist Nazi movement had spread their influence around the world and even in South America where many countries had a large German population. Even America would be polluted with ideology from the Nazi organizations such as Friends of New Germany and the German American Bond or better known as the German American Federation. Germany's deputy Rudolf Hass had given authority to start propaganda schemes in America through Socialist Nazi Organizations.

This attempt to spread a socialist ideology in America failed because most of the people in this period understood that a socialist or communist style of government would only lead to a dictatorship. They understood by allowing government to control economics, industrial, health, and other forms of governmental management would only lead to controlling the people. Germany had also established a network of spies and saboteurs that would spread to major cities across our country. The Nazi Saboteurs mission was to create panic by placing explosive devices in strategic places like shipyards or warehouses. Their attempt was to stifle our nation's ability in sending food and other aid to England as well as the Soviet Union. The Nazi terror ring was successful in five bombing attacks on American soil. What shocked me was how few Americans knew about this Nazi plot to stifle our ability to send aid to our allies. The FBI eventually did infiltrate this terror group and found it was operated by Fritz Duquesne. The FBI had uncovered plots for future attacks and multiple explosive devices, which led to the convictions of 32 Nazi terrorists. The idea that these terrorist attacks occurred before America entered World War II shows how aggressive a dictator style government can be. Another fact you will not find in most history books is the unpatriotic infiltration in our government. Director Hoover warned Pres. Roosevelt about the communist ties to the vice president Henry Wallace. The director also indicated the vice president had many communist friends. This is a good indication on how vulnerable America was to the threat of treason and a threat to every American losing their freedom. By this time in our history we have been attacked with communist or socialist ideology and these ideologies had brainwash several of our politicians, which would lead to corruption in Washington.

Pres. Roosevelt met with Winston Churchill as well as other ally leaders and was informed they no longer have the funds to pay for military equipment and supplies. In 1939 Pres. Roosevelt signed in the land lease agreement, this bill would allow the United States to place army, naval, and airbases in strategic places around the world for the exchange of weapons. On December, the 7th 1941 Japan attacked Pearl Harbor which temporarily crippled the US's Pacific Fleet. America declared war on Japan as well as on Germany and then later Italy. These nations were built on conquest and their only desire was power and they realized by conquering other nations they would not only give themselves wealth but land as well. Japan had already captured most of the Pacific islands and launched a massive invasion in to China. Chinese military were slaughtered in the streets, and many of the people that surrendered were lined up in front of a firing squad. The Japanese army had committed horrible war crimes against the people of China. Italy desired to reestablish the great Roman Empire. Germany and Russia invaded Poland and Germany's motivation was to capture all of Northern Europe. The only European country that was left standing was England. However, through constant aerial bombing England was brought to her knees. Germany then broke its pact with Russia and invaded Russia. The German war machine pushed the Red Army all the way past Moscow.

While many nations recognized America as an industrial giant, most of them did not see us as a military threat. As long as American borders were secured, Americans did not care for a massive military buildup. Their true devotion was to live in peace. Yet, the sneak attack on Pearl Harbor jolted Americans into action. After Pearl Harbor was attacked, one Japanese Captain Yamamoto was asked how he felt about the attack. He replied, "I fear that all we have done is to awaken a sleeping giant and fill him with a terrible resolve." The sleeping giant had awakened. Americans came together and built assembly lines across this nation. They were building tanks, jeeps, ships and planes for the Army and Navy. America had engineered military might overnight. They set up defenses to prevent Germany from invading England and sought their enemies in the oceans. America was at war on two fronts; they were fighting the Japanese in the Pacific and fighting the Germans in the Atlantic. American Marines stormed the islands in the Pacific and through ferocious fighting they liberated island after island. The American Navy had won massive naval battles through the Pacific and continued to push the Japanese Navy back to their homeland. During this time America and our allies had launched a massive invasion on German occupied territories. America and her allies were successful in pushing back their enemy to their homeland. Italy quickly surrendered but Germany was forcefully brought to their knees. America goal was to bring democracy to Europe while Soviet Union wanted to spread communism. A line was drawn across Europe which divided east and west. The battle to prevent communism from spreading had begun.

America and Japan were still at war even though Japan was pushed back to her mainland. Japan no longer had a naval force or an air force to protect her skies. Japan was looking for a conditional surrender whereas America wanted an absolute surrender. They hoped that America did not want a land invasion due to the carnage it would cause. Our military leaders understood that a land invasion would cost many

American soldiers lives. America also did not want Russia to get involved in the Pacific theater. They knew if Russia helped invade Japan they would want their troops to remain there and Japan would find themselves divided as Germany was: one side democratic and the other communist. The carnage of this war was horrific as the American people cried out they did not want to lose any more sons or daughters, so our government needed a quick and decisive victory. President Truman decided to drop two atomic bombs on Japan, forcing them to surrender unconditionally. When Japan had surrendered, Americans cheered in the streets the war was over. The carnage of this war was horrific for so many nations and the genocide of the Jewish people was a crime against humanity. America was exuberant to know their men and women; American soldiers were coming home. Unfortunately, many Japanese civilians and soldiers died a horrible death because of those two atomic bombs. Many more died later due to radiation sickness and the ground along with the fresh water remained radioactive for several decades.

You have to realize, if America was delayed months or even years of entering World War II, the world we live in today would be dramatically changed. Without America's help, England would have been destroyed within a short time. After all, England was having difficulties protecting themselves from aerial bombardment from Germany. American forces landing in England helped prevent a German invasion. England and America combined their strength along with the remaining Dutch and French forces in England and they launched a land invasion into German occupied territories throughout Europe. The Allies landed on beaches like Normandy where they sacrificed so many lives to push the Germans back. American forces also helped slow down the Japanese advancement through China.

It is horrible to imagine, but if America was never involved in World War II England would have fell into German hands and the Nazis would have been able to concentrate their full might onto the Soviet Union. If Japan continued to conquer China at its original rate, China would have fallen quickly and then Japan could have joined in the attack on Soviet Union. The Soviet Union would have found themselves fighting a war on two fronts. It is hard to believe that one country could have ruled all of Europe and Soviet Union. I have no doubt that the Nazi Party would have eventually declared war on Italy, and then all of Europe and North Africa would have been under Nazi control. Japan would have had control over all of Southeastern Asia. You have to wonder where this would have left America. If America had not joined the war when we did we could have been standing alone facing the full force of a Nazi German Empire and Imperial Japan.

Even though World War II was over, the Cold War was about to erupt. America would then encourage freedom and Democracy around the world while Russia and China would attempt to spread Communism. We must realize that Communism's true goal is absolute power and world domination. It's very beastly tentacles seem to reach all corners of the world even in America. I find that communism is very conniving as it attempts to paint its glorious picture and manipulates the world. During the 1950's Soviet Union continues to send communist sympathizers to America to established the Communist Party of America but gained very little acceptance during this time. With this failure to gain support for the Communist Party in our nation they resulted to brainwashing a young. These communist sympathizers invaded our universities to spread their ideology. Their goal was to change American history and to villainize our government. They created an image of America being colonialist and a tyrant to the world. They praised other communist nations as if they could do no wrong. Another stained America patriotism was the allegations made by Major Jordan had indicated that the United States was shipping military equipment, materials to build an atomic bomb, and even whole factories to the Soviet Union after the war, under the land lease act. He also indicated the United States had sent printing plates as well as paper and ink so they may print their own U.S. Federal Reserve Notes which could be exchanged for American currency which cost taxpayers billions. Maj. Jordan attempted to report this to his commanding officer and even the air Corps which was ignored. Maj. Jordan also testified for the Senate which gained very little attention. Maj. Jordan had ample evidence to prove illegal activity in our government, which was a threat to America's security. I sit back in my chair trying to understand why this matter was not taken serious by our government, and media. I encourage you to read Maj. Jordan's Diary and check the facts so you may be certain of the truth.

Our grandparents and past generations understood that communism was a cancerous society, where only the working class were devoured and the people were left in poverty. Where communism had failed, it had succeeded in countries like Vietnam and North Korea. We must realize when the Communist Party gains control; the people have very few rights and work for meager wages. There is no such thing as freedom of the press and what is taught to their children is controlled by leaders the people do not choose. There are no morals and very little care for the people and they are treated as statistics. They live with very little healthcare and their standards of living is extremely poor.

This was like a disease that had struck fear in the leaders of our past, such as John F. Kennedy. President Kennedy understood he could not allow communism to spread throughout the world. I commend him on how bravely he stood during the Cuban Missile Crises. It was where Soviet Union had strategically placed missiles in Cuba and had them aimed at America. I truly believe his actions prevented World War III. I also believe that America as well as Western Europe prevented communism from spreading throughout the world. America did attempt on numerous occasions to establish peace with Russia and China with little success.

While Soviet Union continued to build up their military, as well as its nuclear arsenal, America had no choice but to participate in this arms race to protect our sovereignty. Even the last frontier that is space exploration became a rivalry between America and Soviet Union. America would eventually win the Space Race by sending the first man to the moon in 1969, Neil Armstrong.

America's ingenuity and ability to construct skyscrapers, advancements in aircraft, and even space exploration were outstanding during this time. America's spirit as well as the pride of its people had never been stronger. America was not only on the edge of exploding industrial might; we were on the cutting edge of science and healthcare. The feeling of security and greatness had filled our nation, although this was not without challenges.

Even though America was a free society it was not without its flaws. All races of people were still not treated equally and women would have to continue to fight for their rights as well. But America was on the brink of change. Great leader such as Martin Luther King Jr and Clara Barton showed us the errors of our ways.

Racial ideology had poisoned our great nation from its very beginning. Many of our forefathers did not believe in slavery for they believed all men were created equal. Unfortunately, many more of our forefathers did believed in slavery and it took a century to correct that horrible mistake. It is horrible to know that another century had passed and people were still fighting for equality. To stop racism, you must first stop there lies with honesty and meet the hate in their heart with love. This is the only way to stifle the spread of racism. Still this rhetoric has continuously spread throughout our nation. I truly believe we can become a true and equal society but first we have to dissolve these secret and racial organizations that only spread their hatred. For these organizations have one agenda and it is to change the political structure of America. These organizations are either motivated by political control or racial dominance.

Our ancestors and grandparents fought against their evil intentions, but still they spread their propaganda. Throughout the years, many nations have proclaimed that they will destroy America from the inside out. They realized how America was a superpower with a strong military might, so they strategized new ways to cripple our great nation. They sent spies to infiltrate our government and organizations. They sent propagandists, to not only poison the minds of Americans, but also turn us against one another. They use tools such as freedom of speech to spread their propaganda and lies. They manipulate great masses of people with their ideology and turn them against their own government. We must realize that this is a cancer that is devouring our great nation.

We once stood proud at the watch tower and challenged their ideology. Even John F. Kennedy spoke out against these racist or secret organizations and expressed his desire to end such rhetoric. I commend those who stood against Communism, Socialist ideas, and even racism, they were true patriots. So many people had sacrificed to preserve our great nation, from our grandparents, great grandparents, and all the way to our forefathers. Many had even given their lives for our great nation. Let us not allow the sacrifices of so many or the heroic acts to go in vain.

While America Slept

While America slept communism and socialism rooted their
ideology deep within our society. For decades, the socialist and
communist movements infiltrated our government through many
departments. They spread their ideology through the Department of
Education, Workers Unions, and have even attempted to control media.
This battle between the Communist and Socialist Party's for supremacy
over our nation has continued for decades. The socialist movement
infiltrated the Democratic Party through the liberal movement and for
years they met in secret to deceive the people. With communist and
socialist ideology being spread like a disease many Americans began to
question the longevity of our country. There deeds went unnoticed for
years as they plotted their evil intentions behind closed doors. Those
who desire to smother the flames of democracy are not just from this
nation but nations abroad. They came with one agenda: to manipulate
enough people to establish a foothold in our government for political
reform.

Pres. Kennedy warned America about secret organizations within
our society when he stated "The very word secrecy is repugnant in a
free and open society." Pres. Kennedy was not just warning America
about the threat of the communist or socialist movements he was
warning us about the threat of the illuminati and other secret
organizations. This is no conspiracy, for the illuminati are real and
Rockefeller admitted in his self- written biography he was a member of
this secretive organization. There is a tremendous amount of
documented evidence to prove the year the illuminati were formed and
their ranks were filled with those in the elite circles.

Today there is evidence around the world that proves their
existence with illuminati symbols on governmental buildings and even
our own currency has symbols of the unfinished pyramid. The
illuminati's goal was to abolish religion and to create a New World
Order. The elite has masterfully plotted their position to be our masters

in the one world government. A half a century has passed since those elite bankers had empowered themselves to write the Federal Reserve act. Through the manipulation in our government they have become extremely powerful and they have obtained a tremendous amount of wealth. Through their power the elites are trying to establish a world central bank for more dominance over the world. They have adopted the framework of socialism as a structure for the New World Order. They plotted to destroy America's currency decades ago by removing the gold standard from our currency to establish their own worldwide currency. They have plotted to destroy religion through our educational system with false teachings in evolution. Their goal during this time was to remove prayer from schools and to abolish the Commandments from our society. They have infiltrated our universities to brainwash our young with their sickening ideology. Their intent was to spread their socialist ideology while distorting our own history. They systematically passed laws to change the political structure of our nation. America for us to bring honor back to our nation, we must reveal the truth and uncover the damage these secretive or radical groups have caused.

A few years after World War II, the Soviet Union began to send communist sympathizers as well as spies to our nation. Senator Joseph McCarthy had accused many in our state department and even governmental officials of being involved in the Communist Party.

"I have here in my hand a list of 205 names that were made known to the Secretary of State as being members of the Communist Party and who nevertheless are still working and shaping policy in the State Department. "Sen. Joseph McCarthy, February 9, 1950.

The McCarthy Hearings were a series of hearings held between March and June 1954 by the US Senate's Subcommittee on Investigations to investigate accusations of Senator McCarthy against the US Army.

He had shown evidence along with communication transcripts from the Soviet Union to these communist sympathizers. He gained little ground due to the fact he could not reveal his source or how he had obtained such evidence. The agencies that were monitoring these transcripts did not want it revealed to the Soviet Union they were listening or had the ability to break their secret code. Later the C.I.A released documentation showing that Senator Joseph McCarthy and most of his evidence was valid. Even the FBI was investigating this manner. In 1960, Director J. Edgar Hoover warned the president as well as the American public on national TV that communism was a real threat to America's security. Director Hoover stated "We must now face the harsh truth that the objectives of communism are being steadily advanced because many of us do not recognize the means used to advance them... The individual is handicapped by coming face to face with a conspiracy so monstrous he cannot believe it exists. The American mind simply has not come to a realization of the evil which has been introduced into our midst." Director J Edgar Hoover was a true American patriot. While director of the FBI, he spent his years battling communist threats and the mafia. Pres. Kennedy attempted to warn America about the threat of communism and secret organizations.

In 1963, John F. Kennedy was assassinated by a communist sympathizer named Lee Harvey Oswald. This horrific deed awoke the American public to the threat of communism. Our government and the FBI began intensive internal investigation to shut down this attack on America. This Communist threat would not simply vanish throughout the 1960's. It would lay in wait in the darkest corners of our nation. The Communist propagandists went underground, keeping their true agenda secret. Through the decades Russia continued to send communist sympathizers as well as spies to steal our technology. Communism was a severe threat for the whole world and after John F. Kennedy other presidents such as Lyndon B. Johnson, Richard M. Nixon, and even Gerald R. Ford fought against this threat.

During the 1960's, many other threats had emerged. The ideology of a Socialist society started to spread. Socialism is the redistribution of wealth where everyone is equal and receives the same benefits. This is completely unjust. The idea of taking wealth from a hardworking individual and sharing it with those who don't work is wrong. This idea of a socialist society compares with utopian beliefs where everyone has a house and once again there exists a distribution of wealth. The very idea of distribution of wealth or where everyone receives the same benefits is ludicrous. We must realize this will destroy our competitiveness and our willingness to try harder for a better life. They believe creating a society where everyone has the same will eliminate crime, but what about those who want more? Other ideas were emerging in the sixties such as anarchy and Marxism. The idea of anarchical society is not only reckless but also dangerous. A society without a leader or without the ability to vote, would eventually lead to dictatorship and a criminal society. Marxism is an idea from Karl Marx that would lead us to a socialist society. You must also realize that communism, socialism, and Marxism would destroy capitalism. Their desire is for all industries and businesses to be controlled and regulated by the government, which would destroy competitiveness. With government controlled industries your right to bargain would be no more as you have no option but to purchase items from these governmentally controlled industries.

I found myself asking why so many people during this decade had a desire to change our political structure? I feel they did not have the will of the people nor do I believe they understood the true meaning of a democratic society. These radical ideas of a utopian society were being taught in universities and would eventually lead to the Hippy Movement. Not only did they spread these radical ideas throughout our nation, but they ripped the moral fabric of our society. With their ideas of a sexual revolution developing and a drug culture had truly stained the moralities of America. The Hippie movement not only tried to spread their idea of a utopian society, they even tried to live it by creating hippie communes. The majority of the hippie communes that were established failed miserably within a short time. The idea that they would equally share everything, including chores did not work. For example, one would grow their vegetables and succeed, while the other failed or didn't even try. If their ideology of an equal society cannot work on a small scale, what makes them think it will work on a large scale? We must realize, for most people to obtain wealth and security, you must work for it. The hippie movement, as a whole, did not believe in capitalism and a good majority willingly or unwillingly supported socialism. The idea of utopian society could have never been established without redistribution of wealth, which gives a government tremendous power to take wealth from the working class and the power to decide on who receive these benefits. Their evil deception will lure millions to the bosom of welfare and there they will be trapped in a life of impoverishment. Left abandoned to poverty and brainwashed, they dance to the false songs of those politicians who support socialism. During this era, the welfare system had grown immensely, becoming the beast that absorbed our nation's wealth. The socialist movement has resulted to a large government with tremendous power.

Our government began to empower themselves with controls over the food industry, health industry, education, economics, transportation, and with such a demand for control will only result to a big government controlling us all. America, we must look at how corrupt our government had become by the 1970s and we have paid for their corruption through over taxation or through intense regulations. These radical socialist or communist groups laid out an assault plan that was political and social. Their political plan was to infiltrate different parties or organizations to spread their ideology. Socially they use false propagandas to fuel riots and create more division within the people. They infiltrated our educational system to spread their socialist ideology and censored our history to destroy patriotism. These radical organizations had assaulted our Christian faith by accomplishing their goal in the removal of the Lord's prayer from our schools. During the 1970s many school districts had in doctrine courses in evolution and the goals of the illuminati or communism was to replace religion with humanism. By removing prayer from our schools and replacing God's word with false teachings in evolution have placed our nation on a dark path.

The hippies were also known for protesting the Vietnam War, which was their right to assemble and protest in a war they did not believe in, but what I strongly disagreed with was those who spit on our soldiers and mocked them. This was not only an unpatriotic act but it was cowardly. Our soldiers were not draft dodgers unlike so many hippies; they chose to serve our country. My objective is not to bash all hippies or to destroy their credibility, but we have to accept the fact that the hippie movement was a strong political movement for socialism. Their delusion of a utopian society was heavily influenced by faults propagandists in universities across our nation throughout the 60s and 70s. The hippie movement was hypocritical as they call out for peace they strategize for revolution. When their cries for revolution lost momentum, they then strategized on infiltration in our political system, seizing control over education, control media and infiltrate worker unions or organizations. The hippie movement faded into history by the mid-70s and a greater monster had risen field with deception. The great beast of socialism had infiltrated our political system to fulfill their evil deeds.

I had the opportunity to meet a hippie from the 60s and I asked him what this decade was like. He started telling me how sexual everyone was and how everyone was doing drugs and taking hits of LSD. (Everything was just groovy.) He then told me about Woodstock. I then commented that the very government they protested against had to come in to rescue them during the Woodstock festival. They had to bring everything from food, water, medical supplies, and porta potties at taxpayer's expense. I asked him how he felt about the fact that the organizers of this event were sued by the surrounding farmers. He didn't give me a reply; he just commented the hippie movement did a lot of good for our country. I then asked what good had come out of it. He said they stopped the war on Vietnam, where so many soldiers had died and started many environmental movement. He went on and told me about how much fun they had at these peace rallies. I then wanted to know what he meant by fun during these peace rallies. He smiled and said they would get high and take hits of LSD and start tripping. He accused our government as well as our soldiers who fought in the war of being murders. This aggravated me. Several of my uncles had fought in this war and for him to diminish their patriotism is wrong. I quickly realized this was a man who knew nothing about history. Because when I asked him how he felt about us abandoning the South Vietnamese when they needed us the only response I received was a puzzled and confused look. Before I walked away I told him that the South Vietnamese called for our aid and when we abandoned them millions of Vietnamese were slaughtered by the North Vietnamese. His only reply was, "That was heavy."

This is another example on how people express their points of views without knowledge of history or without understanding. South Vietnam truly desired freedom and democracy but Communist Russia as well as China had infiltrated their country and spread their ideology. I do agree we do not have the means or the ability to police the world, but we must realize the severe threat of the spread of Communism. Rallies to end the Vietnam War were not all peaceful. Several groups and organizations turned to terrorists' attacks against our nation. Domestic terrorist group such as the Weather Underground terrified our nation with bombing attacks. Bill Ayers, one of the founders of the Weather Underground planted bombs that exploded at the New York City Police Department, Pentagon, and even the capital. These ruthless cowardly acts horrified the public. This was the first time our capital had been attacked since 1814 when the British burned it down. Bill Ayers showed no remorse and he was proud as he commented, "We are all a guerilla organization. We are Communist women and men, underground in the United States for more than four years." 1974 Published in Prairie Fire: The Politics of Revolutionary Anti-Imperialism.

As I ponder, I try to understand the mindset of such madness. If they believed in a Communist style of government, then they should have relocated to Communist China or Soviet Union. I find that all those who desired to change our political structure were self-centered. Had they foolishly thought their ideology superseded the rights of the people? The sixties were a time of great turmoil in America. Many cities throughout our nation erupted with violence and those who wanted to change our political structure. This weakened the morale of the people. The sixties could have been a glorious decade. It was an opportunity to right the wrongs of our past in regards to civil and women's rights. Civil rights organizations and women rights organizations had fought for their rights for well over a century. I find it shameful that it took so many years for our government to realize that everyone deserved equal rights in our society. Even Martin Luther King Jr. was met with extreme hostile opposition. The Democratic governor of Mississippi, Ross Barnett and the Democratic governor of Georgia, Ernest Vandiver fought Martin Luther King Jr. on many fronts to end the Civil Rights Movement. Martin Luther King Jr. also met aggressive opposition by Democratic governor George Wallace of Alabama, who stood on the steps of a University in an attempt to stop segregation. Many attempts were made to silence his voice, but neither his spirit nor his conviction could be broken. In 1968 Martin Luther King Jr was assassinated. This despicable act was carried out by a racist James Earl Ray. It is unimaginable how many greater deeds could have been accomplished if this tragedy had never happened.

Americans were once again brought to their knees when they witnessed the war crimes in Vietnam not just in photos but on television. To witness such carnage of bodies lying dead in the streets, or the aftermath of carpet bombing was intolerable. The devastation of this war was not just witnessed on TV; it was witnessed through small towns across America. Soldiers were coming home in body bags and some were severely wounded. Many of the problems America was facing had continued into the seventies with the recession and the oil crises. The spirit of our nation was dwindling and so many were left questioning our future.

In 1974, America began to question the credibility of the government with the resignation of Republican President Richard Nixon. If Richard Nixon had not resigned, he would have been impeached for obstruction of justice and abuse of power. I have no doubt in my mind that Richard Nixon was guilty. He had secretly recorded over 3,000 hours of meetings and phone conversations. He also had five people of his committee break into the Democratic National Headquarters to obtain information and evidence and had secretly planted listening devices. When the five men were apprehended by authorities Richard Nixon denied any knowledge of their criminal act. He continued to manipulate and lie to the authorities and even attempted to commit bribery to hide his involvement. I do not only question his abuse of authority but played a major role in the actions orchestrated in Vietnam. Richard Nixon should have not only been impeached but put on trial as a war criminal. I found myself trying to find understanding and the more information I obtained the more questions I was left with.

As I was reading about Republican President Gerald R. Ford pardoning Nixon, it left me puzzled. They had ample evidence to show Nixon's guilt and the fact that he attempted to obstruct the FBI's investigation was un-American especially for a president. I even read the interview that Mr. Frost had given Pres. Nixon, and the one thing that was left out was a motive. Behind every action there is a motive! I continued to do research to find his motive, but only found speculation. I read reports that accused Pres. Nixon of being paranoid or insecure, or he was trying to find their democratic campaign strategy to win his presidential election. I recall reading another report claiming he was delusional. Well, doubtful, doubtful, doubtful. President Nixon was not paranoid nor was he delusional. I also do not believe he was insecure. He was an overconfident, very proud man, and probably had a dominant personality. If we look at the evidence, we know Richard Nixon is guilty and even in the Frost interview he admitted he was guilty. When Frost asked Pres. Nixon why he did not burn the tapes he had recorded he did not respond to the question. David Frost then asked Nixon why he felt he had the right to secretly record others. Nixon only rationalized it by claiming other presidents had made recordings as well.

We must realize that Richard Nixon had accomplished many things in his life. He got a scholarship to Duke University where he studied law. He then opened his own law firm after graduating college. In 1942 he served the U.S Navy as a lieutenant and in 1946 he was elected to Congress, and then to the Senate in 1950. Later he had the honor of being vice president in 1952 and won the presidency in 1968. To say this man was anything less than accomplished would be a massive understatement. To proclaim that he was paranoid, insecure, or delusional has no merit. Nixon even served on a committee in which they investigated Communist spies.

I do believe Nixon was over confident and believed he was above the law, especially in the interview with David Frost, were Nixon commented, "Well, when the president does it that means that it is not illegal." The very question that was left out of the interview is why did Nixon secretly record so many conversations or send people to break into the Democratic Headquarters. You must realize, before David Frost was allowed to interview Richard Nixon he had to meet with lawyers that represented Nixon. This led me to believe Nixon's lawyers pressured Frost into not asking certain questions and if he did so he may have faced a great deal of blowback. Much of the evidence was not allowed to be viewed by the public and very little of the 3,000 hours plus of recording was released.

Another question I think is equally important is what was the objective of the five men that Richard Nixon sent to break into the Democratic Headquarters looking for? I do not believe that Richard Nixon would send five people from his personal committee to the Democratic National Headquarters to spy on their campaign strategy. Another good question was why were the American people misled by the government and media into believing these five men broke into Watergate Plaza instead of the Democratic Headquarters? Was this an attempt to take suspicion off the Democratic Party, so this scandal would fall only on the Republican Party. This leaves me with a bigger question now, what information where they looking for? We may never know the answers to these questions due to Gerald Ford pardoning Richard Nixon as soon as he took office. There was an overwhelming demand for Richard Nixon to resign. Even if he had evidence or the secret recordings revealed information he realized he had no choice and it would be inadmissible in court because it was illegally obtained. This left the American public with so many questions and shattered the trust in our government. America's patriotic pride had never been lower. We had lost our first war while going through a massive economic recession and faced an oil crisis. America was also facing the threat of a nuclear war along with the fear that more Communist spies had infiltrated our country. These were hard times for America. In 1975 our government abolished the un-American activities committee which was established in 1938. This committee's responsibility was to investigate Communist and Socialists activities in our Nation. Our government then transferred this responsibility to the Judiciary Committee which seem to passively sweep this matter under the rug. Communism and socialism had started in America in the early 1900s which gained very little support. Many patriotic people and representatives of our government spoke out viciously to end this assault on our nation. Through the onslaught of these propagandists we heard the alarm loud and clear from our senators, congressmen and women, Pres. and even the director of the FBI. In decades to come the alarm to warn Americans had fallen silent as a Socialist Party had begun to take over our nation.

I remember when I was a young child my parents and grandparents watched the news in disbelief. It seemed as if everyone was worried about a war or feared that our country would collapse. Liberal points of views started spreading throughout the seventies along with the desire of other radical groups to change our nation. America was desperately looking for hope, but sadly it would not be found through the Carter administration. I feel that Democratic President Jimmy Carter did not have the strength of character or the leadership to lead our nation, but I do give him credit for his stance on the Civil Rights and Peace treaty between Israel and Egypt. He could not create economic stability and his stance on the Iranian hostage crisis was very weak. When extremists captured the American embassy, they held captive 52 Americans. The hostages were held captive for 444 days in Iran. To know these poor people were held hostage for well over a year is horrific. This had weakened the confidence of the American public and severely questioned the strength of America's conviction.

During and after his administration Jimmy Carter supported dictators like Pakistani General Zia al Huq, Fernando Marcos, Saudi King Faud and many others. You must realize how devastating it is for a Democratic nation to acknowledge or praise such dictators. These leaders had violated human rights; they had suppressed their own people and even committed murder. The people as well as the land had been robbed of their riches and those who stood up against tyranny were executed, tortured, or raped. I have heard these horror stories for myself from my aunt Cecilia who fled from Cuba after it was captured by Fidel Castro and his forces. She told me how her father was riddled with fear because he worked for the previous government of Cuba. Fidel Castro and his men were executing anyone who supported the prior government so my Aunt Cecilia's family had no choice but to flee to America.

During Cuba's Revolutionary War, Fidel Castro promised the people a democratic government. Not only did he deceive the people when he became a dictator he brought a communist style of government. America tried to stop the spread of communism throughout the world. We stopped the advancements of communism into South Korea and we lost the battle in Vietnam. There's no doubt in my mind that a communist society has a thirst for power and desire for conquest. It does not matter the destruction they leave in their wake, such as communist China's invasion into Tibet or Russia's invasion in Afghanistan. Communism would spread throughout the world into the Western Hemisphere challenging the stability of democratic society. The idea of a democratic society is where people have the freedom to choose their own destiny, and even that was being questioned. Not only did Americans question their future, but the world questioned if this style of government would last. America's confidence had weakened in the belief in our government and the strength of our military.

America had gone from a proud independent nation to a weakened dependent nation due to the environmental movement and intense regulations. I find it shocking how many Americans have forgotten or have no clue how hard life was back in the seventies. It was unimaginable, the stress, and uncertainty that Americans were facing. Gas stations across the country were running out of gas, and the few that had gas had tremendously long lines. Arguments and fights had broken out over this valuable resource. Americans were being limited on how they purchased gas through the Carter Administration. The idea that they could purchase gas every other day, and was restricted on how many gallons they could receive created tremendous uncertainty. People lived in fear of having their gas stolen out of their vehicles so they stood on their porch or camp in their yard trying to protect what little gas they had. Across the nation, street lights were turned off and stores were cutting off their lights trying to preserve energy. I was just a young child, but I remember the long lines at the gas pumps, and fighting that broke out in the streets during this time. The fact that the gas was rationed must have sent a shockwave of fear across our nation.

During this time, we were already in a recession, and with the fear of running out of gas it only heightened people's fears of it worsening. Our government seemed incapable of resolving the gas dependency issue, and the hostage crisis was in total disarray. Our military was left handicapped with the major cutbacks by the Carter Administration and the fear of a nuclear war was part of our daily lives. I remember as a child watching the cartoon Duck and Cover. It was where Bert the turtle taught us how to prepare in case of an atomic explosion. During this time, the question was not "are" we going to be attacked, but "when"? Many children were left in fear as they taught these lessons at school.

Due to America's dependency on foreign resources we began to submit to the will of other nations and compromise our own morals. America was in desperate need for a strong leader, one who could bring pride and prosperity back. We needed a leader that would fortify the belief of the constitution once again, and bring vigor with honor back to our military. We needed a president that could restore our economy and rekindle the spirit of American pride. America would find such a leader in the Reagan administration. If we were ever in need of a great leader this was the moment for one to emerge. America's credibility around the world had been damaged. The confidence and the strength of our military had been weakened due to the Vietnam War and the severe cuts to our military budget from the Carter Administration. Communism had spread throughout Asia, Africa, and even the Western Hemisphere with Cuba.

During the 1970's America was cutting back on their military and Russia was expanding theirs. Dictators were controlling the Middle East, which led to the oil crises that was crippling the United States. The very spirit of what it was to be an American was dwindling. Many wondered if we could even stand up to the might of Russia or other rogue nations. The perfect example was the hostage crises we were facing with Iran. We were not being taken serious as a nation. This all changed with the Reagan Administration. As soon as Ronald Reagan was sworn in, the American hostages were released. Many have claimed that Reagan should have not received credit for the sudden release of the hostages, but I strongly disagree. I believe the dictator of Iran understood, that the Reagan administration would not delay or hesitate to send military force in too free our hostages.

Republican President Ronald Reagan's first executive act was to remove the price control on oil, oil production, and the sanctions that were placed on American's by the Carter Administration on how they purchase gas. President Reagan's policy on removing price controls on oil and its production had paid off tremendously. Oil prices had dropped by fifty percent and Americans were relieved to pay less at the pump. By removing the sanctions or the rations on gasoline it started to restore America's confidence. President Reagan truly understood to bring confidence back American's had to feel secure on their own soil and around the world. He gave our military men and women a pay raise while raising their standard of living and better housing.

Before the Reagan administration the military lacked in weapons and equipment, and was under funded. Many soldiers still carried weapons from the Vietnam era. It was ridiculous. With advancements in weapon technology he quickly upgraded our military to handle any threat. His most ingenious program was the SDI (Strategic Defense Initiative). This missile defense would not only bring the Soviet Union to the bargaining table, it also broke their grip over the world and ended the Cold War. Reagan and his administration had a can-do attitude. He would not compromise American morals, nor was he willing to sacrifice our freedom. He understood that communism was a cancer with the intent to devour the world, and socialism was a disease that would eventually lead to communism. I was a young teenager, but I can still remember his speech, "We Must Fight."

We Must Fight

"Now let's set the record straight. There's no argument over the choice between peace and war, but there's only one guaranteed way you can have peace and you can have it in the next second surrender. Admittedly, there's a risk in any course we follow other than this, but every lesson of history tells us that the greater risk lies in appeasement, and this is the specter our well-meaning liberal friends refuse to face that their policy of accommodation is appeasement, and it gives no choice between peace and war, only between fight or surrender. If we continue to accommodate, continue to back and retreat, eventually we have to face the final demand the ultimatum. And what then when Nikita Khrushchev has told his people he knows what our answer will be? He has told them that we're retreating under the pressure of the Cold War, and someday when the time comes to deliver the final ultimatum, our surrender will be voluntary, because by that time we will have been weakened from within spiritually, morally, and economically. He believes this because from our side he's heard voices pleading for "peace at any price" or "better Red than dead," or as one commentator put it, he'd rather "live on his knees than die on his feet." And therein lies the road to war, because those voices don't speak for the rest of us. You and I know and do not believe that life is so dear and peace so sweet as to be purchased at the price of chains and slavery. If nothing in life is worth dying for, when did this begin just in the face of this enemy? Or should Moses have told the children of Israel to live in slavery under the pharaohs? Should Christ have refused the cross? Should the patriots at Concord Bridge have thrown down their guns and refused to fire the shot heard 'around the world? The martyrs of history were not fools, and our honored dead who gave their lives to stop the advance of the Nazis didn't die in vain. Where, then, is the road to peace? Well it's a simple answer after all. You and I have the courage to say to our enemies, "There is a price we will not pay." "There is a point beyond which they must not advance." And this is the meaning in the phrase of Barry Goldwater's "peace through strength." Winston Churchill said, "The destiny of man is not measured by material computations. When great forces are on the move in the world, we learn we're spirits not animals." And he said, "There's something going on in time and space, and beyond time and space, which, whether we like it or not, spells duty." You and I have a rendezvous with destiny. We'll preserve for our children this, the last best hope of man on earth, or we'll sentence them to take the last step into a thousand years of darkness.

President Reagan was truly the "Great Communicator." He not only rekindled what it was to be an American, but also gave many the courage to fight. To this day, there are times I go back and listen to his speeches and still his words inspire me. "Mr. Gorbachev, tear down this wall!" This was bold and showed true courage of what it was to be an American. Pres. Reagan telling the USSR to tear down the Iron Curtain and to unify the German state was a huge leap towards ending the Cold War. The massive blow came from deploying Pershing and cruise missiles into Western Europe. Reagan would not be detoured even with members of the Democratic Party standing against him and Soviet Union walking away from the arm control talks. Pres. Reagan stood by his plan and deployed the SDI program.

I find it shocking that a member from the Democratic Party, Ted Kennedy, went behind Reagan's back and offered assistance to the Soviet Union. Ted Kennedy's goal was to stop President Ronald Reagan from deploying missiles into Western Europe and ending the SDI program. Not only did he plot against Reagan he deceived America. Ted Kennedy denied any involvement with this scandal. This too would be revealed as a lie years later when the KGB files were released. Another thing that I found shocking was how hardly any media reported on this scandal. This goes to show how Liberalism had infiltrated the media and how far back they have gone to control what Americans learn. We must realize how dangerous the USSR was during this time. Many will tell you to understand a country; you must first understand their history. They invaded numerous countries such as Poland, Hungary, Austria, Czechoslovakia, and many more. In 1939-1940 they invaded Finland just to obtain a seaport in warmer waters. President Reagan understood how dangerous the USSR was and their past indicated they had a desire for conquest and enslaving those they had conquered. If anyone opposed the USSR in this Communist regime or conquered territories, they were sent to prison camps.

Even Joseph Stalin made a pact with Adolf Hitler on how they would invade Poland and split the territories between the USSR and Nazi Germany. President Reagan continued to put pressure on the USSR while continuing to focus on problems we had here at home. It amazes me how he was capable of handling so many issues at once. After resolving the oil crisis our economy started to improve dramatically but it was Reagan economics that enriched our economy the most. He encouraged industries to upgrade their machinery and tools to give them a competitive edge on the global scale. Businesses began to expand while new enterprises were born overnight. He truly believed in a free market and understood less governmental restrictions and taxes would create growth. With tax cuts our economy seemed to change overnight. President Reagan also granted tax credits that encouraged industrial growth as well as upgrades for new machinery which also helped boost our economy. President Reagan truly understood by lowering taxes and deregulating industries would have a significant effect on lowering a hidden tax called inflation. We must realize every time you raise taxes or regulation fees on industries, it significantly raises the cost of living for every American.

Reagan's economic boom continued to grow into the turn of the century. President Reagan's policies aided America win the Cold War and through his administration we saw the USSR collapse. The wall that divided Eastern Europe from Western Europe was torn down while millions won their independence from USSR. Finally, nations like Georgia, Lithuania, Bosnia, and many more had their independence from the Soviet Union's horrible iron grip. We even saw Afghanistan defeat the Soviets. Many criticized President Reagan for giving weapons to Afghanistan or training the Afghans on how to defend themselves. I have heard them claim that Reagan's policy when training the Afghans had resulted to training such groups such as the Taliban. I strongly disagree.

Reagan did not believe that the training these people were receiving would lead to the results of them committing terrorist acts toward America. He gave the opportunity for a third world country to stand up against a superpower. I do not agree with the weapons that were being secretly sent to Iran which was later called the Iran-Contra Affair, but I understand his reasoning for Iran was not faring well with the war against Iraq. The realization that if Iraq defeated Iran they would have had control over a great percentage of the oil in this area was crucial in deciding to supply Iran with weapons or not. Iraq would have become a superpower and could have led to them conquering the surrounding nations.

The oil crises that America faced during the seventies led to a lot of the policy decisions our government made and would make through other administrations. President Reagan stood by his morals and led by his Christian principles on many bills such as abortion. I believe that Reagan was one of the greatest presidents we ever had. He belongs in the category with George Washington, Abraham Lincoln, John F. Kennedy, and other great presidents. He believed in America, stood up for the Constitution, and he repaired so much damage that had been done by prior administrations. One of his most amazing accomplishments, was the friendship that began toward the end of his administration between America and the new Russia. Who would have ever thought within eight years, two nations would go from sworn enemies, to friends.

I remember well, when Pres. Reagan's eight- year term ended. I can still recall his farewell speech and even remember how I felt when he left Capitol Hill for good. I felt worried and uncertain to see such a great leader leave office. By this time, throughout my young life, I had seen the hard times of the seventies and the prosperous times of the eighties. This one administration changed so many of our lives and by understanding that caused great concern for the next administration. Many Americans had great hopes for our next Republican President George H. W. Bush.   He was a war hero from WWII and served as governor and head of CIA. He was already well known for serving the Reagan Administration as Vice President. Many hoped he would continue the policies from the Reagan Administrations. President George H.W. Bush seemed more concerned with foreign affairs than domestic. Our relationship with Russia continued to grow and President Bush had the opportunity to open up many doors with other nations. A lot of things happened during his administration.

In 1989, he sent U.S forces into Panama to liberate the people from the cruel dictator General Manuel Noriega. After General Manuel Noriega was removed from Panama and sent to the U.S to stand trial many Panamanians came forth with horror stories on how they were brutally treated. There is one thing I do question: why was General Manuel Noriega on the CIA payroll? The U.S forces went in to liberate the Panamanians as well as take control of the Panama Canal from the evil dictator. You have to realize for a dictator such as General Manuel Noriega to control the Panama Canal was far too much control. Gen. Noriega increased the rates for passage through the Panama Canal. This would have increased the cost of goods worldwide and would have led many more to poverty. He also had the ability to stop nations from entering the Panama Canal, which would force them to ship their goods around South America. This would have caused the prices of the goods that were being shipped to increase dramatically from the extended time of delivery and fuel usage. Once Panama established a government we returned the Panama Canal back to their control.

Shortly after the liberation of Panama the Iraqi military invaded Kuwait. Kuwait quickly pleaded to America and the world for assistance. America responded rapidly, and President George Bush Sr. condemned the actions of Iraqis dictator Saddam Hussein. America as well as the United Nations continued to put pressure on Saddam Hussein. They repeatedly gave him opportunities to withdraw his forces peacefully from Kuwait. While Saddam Hussein continued to refuse to withdraw his forces the U.N had no choice but to agree to mobilize forces to liberate Kuwait. This was such a huge leap to see so many nations voluntarily working together too free one nation from the powerful grip of a dictator. Kuwait was quickly liberated and Saddam's Forces were pushed back to Iraq. Many Americans were aggravated with President George Bush Sr. for not sending U.S military forces into Iraq to apprehend Saddam Hussein and put him on trial for war crimes; but I personally agree with President George Bush Sr. for his decision on not to pursue Saddam Hussein and his forces. You have to realize this is one of the first times the U.N was capable of assembling such a large force from so many nations. It gave the world a glimpse of how we could work together and solve major problems. The U.N council only voted on liberating Kuwait they did not agree to go into Iraq and apprehend Saddam Hussein. I'm sure President George Bush Sr. wanted to liberate the Iraqi people from this horrible dictator and charge him for the war crimes he committed against Kuwait. This decision would haunt him until the next election.

There were many other problems happening around the world during this time. Terrorism started to spread across the Middle East with the Taliban and other terrorist groups spreading their influence around the world. Riots were breaking out in the streets of Russia and China. In the streets of Russia, Communist sympathizers were rallying forces to bring back Communism. While in China, college students were protesting for Democracy. You can see how Bush's hands were tied with so many problems happening around the world. He did pass several bills. One such bill was the American Disability Act, and he reauthorized the Clean Air Act. I wish President George Bush Sr. had paid more attention to Reagan's policies on a free market, but instead he broke his word and raised taxes. He also paved the way for the NAFTA Treaty (North American Foreign Trade Agreement). This would become detrimental to the American workforce. The only way you can establish free trade for nations around the world is to ensure a fair-trade system. By making it a requirement for nations who desired free trade to have an equivalent minimum wage would raise the standards of living around the world. A tremendous strain had already been imposed on our industrial might through overtaxing or horrendous regulations. The NAFTA treaty would have a dreadful impact on our economy and would result to millions more Americans working for lower wages. America, I plead with you to take heed, for this is an attempt for the super elite to pull their strings on the world stage. There is no way the NAFTA treaty could benefit the American people, if our politicians are truly representing the people, then tell me why would they support such a treaty? This is a good indication that shows our politicians are supporting the super elite.

I believe the NAFTA treaty was a strategic plan to help usher in the New World Order, and bring forth a cheap labor force. A century ago the super elite had manipulated our government to control the banking industry through their Federal Reserve Act and now they are plotting to control the world's economy. Without a conscious, our politicians pass bills with intense regulations. The EPA has imposed their might, and our governments intense taxing system has left a path of destruction with broken impoverished families. We must realize that what truly made America great was a free capitalist society. I do believe employee rights as well as a required minimum wage. I also believe in the requirements that OSHA has established to ensure employee safety, and I believe it is our responsibility to protect the environment. Our government has overstepped boundaries in their attempt to control our industrial might through governmental controls or by imposing intense regulations. The super elite evil plot for world dominance has manipulated governments to control the world economy and the banking system. They control a tremendous amount of the world's wealth and they have monopolized the oil, gold, steel industries to obtain more wealth and power over the world. In the past the elite has infiltrated and manipulated groups such as a socialist or communist to do their bidding to obtain their goal for a New World Order. Their devious plans were deceptive, for the elite strategized their plots to control what we hear through the media networks they own. There evil plots fell into stages with their attacks on our Christian faith for well over two centuries, and there devious bidding to corrupt our politicians to sell away our freedoms. Make no mistake America, the elite class is the mastermind behind the socialist and the communist movement.

America Under Siege

Today I call out for all Americans to take heed for we are being attacked on all fronts. The very meaning of what it is to be an American is being distorted. The very structure that has established our freedom and liberty is being removed stone by stone. Today, Lady Justice's scales have tilted where unfair laws are being passed without question. Even Lady Liberty's torch is dimming as the gateway of opportunity closes on us all. The people are overwhelmed through over taxation as disparity grips the land. The wealthy are uprooting the industries and even the factories that gave us prosperity have abandoned us for faraway lands. It is as if though darkness has fallen upon our great land and has left us in poverty. The corruption of our leaders has devastated the spirit of America. Even freedom of speech is being restrained or abused and the freedom to just be oneself is no more. I look upon the masses and they seem dazed and confused. Hope is being devoured by hopelessness while filling our hearts with despair. I cry out to the people "Do you not see what is happening?" and so many reply "it is useless for they have taken our voice." How have so many people simply given up without a fight? For I know I do not stand alone. I have heard those who valiantly cried out "They are trampling on our constitutional rights!" America make no mistake the elite is the grand puppet master as they have already asserted their dominance over us all. They have filled the ranks of their army with bought politicians and judges. Our nation has become fractured as the people are divided. We must all open our eyes for evil deeds have gone unseen for far too long! Hatred has filled our hearts to turn brother against brother. We must realize a divided people can be easily controlled. Even the truth has been distorted to poison the minds of us all. I say no more, for we must rise to unravel this beastly tongue to bring honor back. No longer shall we carry hate in our heart for it only brings sadness. Let us carry hope and valor like a shield as we vigorously fight to bring back morals and Christian principles.

All these problems may not have occurred in your generation, but they are still bearing down on you today. We can no longer pretend this madness is not occurring. Let us bring light into the darkness for we may see the faces of those who are committing injustice. We can no longer be in a state of denial; nor can we procrastinate on these issues any longer. We must endeavor to unravel the truth and break the hold of despair. I truly believe deception and disparity rooted itself a little over six decades ago. We must unveil these dark forces and unravel their tentacles that are choking our nation. I call out for all Americans to gather up your courage. No longer should we be divided by color. Together we must find our voice and speak out with boldness. These rights that have been trampled upon do not just belong to us but to our children. Let us not be the generation Democracy dies. Let us ensure our rights are protected for many more generations to come. America, we must expose this madness for the truth has been entangled in lies. The minds of our young have been polluted for far too long. During the Presidential elections of 1992, I wish that George Bush Sr. and Bill Clinton would have listened to Ross Perot. He was an independent running for president, and he warned America of the dangers of the NAFTA Treaty. He stated this during one of the presidential debates:

"If this agreement is signed as it is currently drafted, the next thing you will hear will be a giant sucking sound as the remainder of our manufacturing jobs-- what's left after the two million that went to Asia in the 1980s--get pulled across our southern border. We need jobs here, and we must manufacture here if we wish to remain a superpower. We must stop shipping manufacturing jobs overseas and once again make the words "Made in the USA" the world's standard of excellence. We can do it. The question is--will we? It's up to us, the owners of this country--THE PEOPLE."

-Ross Perot

Democratic President Bill Clinton would win the 1992 Presidential Election. The primary reason he won the election was the fact that the Conservative votes were split. In the presidential campaign,

Conservative Republican George Bush Sr. and Conservative Independent Ross Perot were running against Liberal Democrat Bill Clinton. Even though President Bill Clinton won the electoral votes for president, he only received 43% of the popular vote. What really destroyed my political confidence in American voting in this election was not just what I heard on TV but also what I heard from the people around me. People admitted to voting for President Bill Clinton because he was young, cool, good looking, and played the saxophone. I know that Liberal Americans supported his policies but to hear that so many young people were voting in this manner was disturbing.

America, we must make our vote count and do our homework. His agenda for being on TV in sun glasses while playing the saxophone was to attract the younger audience. A campaign for such high office should have never been run in this manner. We should have never based our votes on appearance. What is important is the character and policies of the candidate and how they plan to lead our nation. Their past accomplishments and how they served our country gives us the ability to predict how they will serve us in office. If you look at his past accomplishments while he was Governor of Arkansas, you will see he did some good. While serving as governor he improved education rankings slightly but academic rankings and teachers pay were both still ranked near the bottom. He improved job growth in the state, but most would claim that he created low paying jobs. This statement is true; Arkansas was ranked very poorly in personal income growth.

I personally did not vote for Bill Clinton when he ran for president in 1992. I did not agree with his policies while he was governor and because of the fact he attempted to avoid the Vietnam draft. I feel if anyone refuses the call of duty to serve their country, it is not only cowardly, but also dishonorable. They do not deserve the opportunity to serve in office. Although Bill Clinton did not flee to Canada he danced through many loopholes to avoid the draft. What truly disturbed me were President Clinton's ties to Communist or Socialist groups. According to Sunset Research Group and FBI files, President Clinton is connected to groups such as IPS (Institute for Policy Studies), SDS (Students for a Democratic Society), and NACLA (North American Congress of Latin America) which is associated and helped founded by SDS. The NACLA is a tool for SDS recruitment as well as spreading propaganda for revolutionary changes abroad and domestically. In 1969, SDS leaders claimed they were responsible for the riots and the fires that were started in many universities across our nation through this era. IPS, the largest pro-Marxist group, was founded by Marcus Raskin and Richard Barnet in 1964. This organization has many faces. While most support Marxist or Socialist ideology, there are those who support Communist as well. Their agenda is to weaken America's foundation, control the media, and manipulate the citizens of America. They spread their ideology for revolution to change America from a Democratic to a Socialist society.

Richard Barnet, leader of IPS, helped Nicaraguan, North Vietnam dictators and traveled to North Vietnam where he personally supported Communist leaders. America, we must realize how conniving, manipulative, anti-American their true agenda is. They have infiltrated our government, as well as the media. They have spread propaganda to confuse the people through asserting control in our education. How powerful these organizations have become cannot be ignored for they have not only influenced our politicians, but they have reached all the corners of the planet. Pres. Clinton is linked to IPS though his friend, Derek Shearer, who claims Marxism will help us humanize. I do not know how Derek Shearer can come up with such an assumption, for Marxism is the same monster as Socialism. It does not matter how you dress it up, their political ideology is the same. Their dark agenda has unfolded before us, for they have asserted their dominance over our financial system, healthcare, education, and transportation. Their plan for a utopian society has unfolded before us through their plans for redistribution of wealth has left millions more in poverty. To take money from the wealthy and to redistribute is wrong. It destroys drive and motivation.

Tell me, why would one desire to be wealthy if he or she knew that their wealth would be taken from them? How would we motivate our children in school to achieve great academic standards for them to only realize they will receive the same as everybody else? We must realize that a Marxist and a Socialist society destroys motivation and drive and kills dreams as well. If you use common sense, you could easily see what horrors wait for the path that we are traveling. A dictator style government led by an extremely small wealthy class, and through their dominance we will be left shackled.

This monster's agenda is to control the economic structure of the world by governments regulating businesses as they sink their claws in for total control. Their ideology pushes for more social welfare programs, which is not only bankrupting our government, but governments around the world. It does not take a mathematician to understand that the more welfare programs created will only increase the numbers of those who will take advantage of these benefits. If the Liberal or Socialist movement is so interested in humanizing the world, then how do they answer to the millions upon millions of babies that have been murdered through abortion? Their strong stance to support abortion is just another form of genocide. They have raised taxes to pay for their immense size and a welfare system that is severely corrupted. The dramatic increase in taxes has resulted to the increase in the prices of goods sold around the world, which has left more people in poverty.

We must realize the true agenda of the Communist and Socialist groups is to dismantle America brick by brick destroying our foundation from the inside out. They were intent on revolution in the sixties but failed miserably. Now their intent is to infiltrate our government to bankrupt our economy and change our political structure. Researcher of the IPS, Karl Hess, agenda was to destroy our foundation. He was appointed as chairman by Pres. Clinton and Chairman Karl Hess believed that businesses could be controlled and our government could be dismantled. The FBI even warned that IPS as well other Socialist and Communist groups had infiltrated our government and political groups.

Rush Limbaugh, in 1992, warned America about Clinton's connections with these organizations. I find it disturbing, how someone can become president of the United States with so many anti-American Communist connections. But I will be honest, like so many others in the 1992 Presidential election, I was not aware of this information. What shocks my faith even more is the fact that Bill Clinton received campaign money from the mafia as well as credible statements accusing him of being part of money laundering and drug smuggling while he was governor of Arkansas.

Another thing I find disturbing is the disappearance or murders of many people who had information about these crimes. There are also many questions unanswered about ADFA (Arkansas Development Finance Authority) where alleged drug money was being laundered through other banks. Dan Lasater, one of Bill Clinton's good friends, and Roger Clinton were found guilty of drug related crimes. Chief Delaughter was investigating the drug smuggling ring as well as sexual abuse allegations and during this investigation he was harassed by members of his own police department. I know this is speculative but there have been those who have come forth and given statements accusing Bill Clinton of having connections with organized crime. I will be the first to say just because you know a criminal does not make you one and the fact that he was acquainted with Marxist or Communist supporters does not make him anti-American. You can come to your own conclusions about his character from the individuals he surrounds himself with. This demonstrates how the Liberal media controls what we see and hear and those who have connections or power can escape justice. I ask you not to come to the conclusion of what you have read, but to do your own research to empower yourself.

I will give credit where credit is due; President Clinton did achieve good things while serving as president. He raised educational standards as well as increased the budget for education. This gave schools the opportunity to purchase new computers as well as other learning tools. He had a tough stance on crime and created a drug free zone policy for schools; yet drug abuse in schools continued to increase. President Clinton also cut taxes which helped stimulate the economy and created almost six million jobs. He also dramatically lowered the number of those who were unemployed and even had a part in balancing the budget. I do give credit to President Clinton but you have to realize, most of the credit goes to Reagan economics. You have to understand the results of a president's actions or policies does not have their total effect at that moment or through their administration, but the result of their political decisions will continue for years. It takes time! Small changes in policies can have great affect over long duration of time.

Old industries began to grow once again; opportunities for growth opened up for small businesses, and even new businesses began to rise. There is no doubt that this new growth was spread by Reagan's administration that would carry on through the Bush and Clinton's administration. Personal growth was felt across our nation with higher wages, which helped fuel the economy. The years are limited for our president but their policies and political decisions can carry on for several decades. The wealth that was achieved during the Reagan Administration for major industries had inspired new industries in small towns where new businesses flourished. Pres. Reagan's policies had created a trend of new growth through his political decisions, that continued with new growth for small businesses into the next decade

Creating such growth did not last long. Pres. Clinton's long term policy would have lasting effects and our economy would become crippled. When President Clinton passed the NAFTA treaty I was left in a state of shock and disappointment. President George Bush Sr. paved the way for the NAFTA treaty which I firmly disagreed with from the start. How can there possibly be free trade between nations that do not have a comparable wage, employee rights, or benefits? Is that not rewarding these nations who do not support employee rights? Or use a child labor force? In many nations around the world if an employee was to be injured while working he or she would be responsible for their medical bills and possibly still lose their jobs. What about the nations that violate human rights or force people into slave labor? Committing to such free trade would not only cripple America, but it would be a crime to people around the world. What amazes me is that two presidents would support such an act. How did they possibly expect to compete with such low wages around the world? America the NAFTA treaty has destroyed industrial growth and has left more Americans working for minimum wage. The elite are the primary owners of many of these corporations and has profited immensely on cheap labor at the destruction of the middle class. Our crooked politician's pathway for socialism has empowered and enriched the elite. This grand puppet master hid their agenda through secret organizations or un-American political groups.

You must realize the disadvantage this has put our country in. How would it be possible for our industry to compete with industries around the world with low employee wages? This also opened the door for greed. Small and large industries would uproot the heart of small towns across America. I don't know how President Clinton or Bush can live with the fact they cost millions their jobs while factories moved across oceans. This would also result in towns filing for bankruptcy across America. Even populations in small towns dwindled because families left their hometowns in search of employment. America, we must wake up! The NAFTA treaty was anti-American. Another thing I firmly disagree with was Bill Clinton appointing people with Socialist or Communist background to his cabinet. He also appointed Morton Halperin to National Security Council which he had strong Socialist points of views. Another unpatriotic decision on Clinton's part was appointing Sam Brown as ambassador who had strong Communist ties.

At times Bill Clinton, did seem conservative, especially with him cutting taxes, but his Liberal agenda would not go undone. His policy on redistribution of wealth as well as his policy to help social programs would be revealed. He would raise the bar for those who were receiving earned income credit so more could receive benefits which would cost taxpayers 24 billion dollars. There are many programs I accept as redistribution of wealth such as government housing, Food Stamps, etc. Even these programs should not be permanent. The goal should be to give a hand up, not a hand out. We need to help these people out of poverty not keep them there. Educating and teaching job employability skills would induce confidence and teach the skills needed for today's market. But I firmly disagree with the benefits of earned income credit. This is redistribution of wealth on a massive scale. To take money from one group of people because they are successful and to give to ones that are not is wrong. This act is Socialism. Our government is passing a Socialist style government piece by piece or bill by bill.

While I was a manager, I had several employees who received earned income credit. They bragged about receiving up to seven to eight thousand dollars back from the IRS through earned income credit and other credits. A large percentage was receiving all the taxes they paid in the year while receiving earned income credit as well. This shows that the IRS is nothing more than a tool for our government to redistribute wealth. I have also had employees deny pay raises, promotions, or even asked to have their hours cut in fear they were going to lose their welfare "benefits." Today in our society there are so many people manipulating the welfare system. As a manager, I would attempt to inspire people to be independent and not to depend on government welfare but this message fell on deaf ears as many continued to stay on welfare even if it left them in poverty. I sit back in my chair and try to understand why our government was leaning towards a Socialist style of government. I do not believe that most politicians support a Socialist style of government. Their Socialist or Liberal policies are strangling Democracy and bringing her to her knees little by little. I do wonder at times if American politicians are following a more of a European style government where Socialism has taken over. America, we must realize that this style of government will not work. Today you look at Ireland, Spain, Italy, Greece, as well as many other nations who are collapsing. Their idea of a government ran health care which provides free healthcare for people taking advantage of welfare as well as other social programs are bankrupting Europe. Another thing that I firmly disagree on is the fact Clinton undid the restrictions on abortion that President Reagan had passed. There is no telling how many lives were lost because of this horrific deed.

With the NAFTA treaty, along with other unfair trade agreements, and so many Social Welfare programs making it through the White House has put us on the path for economic collapse. Even at this time, our rights have been stepped on as Americans. This attack on our freedom did not just start with the Clinton Administration. With each administration that has come and gone they have passed bills that have put a stranglehold on our very freedoms and free market. It is easier for law enforcement to attain a search warrant and some government agencies don't even need one to enter your home.

The perversion of the laws that has violated our constitutional rights has led to violations to our privacy and has allowed our government to listen to cell phone conversations. With supercomputers, the government has the ability to know your entire history. The illusion of the Privacy Act that was signed in in 1974 gave the appearance this bill would protect our rights for privacy, but was that not the responsibility of our Constitution. Amendments to our Constitution has violated personal rights. According to the fourth amendment, is illegal to search your property or papers without a search warrant, which is due process. The privacy act has been changed or molded as new amendments dictates our privacy, which is a loss of a right! Who paid for all this control? We, the taxpayers. We have become a society that is paying a large proportion of our income to taxes and today we have to purchase a license or a permit for everything in life. Tell me America are we truly free, besides walking or breathing our government has implemented their control over every aspect in our lives through over taxation's, regulations, or laws that violate our constitutional rights.

Another bill that President Bill Clinton passed was the Fair Housing Act, which would have long term effects on our housing market and banks. Attorney Barack Obama, as well as ACORN had a hand in pushing this bill through. Attorney Barack Obama represented ACORN to pursue legal actions against American banks, for not giving housing loans to lower income families. President Clinton would pass the Fair Housing Act, allowing unsecured loans, or loans with little down payment. President Bill Clinton's attorney general Janet Reno was appointed to put pressure on banks and even threaten them with legal actions. The Clinton administration also put severe pressure on Fannie Mae and Freddie Mac. They were left with no choice as they were pressured to accept unsecured loans. Loans were approved that should have never been accepted. To be bullied in this manner was ignorant on our government's part.

In 1999, President Bill Clinton appointed Franklin Raines who was a member of his administration in command of Fannie Mae. The fact that our government can seize control over a private business or federally regulate it is a disgrace to the free market. This control started with Fannie Mae and Freddie Mac in 1968 where they were regulated by U. S. Department of Housing and Urban Development. America, you must realize this is not a free market when any American business or banks can be bullied to make risky decisions. In many ways, President Clinton had undone many of Ronald Reagan's great deeds and pushed us far into a Socialist style of government.

Another bill that was passed by President Bill Clinton while being supported by Vice President Al Gore and Senator Barack Obama was the mandate to add 10% ethanol to our fuel. I do agree with this bill but common sense must have been absent while they constructed this bill. You must realize that there was already a tremendous amount of stress on farmers who grew corn. This crop provides us with a large variety of different foods such as bread, cereal, and corn syrup. You also find corn in many feeds for livestock animals and even pet foods. This shows the ignorance of our politicians and their inability to conclude the aftermath in passing such a bill. Due to high consumption of corn made products in our country and the burden of the mandatory ethanol bill has put a tremendous strain on our corn crops. By increasing the demand on corn crops Americans would have to pay the price at their local supermarkets. This would increase the price for pork and chicken due to the increasing costs for their feed. Many farmers abandon their hay crops for more lucrative crop in corn, which increased the cost in beef. America, we have to realize how many millions are starving while over 20% of our corn crop goes to making ethanol. I want to know where the experts or the advisers were before passing such a bill. President Bill Clinton should have given incentives or grants for new or existing farmers to expand their farms to prepare for such a demand.

Another huge blunder of the Clinton administration was the selling of technology to China. The selling of supercomputers or the furry chip that NASA had created had given China a huge technological edge. Not only would this become a threat to our economy but America's safety as well. The selling of satellite technology had not only given them the ability to reach the frontier of space but to also send nuclear missiles at any target around the world. How can we possibly have a strong economy or secure borders if we continue to sell or give away our technology?

The Clinton administration was involved in several scandals. The one that seemed to haunt him throughout his administration was the Whitewater Scandal. In 1978, Bill Clinton and Jim McDougal purchased into the Whitewater real estate venture. It was made up of shady deals that horribly treated many of the people who purchased into this deal. If they were late on their payment, even if it was just a few days late, the land would be seized and the title would be returned to Bill and Hillary Clinton and other partners in this financial partnership. It did not matter how close these poor people were to paying off their loan, nor did it matter if their payment history was perfect their land was seized. This unethical way of doing business not only drew media attention but was investigated by Kenneth Stars, who had subpoena Bill and Hillary Clinton's records on these matters. The Clinton's claimed they lost the files, but two years later these files mysteriously appeared in the White House after the suicide of Vince Foster. The files were found in his office and were later sent to their attorney five days later.

President Clinton then requested that Janet Reno seek a prosecutor to investigate this matter in the Whitewater Scandal. Kenneth Starr was then later appointed to investigate this manner. He found that Bill Clinton had exerted pressure on a business partner David Hale so he would make a loan that would benefit Clinton and his other partners from Madison Guaranty. Madison Guaranty loans and savings would then go bankrupt in 1989. You must realize this is a pattern with President Clinton. Even before he was President he was putting pressure on banks as well as savings and loan businesses. Throughout his administration he also put pressure on banks and threatened them with legal actions if they did not approve of risky loans through his Fair Housing Act. Bill and Hillary Clinton continued to indicate they were innocent of the Whitewater Scandal. The investigation also uncovered that an Arkansas bank concealed records showing transactions of Bill Clinton's campaign fund while he was running for governor. Prosecutor Kenneth Starr was then replaced on this investigation by Robert W. Ray. He quickly dismissed the case due to lack of evidence. Several of President Bill Clinton's business partners were either found guilty and sentenced or they were acquitted. The thing that puzzles me the most is why was there such an outcry from the Liberal left as well as the Liberal media to stop this investigation. Even members from the Democratic Party came out and protested to stop this investigation. I do agree there was a lack of evidence but this case seems extremely suspicious. Why did the Clintons not turn over the files? Why were the files claimed to be lost but later found in the White House?

Another scandal that shocked America and the world was the Monica Lewinsky Sex Scandal. He lost the trust of the American public as well as those around the world when he lied about his marital affair. Many people thought we should have impeached President Clinton but many others rushed to his defense. I do think President Clinton should have been impeached but not only for his marital affair but for his policies. President Clinton's poor decisions and reckless policies would devastate America as well as the future administrations far into the next decade including his opportunity to seize Osama Bin Laden. Not only did

Sudan offer to release Osama Bin Laden to our custody we had many opportunities to apprehend him. This would be another mistake America would severely pay for.

Once again America needed a great leader. We needed someone who would come in and undo this madness from the past administrations. The 2000 Presidential elections were a very tough and close election between Republican George W. Bush and Democrat Al Gore. President George Bush Jr. would win this election by a small margin. You have to wonder what would have happened if Al Gore would have won the election. I truly believe it would have been a disaster. Al Gore would have passed more bills for Socialist reform as well as intense environmental laws, which would not only choke the growth of America but destroyed the American economy. I understand this is merely speculation but if you review his history and his stance on environmental issues coupled the fact he served as vice president for President Bill Clinton you could come to this conclusion as well.

Pres. George Bush records was not without blemish either. He became the first president to serve with a criminal record, but the extent of his crimes does not give me a reason to question his morals. When he was young he was arrested for disorderly conduct and had a record for misbehaving. I don't question this because many great leaders have had a history with misbehaving when they were young. The one thing I do question is his membership in the secret organization of Skull and Bones. This is another secretive organization that stretches back to the 1830's. During their long history, they have had many members in high office, such as former presidents of the United States, Presidents of banks, and CEOs of large companies. To be honest this concerns me greatly, for there have been several secretive organizations field with dark agendas. These secretive organizations such as the Freemasons, the Illuminati, and other political organizations have reshaped the world governments through their manipulation. Their thirst is unquenchable for power as they strive to change our society for total control. The words of John F. Kennedy say it best, "In a free society, why is there need for secret organizations?"

For these organizations, be so secretive we must ask a serious question what are they hiding? America, we have submitted our will as we have fallen under the control of the grand architect. The elite has risen as the monster of the world and they have asserted themselves over us all. We must not forget the Illuminati's goal was to abolish religion and to establish a One World Government. Today too many people have surrendered their faith for the will of the elite without knowing. This monster has many tentacles as it operates through many secretive organizations or anti-American political groups. By this time, they have abolished religion in schools while asserting Islamic teaching. For a century, the evil deeds of the elite have gone unnoticed; they infiltrated our education through teaching their own ideology in evolution or socialism. They have spread their own ideology while distorting our own history to destroy patriotism. They monopolize the media through purchasing almost all networks to ensure they control what we hear. Through their manipulation of our own government had assisted in establishing a central bank within our nation to gain control over our banking industry. They have gained control over our economy as well as the world's economy through the NAFTA treaty. America, we must become alert for they have stomp out our voices through bribing our politicians as their path of corruption is smothering our constitutional rights for their thirst for control. The super elite proclaimed a New World Order would be best for humankind because it would end wars and unify all people under one flag. They want to destroy our faith in God by abolishing religion and transferring our faith to humankind. Their goal is to redistribute the wealth around the world, excluding the elite's own wealth.

America, I plead with you to do your own research for the elite has profited immensely through wars from the past and many of these wars were instigated by their own evil intents. This evil plot to unify the world under one flag is to unify the world under a dictator and the abolishment of our faith is an evil plot to transfer our faith to a dictator.

This evil plot is playing out before us all as our freedom has been trampled on by the beasts that has devoured our faith. America, we must take heed for the union of the super elite's dark agenda has merged with socialism and together they have committed their war to take over the world.

President George W. Bush Jr. had accomplished many great things in his life. Not just in education but in his business career as well. He also became part owner of Texas Rangers Baseball team and then became governor of Texas. He was voted very highly as one of the best governors in TIME magazines. While governor of Texas he improved education, and cut taxes which helped improve the economy. He also had a tough stance on crime and the fact he served our country in the military gave me plenty of reason to support him as our next president. President Bush brought prestige and honor back to our capital. He was a firm believer in God and had strong stance on Christian principles. The thing I admired the most about him was the strength he had to stand up for what he believed in and his fearlessness to undo the wrongs of the past. He stood boldly not only to preserve the rights for the people but to save the lives of infants that were inches from birth. In 2003, President George Bush signed in the Partial Abortion Ban Act. I only wish he would have done more to restrict the access to abortions.

America what I am about to tell you, shook my very foundation, cracked the rock I stood upon, and took my breath away. To be honest I never understood what partial abortion was but after doing research I was left speechless. I will now make it clear I am Pro-Life but I do support abortions for medical reasons such as: a woman's life is in jeopardy or there is no way the child will survive. You have to realize if a mother's life is in danger and already has children it would be wrong for anyone to expect her to carry on with her pregnancy. Also in cases of rape or incest I believe it's a victim's choice to carry the baby to full term or terminate the pregnancy. To expect a woman to carry a baby that was conceived from a violent crime is wrong. Demanding such action could create psychological trauma for the mother and it would be wrong to impose that on her. I do understand the argument one horrific crime should not lead to another but it should not be your decision but for the victim to decide.

What I strongly disagree in is those who seek out abortions as a form of birth control. The deception that abortion is a harmless act is not only a lie but a crime. I could use the Bible to argue my point and quote verses such as: "Now the word of the Lord came to me saying, "Before I formed you in the womb I knew you..." (Jeremiah 1:4-5). But sadly, many will choose not to listen and continue in their selfish ways so instead I will seek your humanity. I will tear down the walls so many have fortified their hearts within. I have met so many people in my life that were Pro-Choice yet many did not know the consequences or actions that were taken to abort a baby. The techniques to abort a baby all have the same results. The unborn child suffers a horrible and painful death. One technique is salt poisoning. I will tell you this is no harmless act and how dare anyone declare otherwise. The injection of saline solution into the mother's womb is not only swallowed by the fetus and burns the flesh from the inside out. This horrible act can take up to twenty-four hours and even then, there is a possibility of the infant being born still alive. In many cases the baby is abandoned on the cold table to suffer a lonely painful death.

Another form of this murderous act is suction aspiration abortion. A tube is placed into the mother's womb and literally rips the baby into pieces. I have unfortunately seen the photos of the horrible aftermath. These poor infants did not have a voice to cry out nor can they tell you about their short journey through life. You don't have to hear their little voices to understand this crime. I ask you to do your own research and don't take my word for it. Do not pass this off as a subject you do not want to know about for it is not a subject, it is genocide against our own children. The truth may be painful but will set you free and you will come to the same conclusion. I have reviewed photos and witness those horrors from this form of abortion. I will never be able to escape the horrible image I witness of an aborted infant that was ripped to shreds. I could not make out the form of the little infant nor tell if the baby was a boy or girl but I will never escape the image of a little hand that was reaching out.

President Bush's boldness in standing up against abortionist advocates to ban partial abortion was definitely humanitarian. He became the voice of these tiny infants, and there is no telling how many thousands of lives he saved. For me the idea of Partial abortion to have been legal is unimaginable. It shattered my faith in not only our government but in our society. What I find even more shocking is that so many people were like me and did not know of the procedures that were taking place as we went on through our daily lives. A partial abortion is when a child is inches from birth or even partially born. Before the head is fully out they puncture a hole into the back of the infant's skull and insert a suction tube and remove the brain, then completing the delivery. Women have had mental breakdowns or have even lost the chance to conceive because of these procedures. Through Pres. Reagan administration had passed many restrictions on abortions which were later was appealed by Pres. Clinton.

Throughout my life I have discouraged many women from seeking abortions. One particular case stands out the most. A young woman I went to college with had gotten pregnant and was being pressured by her boyfriend to have an abortion. She came to me for advice and I expressed to her she had a miracle growing within her womb and who knew what destiny held for this child. I then sat down beside her and reassured to her this was not just a problem or an inconvenience but a human being. This case stands out to me because after six years had passed I ran into this young woman and had the opportunity to meet her beautiful five-year-old daughter.

Another incident that helped formed my opinion on abortions came in the form of comment from an extremely liberal professor. There were a few of us debating this issue after class and I heard his closing comment, "It helps weed out the degenerates." Hearing this comment shocked me. I then asked who the degenerates were. He chose not to answer my question as he closed his briefcase and stated "That is all for the day." I understand the arguments of Pro-choice and I do agree it's a woman's body but what about the little infants? For me to judge if a society is humanitarian or civilized is by their actions. By allowing this criminal unjustifiable abomination of abortions to be legal is a violation to humanitarian laws. I deem our society no longer civilized for the mass murder of the defenseless. How can we possibly call ourselves humanitarians if we are slaying the innocent and defenseless? We must realize how precious life is as the cradle of life was created under the mother's heart.

President Bush also rejected Clinton's bill on ergonomic rules which would allow Occupational Safety and Health Administration to regulate and place intense restrictions on all businesses. These intense rules would have shut down most home businesses and would have made it almost impossible for small businesses to compete. It would have even put a large burden on large businesses such as industrial, chemical plants, and factories. America, we must realize that these regulations our government continues to impose on our businesses are crippling our economy. President Bush also killed Clinton's CO2 policies which resulted in an electricity crisis in California. Clinton's liberal policies along with the Environmental Protection Agency restrictions led to the rolling blackouts in California in 2001. The electricity companies pleaded for more time to update their equipment but were repeatedly turned down. California was once a very prosperous state and still is in some ways but the Liberal movement as well as the EPA is bankrupting the state.

America, we must realize how many factories as well as industries have left our country because of the complex regulations and pressure from the NAFTA Treaty and strict rules from OSHA and EPA. I only wish President Bush had the opportunity to challenge more of Clinton's policies. President Bush was met with intense opposition not only from the Democratic Party but the Liberal media for challenging Clinton's policies.

During his administration, many factories were leaving our nation for countries with less restrictions and lower pay wages. Even though companies were leaving President Bush still created jobs in America, and gave incentives for companies to better train their employees. He also passed two of the largest income tax cuts in American history. He also cut capital gain taxes which helped revive our economy. He also raised educational standards and created the No Child Left Behind act. President Bush strengthened our military and signed the largest arms treaty reduction in history with Russia titled The Moscow Treaty.

President Bush did many great things but there is no telling how much more he could have done if it wasn't for the tragedy of 9/11. On September 11, 2001, early in the morning, 19 Al Qaeda terrorists boarded American and United Airlines flights carrying box cutters and knives. These terrorists split up and hijacked four planes with only one agenda: to commit murder on a massive scale. When the first plane hit the twin towers I can still recall where I was at and what I was doing. Like most American's I thought this was an accident. As I wondered how such an accident could occur. The feeling of sorrow and sadness overcame me. When the second plane hit the Twin Towers I was left in disbelief. I was then filled with anger for I knew this was no accident. As I watched this unfold on the news, I was left depressed. I felt so helpless. I wanted to help these people.

To see these poor people, jump from a window to their death to escape the burning buildings or the collapse of the Twin Towers left me heartbroken. I was filled with rage and a strong desire for justice for this was a cowardly act. I then saw the Pentagon had been attacked. It wasn't that fear had gripped me but I couldn't help but to wonder when and where the next attack was. The fourth plane went down in a field in Pennsylvania where several of the passengers had fought to gain control back after hearing what had happened in New York. My heart truly goes out for those brave men and women. Nearly 3,000 innocent people lost their lives to this cowardly act. Even thinking about this today I am still left in disbelief. How many people will never see their love ones come home and how many children will never feel their parents embrace after that horrible day.

I would like to commemorate all the fallen heroes, especially the New York Fire and Police Department. These brave men and women boldly ran into these burning buildings without hesitation. They only had one agenda: to do their job and save lives. New York Mayor Giuliani deserves a lot of credit for his ability to lead and organize rescue efforts and bring order to this chaos. What I find shocking is how fast the liberal media was to blame or criticize President Bush. I truly believe he was left in shock just like the rest of the country was. Another fact was he was gathering intelligence and had to find out who orchestrated this terrible act. In my opinion he made all the right calls. He shut down all airports and created a no-fly zone across our nation. He put the military on alert and ordered jet fighters to patrol our skies. He was in constant contact with Mayor Giuliani while giving resources to aid and rescue. President Bush re-established order in our nation while he reassured that we were safe and justice would be served to those who perpetrated the attack. What I find disturbing is how the Clinton administration did not act when they had the opportunity to arrest Osama Bin Laden. Osama Bin Laden had openly admitted and even took credit for several terrorist attacks and yet the Clinton administration turned a blind eye to the opportunity to bring justice to him. I ask you to do your own research. There are many documented reports on this case. The Sudanese offered to arrest Osama Bin Laden and transport him to America so he could face justice for his crime but the Clinton administration neglected this opportunity. This was a weak and cowardly act on the Clinton administration but the Bush administration would not make the same mistake. He would seek justice for America.

George Bush 9/11 attack speech:

"Thousands of lives were suddenly ended by evil, despicable acts of terror. The pictures of airplanes flying into buildings, fires burning, huge structures collapsing, have filled us with disbelief, terrible sadness and a quiet, unyielding anger. These acts of mass murder were intended to frighten our nation into chaos and retreat. But they have failed. Our country is strong. A great people has been moved to defend a great nation. Terrorist attacks can shake the foundations of our biggest buildings, but they cannot touch the foundation of America. These acts shatter steel, but they cannot dent the steel of American resolve. America was targeted for attack because we're the brightest beacon for freedom and opportunity in the world. And no one will keep that light from shining."

When Pres. Bush called all these terrorist groups evil he was right. They operate by installing fear and the killing of the innocents. It does not matter if they are children or if it's the elderly, they have no heart. Their mission is absolute control. They never dreamed this cowardly act would unify Americans as we boldly cried out no more. It did not bring the American people to their knees like they had hoped but instead we came together as one. So many heroes rushed to the aid of the victims to dig through the rubble to find survivors. I've often heard you can judge a person's character in a moment of crisis. Well in that moment, Americans proved we have a strong character and good morals. We stood shoulder to shoulder with no indifference to the color of skin or religion. We were angry that our own people were attacked in such a manner and the fact that these terrorists entered our nation under false pretenses. America, I do feel like our politicians has failed us and needs to do a better job in screening those who entered our nation. Our government has continuously failed us through the past decades and this tragedy is another example of their failure, for it is the government's responsibility to ensure the safety of all Americans.

Pres. Bush showed tremendous strength while executing two wars at the same time. The strength of our military and its capability were both shown here for the world to see. Afghanistan was liberated from terrorist groups such as Al Qaeda and the Taliban. President Bush's ability to create a collation of nations to not only liberate Afghanistan but Iraq as well was remarkable. Iraq was controlled by an evil dictator who according to intelligence gathered by the US and many other nations had in his possession weapons of mass destruction. Prior to collation forces liberating Iraq, Iraqi pilots were flying mysterious missions to and from Syria. Even after Iraq was liberated Iraqi military pilots came forth and reported that they had taken unknown cargo into Syria. You have to realize Saddam Hussein and his sons were murderous dictators. They killed anyone who opposed them or tortured them severely. They committed horrible crimes against their people and even genocide. Tell me, if Saddam Hussein had no weapons of mass destruction then where did he get the biological weapons he used to kill thousands of his people? The fact that he could commit such a crime against his own people by attacking Kurdish towns in Northern Iraq shows his madness. I do believe this war was justifiable in many ways. Saddam Hussein was a threat to his neighboring countries and even his own people.

America was attacked by the Al Qaeda and the Taliban, and 9/11 was not the first terrorist attack on America. The New York Trade Center was attacked in 1993 by a vehicle loaded with explosives. In 2000, the USS Cole was attacked by a vessel loaded with explosives that killed seventeen U. S. sailors and injured nineteen. Two American embassies were attacked in Africa. Let us not forget how the United States embassy was attacked in 1979 by radicals which triggered the hostage crises. Airlines around the world had been hijacked and unknown numbers had been murdered by these terrorist groups. Even Christians have been beheaded and these radicals' true agenda is to bathe the world in the infidel's blood. They claimed they do not want infidels in their land yet they attempt to spread their radical ideology around the world. What I find shocking is the fact that America helped Al Qaeda free themselves in Afghanistan from the Soviet control and then committed attacks against us. Another thing that baffles me is that there are those in the Liberal movement or media who seem to defend those who believe in radical Islam. This goes to show that there are those that will support any group no matter how radical as long as they stand against America or our values. How else would you explain this? There are no women's rights in many Islamic countries. Women cannot be educated or read their own Bible the Koran. Most Islamic nations will not allow women to show any part of their body except the upper face and their hands. In these countries, a woman is not allowed to drive, vote, or even leave the house without their husband's permission. In some countries, a woman has to carry a note from their husband to show she has permission to be out. Let us not forget what happened in Saudi Arabia where a poor girl was raped and the Arabian court found her guilty and ordered her to be whipped by a cane.

There are horrors being committed today in many Islamic nations against their own people that have Christian beliefs, or those found with a Christian Bible. They are tortured and most are murdered by beheading. One young teenager with Christian faith in Africa was tormented by those with Islamic faith, later he was found crucified to a cross. In my heart, I truly believe that God gave all free will, the right to choose your own path, and for a country or people to dictate your beliefs is wrong. I also do not believe God intended for women to hide their beauty or be subjects to men. The fact that a large percentage of Islamic men do not believe in educating their female population is to assert control over them. I do not believe it is our right to change their beliefs either, it is up to the people of these nations to fight for their own rights. These are serious problems that have been repeated through time. The Catholic Church was bent on religious domination at its conception. One of the reasons the Roman Empire had chosen Catholicism was because it had the same hierarchy as their own government.

Throughout the dark ages of Europe, the church had asserted their control over kingdoms and destroyed other religions through the centuries. They forced whole nations in Europe to kneel before the cross by the sword. Even the American Indians and the Mayans of Mexico met the same fate. The church attempted to control people through biblical manipulation and even burned other biblical books in their attempt for censorship. This was a horror that was committed by the early Catholic Church, but in time we Christians learned the truth. The truth: God is loving and through his love he gave us a precious gift, free will. Even though the war in Iraq and Afghanistan was justified, it is not our right to change their governmental structure or their people's beliefs. As long as America pumps money into these countries through foreign aid or makes them rich by purchasing their oil they will never see the error in their ways. Today our military is scattered throughout this region as our government proclaims it is for democracy and to vanquish the terrorists that are operating within these regions. America, it is time for age of Enlightenment, a time for truth and justice. For well over a century the elite has manipulated and deceived the world for their thirst for power. They have instigated wars to increase their own profitability and through the ages millions were slaughtered for their greed.

The fact that George Bush spent 4 trillion dollars on this military campaign is ludicrous. We built new schools for them and what did we gain from this? So, they can teach their kids Jihad? We rushed to Kuwait's aid but where were we when Georgia pleaded for our help when Russia invaded them in 2008? Georgia was part of the coalition that helped liberate Iraq and Afghanistan. Where was the coalition when they were in need? I do understand why America did not come to the aid of Georgia; it would have ignited World War III. But this did not excuse Russia from invading this nation and committing murder. They lined these poor people up in front of firing squads and still to this day, Russia occupies part of Georgia. I have no doubt that America's oil problem has led us down a path of corrupted and poor political decisions. The fear of the repeat of the 1970's oil crisis has caused America to sacrifice their morals.

I do give Pres. George Bush credit for the Energy Policy he passed but it was not enough and it took far too long. America we should have been looking for new alternative fuel source decades ago. Instead we have allowed our hands to be tied, swallowed our own pride, and sacrificed our own morals. We bribed other nations with foreign aid or border security, and for what? So they can teach hate for America? It is time for America to drill for our own oil. We must not allow the Liberals or EPA to restrict us for if we do not act now we will be placing a terrible burden on our children's future. If we begin today to drill our own oil it could create tremendous revenue which could be poured into research for an alternative fuel source. America, we are responsible for our future, and our actions today will determine what future our children will have. Many have indicated that President Bush has created tremendous debt for our nation from this war, and I do believe the 4 trillion he spent on these wars could have easily paid off our deficit. We can never submit our will through their terroristic threats or attacks, and we must continuously endeavor to protect the safety for every American. I do not agree with all Pres. Bush's policies; in fact, I strongly disagree with his laws that restricted American's freedom. The Patriot Act that Pres. Bush signed in was in violation of our constitutional rights and the fact that he allowed Islamic terrorists to use fear to pervert our constitutional rights is a criminal act. I also strongly disagree with directive 51 that Pres. Bush Jr. signed in to law as an executive order. This gives tremendous power to the executive branch to consolidate all branches a government under presidential authority is ludicrous and is a severe violation to our constitutional rights.

What aggravates me is the Liberal smear campaign that lays all our nation's problems on Pres. Bush administration. It is true that he had the highest bankruptcy in U.S history and during his presidency the Treasury Department had major problems. Two million people lost their jobs and while he was president he cut employee benefits. But like I said almost all of this is propaganda. This smear campaign holds no merit and I implore you to do your own research. The burden of these problems resulted from the incompetent Clinton administration. The highest bankruptcy rate was the result of Clinton's Fair Housing Act. This policy allowed unsure loans for those who did not have the ability or means to pay them off. I don't know if Clinton was intimidated by ACORN or their attorney Barack Obama or maybe he was just in bed with them to. The loss of so many jobs had resulted from Clinton's NAFTA treaty. Let us not forget how he appointed Franklin Raines to oversee Freddie Mae and Fannie Mac, which was later uncovered that Franklin Raines was falsifying reports so he could collect millions in bonuses.

The Clinton administration also appointed Janet Reno to put pressure on banks and threaten them with legal action if they did not accept unsecured loans. The fact that two million people lost their jobs was a direct result of the NAFTA Treaty. In towns across east Tennessee many factories have closed their doors and moved over seas. The people that worked in these factories were not the only victims of this bill. This put a tremendous burden on the surrounding businesses who lost revenue due to the factories closing their doors. Pres. Bush was also forced to cut unemployment benefits because of the sheer number of people with drawing form unemployment. President Bush made tremendous efforts to recover America from the Clinton administration. There is no telling how many more millions of jobs would have been lost if the Bush's administration's efforts had not succeeded. If he had allowed Clinton's CO2 bill or OSHA's regulations, it would have crippled America beyond belief. We must realize the mistakes of one administration such as the incompetence of Bill Clinton can place a tremendous burden on the next administration. We cannot correct the mistakes of our past unless we analyze them first. I have no doubt America will wake up and place the problems that we are facing today where they belong.

President Bush may have not been our greatest President but he faced many difficulties and did the best he could have. I have doubt that one day in our future we will accurately record our history. We will analyze the decisions and policies of each administration and learn from these mistakes. America was still in desperate need for a great leader one who would end the bureaucratic madness in Washington. One who would strengthen our economy and was willing to restrict destructive bills that were passed such as the NAFTA treaty. We needed someone who was willing to stand up to the EPA and OSHA and remove the governmental leash that restricted growth in our nation.

The 2008, Presidential Election was indeed a campaign for change. Senator Barack Obama won the Democratic Primary for his bid for President and chose Joe Biden as his running mate. Barack Obama started his career as a civil rights attorney and then became senator and served for Illinois for twelve years. Joe Biden was a Senator for Delaware with thirty-six years of experience in politics. Senator Barack Obama campaigned on change. He declared that no more bills would be signed behind closed doors. He promised transparency in our government and the passing of the Universal Healthcare Plan. He also campaigned on his strategy on taxing the rich and cutting taxes on the poor. He pledged to remove our military forces from Iraq and Afghanistan and shut down Guantanamo Bay in Cuba.

His opponent John McCain won the Republican Primary and chose Governor Sarah Palin as his running mate. John McCain retired as a captain from the Navy. Not only was he a war hero but spend five years in a Vietnam prison camp. I would like to commend John McCain for his strength and strong morals. When the North Vietnamese found out that John McCain's father was a high-ranking officer, they attempted to offer him a deal for early release. John McCain knew they would use this as propaganda against the United States so he refused to bargain with them because it would violate the military Code of Conduct. Because of his decision he was severely beaten and tortured but still he did not break. After retiring from the Navy, he became senator of Arizona where he would eventually accumulate twenty years of experience in politics. Sarah Palin was governor of Alaska where she had a tough stance on crime and raised educational standards. She improved the Alaskan economy and by the time she was running for Vice President she had been in politics for sixteen years. I also would like to give credit to Sarah Palin because not only was she the youngest governor elected in the state of Alaska but she was the first female governor. Personally, I think she had more experience than Senator Obama or Senator McCain because of the fact, that she was a state governor. Senator McCain and Governor Palin's strategy was to make America more independent by drilling our own oil and finding alternative fuel sources. They wanted to cut taxes to help American families and strengthen the economy. They had an intense job growth plan. Senator McCain had pledged to work with farmers and reduce the ethanol mandate that was set by the Clinton Administration. He pledged to include members of the Democratic Party in his administration and put country over party. He also pledged to work with other countries to catch child pornographers and he had a strong stance on Pro-life.

The 2008 elections were one of the worst smear campaigns I had ever seen. The Liberal media as well as the Democratic Party seemed to focus more attention on Sarah Palin then John McCain. Many indicated that John McCain made a huge mistake by selecting Sarah Palin as his running mate. I firmly disagreed. Sarah Palin cut millions in taxes as governor in Alaska. Many Americans made the mistake of listening to this smear campaign and even Obama was part of this attack when he called John McCain and Sarah Palin liars. It is true that Sarah Palin is Pro-life. She strongly believes in the second amendment to bear arms. She has strong Christian principles and for her family to be attacked in this manner was ridiculous. The Liberals turned against Sarah Palin because she was a conservative female; whatever happened to the right to be? I believe this was a deliberate attempt by the Obama campaign to take the focus off of John McCain and put it on Sarah Palin.

You did not hear John McCain or Sarah Palin change their stance on important issues but Obama changed his stance many times on many issues. I believe Senator Obama was watching how Americans stood on these issues and made changes accordingly. This was an important election for two reasons: this was the first time we ever had a black man run for president and the first time a woman run as Vice President. Another thing that shocked me was how the media gave more air time to Barack Obama than John McCain. We must no longer allow the media to manipulate or persuade our vote. President Barack Obama did indeed win the 2008 Presidential election which was a huge milestone for America because he was the first black man elected as president but was he the best candidate?

First we must ask, is President Obama a natural born citizen? If so, then why did Barack Obama refuse to release his birth certificate and other vital records? What did he have to hide and why was there so much secrecy? There is evidence that questions and supports President Barack Obama's eligibility to serve as our president. The one thing that frustrates me, as well as leaves me confused is President Obama's legitimacy to serve as our President. I have heard the both sides of the argument and it seems the more I hear from each side the more puzzled I become. There are statements that allege President Obama's birth certificate is fraudulent, and the fact that it does not have a state seal supports this. I find this hard to believe. How can someone reach so high in office without receiving an intensive background check? The fact that President Obama traveled to Pakistan in 1991 raises several red flags for me. It would have been impossible for President Obama to have had an American passport and traveled to Pakistan because during this time Americans were not allowed to travel there. He must have had a British passport because at the time Kenya was still under British rule.

Another statement that I find compelling is the fact that Barack Obama received financial aid as a foreign student. If this statement has any truth to it, then President Obama is either not a citizen of the United States or he has committed fraud. To tell you the truth I do not care for those who bring assumptions but I side with facts that can be proven. The problem with our current media outlets is the misrepresentation of facts and allegations. I have seen the Liberals and Liberal media stretch the truth or right out lie. When Bill Clinton was being investigated, the Liberal left came out boldly in his defense without having any facts. The Liberal media spent very little time investigating alleged criminal activity that went on during Bill Clinton's time as governor of Arkansas. During Bush's administration, there is plenty of evidence that shows he cut taxes across the board (for everyone) yet the Liberal media claims he only cut taxes for the rich. They may argue and say they are only bending the truth but any attempt to deceive the American public is a lie. America, I know for many of you this sounds shady but it's not just a question of is he American by birth but is he American by heart? Where is his stance on a Democratic government and does he believe in the free market?

I know during his campaign he claimed his mother Ann Dunham was a conservative from Kansas. America this was a lie. Not only did his mother hangout with Marxists she was a Communist supporter. Ann Dunham met Barack Obama's father, Barack Obama Sr. at a Russian class at the University of Hawaii. Many have indicated that Barack Obama's father is a Muslim. America that is irrelevant. It is not our place to judge for God gave humankind free will and let us not forget one of our foundational American principles: freedom of religion. What is relevant is the fact that anyone can be influenced by their environment and the fact that his father is a Communist supporter could have had devastating effects on President Obama's political views.

Another impact on his political views was his mentor Frank Marshall Davis. America, I plead with you for the sake of our future do your own research! This mentor, Frank Marshall Davis was a member of CPUSA (Communist Party USA). Not only has the FBI released files indicating his Communist ties our Federal government has placed him on a security list. Wake up! This is our President's mentor and he is a security risk to our nation? President Obama's mentor, Frank Marshall Davis, or how our President refers to him as Frank in his book had plans to dismember our government to change our political structure and to usher in a one world order. My question is why is there such a strong connection between those who support a Marxist ideology to those who support Communist.

The reason for this is, there is very little difference between the two. Even these groups have ties to the Socialist movement. The very thing that solidifies these groups, such as IPS, SDS, CPUSA, is simple: the enemy of my enemy is my friend. In the 1960's these organizations plotted for revolution. However, they underestimated the strength of America. They then plotted to infiltrate our government. To not only dismantle our very foundation but to bankrupt this nation through careless spending, social welfare programs, and by creating intense taxes along with governmental regulations that would smother our economic system. America do not listen to the Liberal media or the Liberal politicians for you are seeing through their eyes what they want you to see. America, I ask you to not only do your own research but remember what you have seen through the Clinton administration. The NAFTA Treaty pushed American industries to move across seas. The intense OSHA and EPA regulations choked industry growth and less intense taxing to support a corrupt welfare system has destroyed the middle class.

Before your very eyes the road is being paved for you will no longer see a Democratic government. I ask you: is this your choice? Where were we when these decisions where being made that have so drastically put us on this path? If we continue our present course what style of government will replace our once free nation? Even though we are facing three enemies: Socialism, Marxism, and Communism only one will emerge. But then again don't they aim for total control? If President Obama's father and mother supported Communism as well as Marxism and his mentor Frank Marshall Davis was a member of the CPUSA which endorses him, then where does that leave President Obama's political stance?

A good clue would be to understand more about his mentor. I urge you to look into his book The Communist: Frank Marshall Davis: The Untold Story of Barrack Obama's Mentor by Paul Kengor. To get a better understanding of who President Obama is, you could look into the two books he has published, The Audacity of Hope and Dreams of my Father but I urge you to check the facts. The one thing I did find was the fact President Barack Obama lied about his father being a simple goat herder and his mother being a Conservative. What was the purpose? I believe the purpose was to deceive the American public. By projecting himself as coming from a poor background he was seeking sympathy from the American public. It is also obvious that President Obama projected his mother as a Conservative to mislead Americans into believing he came from a Conservative background. By him misleading the American public, as well as hiding his Marxist and Communist upbringing you must question the moral fabric from which he came from. You must also realize that his character could have been shaped by outside forces but with even saying this I still find reasons to be concerned how his mentor had influenced Pres. Obamas life. Another thing that must have shaped his life was the fact that President Obama attended a black separate church under Jeremiah Wright. America, we need a leader to bring all nationalities together for we have been divided for far too long. Throughout my life, I have tried to be fair and balanced, and I know it appears that I have brought up a lot of bad history on Bill Clinton and President Barack Obama, but I can only give the facts. I have always been an avid news watcher. In fact, my favorite news channel was CNN and then later FOX News. To tell you the truth for many years I was left confused. I have watched the news of Bill O'Riley as well as Rush Limbaugh and then I would watch the Liberal news channel and I would find myself very confused from all the contradictions.

Throughout the years, the fighting between the Democrats and Republicans in Congress and Senate was ridiculous. Their Senate responsibilities were to serve the needs of the people not their own interest. The show that seemed to change my life was the Glenn Beck show. He was a bit eccentric but he gave hard facts. The very thing that I heard him say was, "Don't take my word for it. Check the facts for yourself!" And this I did. America, it is easy to get overwhelmed with the propaganda that the media distorts and trying to interpret truth from lie is difficult. In the past, I have heard many conspiracy theories. Many of them have indicated that there are organizations working behind the scenes, attempting to change or control Washington. For me a conspiracy theory without facts is just a theory. Watching the Glenn Beck show helped me connect the dots of organizations working from behind the scenes to not only control Washington but to manipulate or deceive the people. This brings me back to Richard Nixon. Why was it so important for him to send five men to break into the Democratic National Headquarters? Surely they do not expect us to still believe it was to steal campaign secrets. The better question is why the thousands of hours of secret recordings have not been released to the public as well as the documents that were seized.

America once again, I am not big on theories, but to see so many of our government officials today connected to Socialist or Marxist parties and even Communist groups gives me reasons to worry. Concluding that SDS, IPS, or CPUSA is not a threat when you look at their agenda is outrageous. I truly believe that Richard Nixon and his administration were about to uncover something big. Also, let us not forget, even John F. Kennedy spoke out against Communist groups in our nation. America, we must not only focus on President Obama's past with all that is going on today it is too easy to get mixed up with the debates on his birth certificate. We must not delude ourselves with theories of who his father is or if he is connected to a Socialist or Communist group. We must not be distracted! We must see what his true agenda is for America. If we envelop ourselves with the madness of his past for his intentions for our future shall go undetected. In 1993, attorney Barrack Obama was hired in as a junior associate for Minor, Barnhill & Galland. A majority of his cases were civil rights and he aided voter registration. Attorney Barrack Obama had strong ties to ACORN which would eventually lead to a lawsuit against Citibank as well as other banks to lower their standards for lending practices. Attorney Barrack Obama at this time played a strong hand in pushing Bill Clinton through his administration to pass the Fair Housing Act. I have no doubt that this played a huge role in the debt crises of 2008. The Fair Housing Act not only bankrupted banks but it had a devastating effect on Wall Street which plunged America into a recession. We must ask ourselves what was President Obama's agenda as an attorney to push banks for legal action to take such unsecured loans?

During this time President Obama was connected to many shady characters such as Bill Ayers and Bernardine Dohrn who were both founding members of Weather Underground. America, you must not forget the terrorist attacks that were committed by this Communist organization. Neither Bill Ayers nor Bernardine Dohrn have retracted their Communist statements or believes. There have been allegations that he has been a member of the KGB and both Bill Ayers and Bernardine Dohrn were placed on the FBI's most wanted list. Neither will serve time for their bombings against America but instead were left to continue to spread their propaganda and incite violence and help other organizations such as SDS. Bill Ayers believed in order to create a fundamental change the Left must infiltrate our schools and spread propaganda through the public. He also believes to create social change they must incite violence at street level. His intent is to change the political structure of America.

I find this man completely selfish and arrogant. Has he ever communicated with the American people and truly listened to their needs and wants? I do not believe that the majority of Americans want our governmental structure changed into a Communist style government. So how can he force his points of views on us all? I will give you the very words of Bernardine Dohrn, "The majority of people who are activists have stayed the course in a way or various ways. Devoted to over throwing everything hateful about this government's corporate structure"

I urge you to pay attention to her comment. In the part that she says," The majority of the people who are activists have stayed the course in a way or various ways..." This statement clearly shows that America is being attacked on many fronts. She boldly expresses her passion to overthrow our hateful government or corporate structure. I ask you to look around. Is this not what's happening today? America how have we allowed this injustice to be done to ourselves and future generations? I will be the first to admit that there needs to be changes in our government but many of the changes that need to occur are to undo the madness the Liberal left has created. They call our nation the evil empire; the very nation that gives us the rights of freedom of speech and religion. Our nation protects all of our rights as citizens and in fact there is no other nation that has more laws in place to protect its citizens than our own. America is the birthplace of dreams where the market is free and most important we have the freedom to vote for our leaders. But even these precious gifts that were bestowed upon us by our forefathers are being eroded away. The very fact that President Obama became the State Senator of Illinois with his questionable background which included a circle of Communist friends is shocking.

In fact, this road was paved by them as well as State Senator Alice Palmer. Senator Palmer also supported the Communist Party and was an executive board member of CPUSA. Like Glenn Beck has said, don't take my word for it, research it! For I have no doubt that you will come to the same conclusion as I have. Bill Ayers not only donated campaign money to President Obama when he was running for Senator of Illinois but he even used his own house to throw a campaign fundraising party. I am attempting to not dwell on these facts but I cannot ignore them. There is a pattern which is very clear. You must not only do your own research but you must conclude where this evidence is taking America's future.

As a State Senator President Obama was negligent by either not being present to vote or marking present which implies he did not vote at all. He kept a firm Liberal stance when he voted four times against protection for babies that were born alive after an abortion procedure. As I sit here my heart cries out to all those innocent babies that were abandoned on the table left to die. I feel a rage that burns deep within me for in my beliefs no human being could commit such a cold and heartless act. Even animals do not commit to such horrible acts. I can only conclude those who commit this horrendous deed are evil. I will argue with anyone who will attempt to tell me that President Obama voting four times against this bill was doing it for women's rights. If he was so concerned for women's rights, then tell me why he did not support or even vote for the protection of rape victim's records to be sealed from the public following criminal conviction?

President Obama would quickly go from State Senate to Federal Senate. He helped pass bills for environmental laws, which I do support the EPA but with common sense. You cannot pass laws that will choke economic growth or even put farmers out of work. This has been happening for several decades and has even deprived the California farmers from watering their crops. We all remember how Democratic Senator Dianne Feinstein deprived the farmers in California of water in order to save a fish called the Delta Smelt. I do feel it is our responsibility to be good stewards of the Earth but I ask what happened to the once innovative nation who could solve these problems? America for a long time we have not utilized our resources correctly. We have crippled our growth with intense regulations through the EPA as well as OSHA and allowed government spending to get out of control.

I also support the bills he has helped pass to giving aid to veterans, especially homeless ones. America, it is heart breaking for me as I am sure it is terrible for you to see men and women who so courageously protected our freedoms to go without proper shelter. I believe we must do a better job for those who have served our nation such as job placement skills or even the opportunity for a higher education or attend a trade school. You can continuously give aid month after month or year after year and still these men and women will be left in poverty. The goal should be to give a hand up not a hand out and to give them the confidence to be proud once again as we are proud of them.

President Obama as Senator aided in passing 125 bills for social welfare programs. America if we continue to pass more social welfare programs and the number of those on welfare continue to increase then we are not solving the problem. I'll say it again, a hand up, not a hand out! We must learn to find new ways to create new jobs in this nation and not give away our technology. Another thing you must remember is the fact that Marxist groups from the 1960's as well as Communists have claimed they will break America from within. I ask you to do your research in this matter and ask yourself if they are truly helping those in poverty or are they just keeping them there? Many organizations have told single mothers to not get married because they will lose their benefits. I, myself, have had employees tell me to cut their hours so they would not lose their benefits. Let me get the facts straight, welfare is not a benefit. We must strive to raise the living standards of everyone but to take money from the wealthy because they are successful is wrong. How can we possibly become a society that punishes those who are successful?

If you look at President Obama's record as a Senator, it is like he was paving the way for a presidency. I believe his attack on Senator Hillary Clinton for supporting George Bush after 9/11 was to throw himself into the spotlight. Many Democrats supported George Bush Jr's decision after the 9/11 attack. You have to ask yourself: why would he attack Senator Clinton? I truly believe it was because she was well known. You also have to look at many of his stances when he was serving as a senator. Even though many could see his Liberal stance he often attempted to portray a conservative side. I believe he reached out to the veterans to gain their support. He also claimed he supported gay marriage or even a pathway for illegals to become citizens. During his campaign for presidency he accused Senator John McCain of changing his stance on important issues when, in reality, it was him who had changed his stance. Let us also not forget how he portrayed his mother as conservative and his father as a goat herder. I believe President Obama is a great deceiver and as a senator he held back his true agenda but as our next president his true agenda would be revealed.

America, this book is not just about one president or someone who is serving in our Legislative Branch nor is it about the Democratic or Republican Party. It's about the direction we are heading and the choices we have made. I attempted not to dwell on small issues but on large issues that have had a profound effect on America. I realize that there is deception in our government and our media as well. If you were to go on the internet, you would find that the majority of sites praise President Barack Obama. Even most media networks praise this man as if he could do no wrong. They claim he has restored America's prestige, raised educational standards and brought many out of poverty. They cheer him on for passing Universal Healthcare and passing intense environmental laws. They also accredit him for saving Wall Street and slowing down the recession. They glorify his actions in saving the banks with his massive bailouts.

America, I urge you to do your own research because the truth is out there. We must realize that there are many organizations that are spreading their propaganda and have one true agenda. In the past several decades there has been many laws that have been created that have corrupted our government. From the Liberal media, you will hear a lot about the corruption in the Republican Party. It is true many of the Republicans seem to serve their own agenda or serve to the interest of big business. The truth is that both parties are corrupt. With the lobbying going on in Washington from corporate elite and the massive amounts of money they pour into campaigns funds has resulted to the people losing their voice in Washington. I will prove the Democrats are equally guilty with one fact. In 2010 General Electric profited 14.2 billion dollars while paying no federal taxes. Not only did GE CEO Jeffrey Immelt receive huge tax breaks, Pres. Obama hired him as his business advisor. How can President Obama appoint Jeffrey Immelt as his business advisor when he has out sourced thousands of jobs overseas? CEO Jeffrey has built GE factories overseas as the cost of losing nearly 35,000 jobs in America.

We must realize that, as long as lobbying is legal in Washington or corporations can pour large quantities of money into campaign funds, we will continue to have corruption within our political system. What I find disturbing is how our politicians have become puppets for the corporate elite and make no mistake America as the grand puppet master pulls their strings for total control. There is a darker agenda at hand and if we do not awaken we will be led like sheep to our demise.

There is a movement within organizations that have infiltrated the Democratic Party such as IPS, SDS, and CPUSA. The Liberal media seem to turn a blind eye to these organizations or maybe they are controlled by them as well. The truth is that there are many organizations that are pulling the strings such as MDS (Movement for Democratic Society), and Media Matters. But there are still ways to get to the truth. You can research News Max or go in depth and research our government records such as governmental reports. I also urge you to look into these organizations: IPS, SDS, and CPUSA for they are not secretive about their agenda. Either they believe we are not taking them serious or we as a nation have fallen asleep. I do not believe that most Americans do not care what happens to our country but I do believe most Americans have become too enveloped in their daily lives and simply do not pay attention.

America, we must wake up. Before our very eyes the groundwork that has established our nation is being torn apart stone by stone and is being replaced by socialism. We have even had politicians who have commented we are now a socialist society. The Liberal and Socialist movement may praise Obama for his Liberal achievements but I ask you: are these the changes you voted for? America, take another look for these bold movements will not only change our political structure but their form of social welfare is a tool for redistribution of wealth that will eventually bankrupt our nation. When Obama first took office, he promised transparency yet his first major bill, Universal Health Care, was passed behind closed doors. What baffles me is how our senates could pass such a bill without reviewing its contents. I ask you America: would you sign a contract without reading it first? Then why should senators be allowed to do the same? They have neglected their responsibility to the American people. I will never forget Democrat senator Nancy Pelosi's comment: *"We have to pass the health care bill so that you can find out what is in it."*

Senator Pelosi you have neglected your responsibility to represent the American people. America this is going to cost us 1.5 trillion dollars just in the next decade. It is not just the burden that this will put on the taxpayers, but the consequences of the quality of health care we will receive. America was once a leader but today it seems we follow Europe's lead. We can easily look at Europe today and see what will happen to America's health care quality in the future. The quality of healthcare in Europe has decreased significantly, patients may wait long durations to receive treatment. Something that truly disturbed me is that that there was a council hidden in President Obama's healthcare plan. What is the purpose of this council: The Federal Coordinating Council for Comparative Effective Research? Many have argued that this will raise health care premiums but I have no doubt that taxes will be raised dramatically to offset the health care cost. Obama's healthcare plan is also another form of redistribution of wealth. Those who are making fifty thousand dollars or more will be responsible for this bill. Low income families will receive tax credits that will cover the majority of the health care cost. Even those who are unemployed will receive tax credits to cover the cost of their health care. America this is punishing those who are successful once again.

For those who decide not to participate in Obama Care, they will be fined a penalty and families can be fined up to $2000 for not having insurance. Tell me America are we truly a free society when our government can mandate their policies and demand us to buy their product? I would also like to know who would benefit from the fines of those who refuse Obama care. The government cannot give anything away unless it's taken away from somebody else. You must also realize the financial burden this will put on our businesses as well as industries. They are already overwhelmed from over taxation and governmental regulations. Businesses will have no choice but to lower their number of full time employees and increase their number of part-time employees to offset the healthcare cost. Increasing the number of part-time employees will increase the number of people receiving social welfare. This will result in more people living in poverty and being dependent on our government. America, the reality is our government could truly afforded healthcare for everybody by unify our health care under one universal plan.

America our government spends a tremendous amount of wealth on healthcare at taxpayer's expense every year. We spend well over $1 trillion every year for Medicare, Medicaid, and Veterans Care. This does not include the enormous cost of Obama Care. The problem is the uncontrollable spending in our government and the out of control corruption in healthcare industries. I call it the inverted pyramid, where the revenue is absorbed from the top through corruption and we the people are at the bottom. It does not take a mathematician to understand this. The onslaught of year after year governmental out of control spending continues with over 1 trillion dollars spent on welfare in the year 2011. America, you must realize that it is impossible to spend one trillion dollars in one year on welfare. There are one hundred million Americans receiving welfare. I ask you to do the math and divide one trillion by one hundred million. According the U.S Census Bureau, 49% of all homes in America have at least one person receiving government assistance. Since President Obama has been in office there has been a dramatic jump in those receiving welfare and social security benefits. In fact, one out of three Americans is receiving some form of welfare and since he has been in office 6 million more people are under the poverty line.

Another blunder of Obama's administration that has cost taxpayers nearly 3 billion dollars, was his program Cash for Clunkers. This was a program to get gas guzzlers off the road by offering people five thousand dollars in trade in value for their cars. This is another form of redistribution of wealth where most middle class or upper class vehicles were worth more than the five thousand dollar's trade in value. There was no incentive to buy American made cars through his program; in fact, over half the cars sold through this program were from foreign countries. If President Obama truly wanted to create jobs in America he would have excluded all foreign cars and if he was an environmentalist, as he says he is, then why did he not instead give tax credit for environmental friendly cars? I do give Obama credit for lowering the unemployment rate but you must realize if six million more Americans found themselves in poverty through his administration then this is the result of more Americans taking lower paid jobs. With lower paid jobs, this could contribute to the reason why there are more Americans receiving welfare. You also have to realize that many Americans have given up on looking for work and have turned to drawing their social security which would offset the unemployment numbers. Many Democrats, as well as those in the Liberal movement and Liberal media, have given President Obama credit for pulling us out of a debt crises or slowing down the recession. I've even heard President Obama tell the American people that our economy is going through a recovery. President Obama's plan was simple. He simply threw money at the problem and referred to it as a bailout.

We were facing a mortgage crisis when Obama spent 700 billion dollars to keep banks from going under. He also bailed out the auto industry with 33 billion dollars to General Motors. This was no solution to the major problems we were facing. In fact, what he has done is passed this tremendous debt onto our children. Is he not neglecting his responsibility by passing this off to our children? Throwing money at this massive debt crisis and calling it a cure is not a cure. America is still hemorrhaging from out of control government spending. President Obama's massive bailout plan will cost American taxpayers 1.5 trillion dollars. The purpose for President Obama receiving the bailout funds was to ease the financial stress of mortgages. Instead banks used these funds to buy out other banks. America, not only was Congress lied to but we were lied to as well. However, President Obama is used to lying to the people. President Obama blamed George Bush for the financial crises of 2008 as well as the collapse of the housing market. America let us not be deceived. The very fact that President Obama has the audacity to project the blame on George Bush is ridiculous. This blame lies on his shoulders and his partner Bill Clinton. Do not forget it was Bill Clinton who passed the Fair Housing Act due to the pressure he was receiving from ACORN and their attorney Barack Obama. I ask you to look up these facts for yourself and for those who have access to these records make them public for it was President Obama as an attorney who was suing banks to lower their standards for home loans. This resulted in the highest bankruptcy outbreak in America's history. Unfortunately, President Obama's out of control spending would not end with his bailout plan. His idea of creating green jobs cost taxpayers 90 billion dollars. Such as:

Sun Power 1.2 billion
Bright Source 1.6 billion
Thompson River Power 6.5 million

In fact, there are over thirty companies that Obama has given money through his green job program that are either facing bankruptcy or are facing financial troubles. An example is Solyndra who received 535 million dollars and filed bankruptcy a year later. President Obama's stimulus plan ended up costing American taxpayers 2.5 trillion dollars. To keep up with this out of control spending our government is borrowing more money from foreign countries and our Federal Reserve is printing more money to keep up with the demands of Obama's spending. There is a horrible consequence to this madness due to the Federal Reserve printing more money; it has greatly depreciated the value of the dollar. This will also increase the cost of living for all Americans while receiving less pay for the dramatic tax increase. I ask you: how it is going to be possible for America to pay off our tremendous debt along with Obama Care?

Since President Obama has been in office the world has taken notice to America's financial problems, which resulted to Egan-Jones lowering America's credit standing from an "AA" to an "AA -." America this is the second time our credit standing has been lowered since President Obama has been in office. America's credit standing has never been lowered through any administration before and you must realize by the lowering of America's credit standing will increase the interest that we will have to pay on our debt. I call out for the people to take notice; no other president has raised our deficit six trillion dollars in one term. This is equivalent to President Obama raising our deficit 1.5 trillion per year. I do realize that many American's understand that we are on the wrong path, but if your voice is silent no one will hear you cry out. It is urgent for us to come together, for it will be foolish for us to wait for the elections of 2016. We must realize what Pres. Obama's true agenda is; while many have indicated they believe he is trying to destroy America, others say he is trying to save our country. No matter what his true agenda is; America is falling. This could be easily indicated by the millions that has fallen into poverty; nor can you ignore the fact that one third of all Americans are on some form of governmental assistance today.

We have to realize that President Obama is managing the debt crises in a destructive way. I do agree we cannot allow the banks to go under but the 70 billion dollars was unnecessary. This debt crisis should have been managed in an entirely different way. We should have used incentives for companies to expand or better train their employees. Repairing our infrastructures is another way we could have created a massive amount of jobs that would have truly stimulated our economy. America, we must realize that every time a new industry goes up, it helps the surrounding businesses. By repairing our infrastructure would put many construction workers back to work. By stimulating growth within our middle class our economy would have rebounded by now. President Obama did the opposite. He poured money into banks, Wall Street, and risky investments such as green jobs. If that wasn't enough, Obama also invested half a billion dollars to a car company to make cars in Finland while thousands of Americans were unemployed.

It wasn't just President Obama's bad economic policies that upset me but the fact that he brought his circle of friends or comrades into the White House. These included Van Jones an alleged racist and self-admitted communist as his advisor for green jobs. Van Jones has made several racial comments and for an example I would like for you to review some of the content of one of his speeches in January 2008:

"And the white polluters and the white environmentalists are essentially steering poison into the people of color community because they don't have racial justice frame." -January 2008

Another statement from Van Jones: *"Only suburban white kids shoot up schools; you've never seen a Columbine done by a black child."*

This is a statement by Van Jones that shows his communist beliefs:

"I met all these young radical people of color, I mean really radical, communists and anarchists. And it was, like, 'This is what I need to be a part of. I spent the next ten years of my life working with a lot of those people I met in jail, trying to be a revolutionary. I was a rowdy nationalist on April 28th, and then the verdicts came down on April 29th. By August, I was a communist."

I know that such comments are shocking, and most of you have heard these comments by Van Jones. The question that needs to be answered is why President Obama would bring someone into his administration that openly admits he/she is communist. America, this was no accident. President Obama has brought both Communist and Socialist representatives into the White House such as:

- Anita Dunn- Obama's White House Communication Director (Communist)
- Carol Browner- Communication Energy Adviser (Communist)
- Ron Bloom- Manufacturing Czar (Communist)
- Elizabeth Warren- head of Consumer Financial Protection Bureau (Communist)
- Donald Berwick- Medical Care (Communist)

America, when I first started looking into Obama's past, I question his character and even his morals. I wonder what type of government he would truly stand for because the very fact his mentor was communist and even members of his family supported communism. He surrounded himself with these friends, who were communist, Marxist, and socialist; giving me great concern. The fact that there are those who are serving our nation in the White House who support Communism or are members of CPUSA is alarming. I call out for you to stand up and be heard, for I sound the alarm because America is under siege! When was the last time the people were truly represented? When did we vote to change our nation from a Democratic to a socialist or communist style of government? President Obama I question your ability to lead the people as a president for not only are you corrupting our government but you are eroding our Constitutional rights.

President Obama I also question your ability to represent all people. What did you mean when you commented, "the typical white person?" From what I have seen, white people can be as a diverse as any other race. Another comment that I question is, "white CEOs living in suburbs who do not want to pay for inner city schools." President if you have not noticed there are black CEO's living in suburbs as well as Hispanics and other races. Comments like yours and Van Jones, as well as from other Liberals, and Liberal media, are racially dividing our country. But to tell the truth this is their intention! If we allow this plot to continue, a racially divided country can be easily molded into a dictator style of government, without us ever seeing the treachery that will eventually grip us all.

America, we must realize the more a society becomes rebellious, that fuels rioting will only result to the tighter the grip of the government. I question the motives of these crooked politicians, secretive organizations, and the media for inciting civil unrest. Those with evil intent are seeking out their agenda through dividing the people through racial division and feeling the people with hate for one another. They spread their hate like a dark cloak over our nation causing division between the poor and the middle to upper class. I tell you America the working poor class, middle class and upper middle class works hard for their money, the true evil that seems to escape all this criticism is the super elite, who have taken money from everyone throughout the world. America, we can no longer be divided by religion, party nomination, race, gender or by age, for we must all come together to save our nation.

What happened to serving the people? Truthfully I believe you had your own agenda. My next question is for the Liberals, socialist movement, and for those who support the Marxist idea. Have you ever thought if America fell to a communist style of government what would then happen to the EPA? The leading communist, China practically has no EPA and produces more pollution than any other country. The majority of China's power comes from burning coal. The better question is what would happen to the people's rights and employee rights because in a communist nation where there are none. For those who support a socialist style of government turn your eyes towards Europe. America there has never been a nation where the people have more rights than in America. The Liberal left is pushing for redistribution of wealth but let me ask you: how are we supposed to redistribute the wealth? I tell you, you cannot bring the poor into prosperity by moving the wealthy out of prosperity.

2,000 years ago, Rome had to make a law that it was illegal to quit your job. Rome too had a form of welfare, where their people were receiving food or free bread, while the working-class was overtaxed. The greed of the Roman aristocrats and through over taxation had literally bankrupt their empire. More and more Romans lined up for free food or governmental assistance. The same thing is happening in Europe. You must understand human nature, if there is a choice to work for your living or receive a free living; a great deal of people will choose free living at the expense of those working. Those who are on welfare or other governmental assistance are reaping the benefits of those who have labored. The question is, where is the breaking point for such a society that rewards those who chooses not to work?

This is another indication why socialism, Marxism, or communism could not work in our country. It destroys the middle class and leaves them in poverty. Also for those who support animal rights, do you honestly believe that a communist or a socialist America would support the rights of these endangered species? All you have to do is look abroad. Communist China has very few rights for protecting endangered species and socialist Russia is still hunting endangered whales.

Another lie that President Obama and the Liberal left wants you to believe, is that Republicans give tax breaks to the rich. I am sure you can recall the attacks on George Bush when he cut taxes across the board. The only thing that the Democrats could utter out of their mouths was that he was cutting taxes for the rich. The truth is the top ten percent of income earners pay over 70% of all Federal income tax and the bottom 50% of income earners only pay 2%. President Obama made relentless calls to the middle class to support his raising taxes on the rich while cutting taxes for everybody else.

America, this simply will not work. The records show that every time we raise taxes on top income earners it slows the growth of our economy and the prices of goods go up. The Federal income tax is better known as the Internal Revenue Service used as a form of redistribution of wealth. America, I am calling for the end of redistribution of wealth but we must not abandon the social welfare program. I am calling for limitations on the length that someone can draw welfare. Remember, a hand up, not a hand out. It does sadden my heart to see those who are homeless or those families who cannot afford to feed their children but these services are not free. We must find solutions for better education, job training and creating jobs in this country. Today, Americans are overtaxed. We pay taxes for our groceries, where those who receive Food Stamps pay no tax; we pay income tax, sales tax, and even property tax. Even those who are in the Liberal circle have expressed interest in taxing the churches. One article that I have read in a Liberal paper years ago claim that churches have become too powerful in attempting to use their money for worldly matters.

America, there has been an attack on our Christian principles for well over two centuries. Secretive organizations like the illuminati has set out for their path of war against Christian beliefs. Through the ages, their evil deeds were orchestrated by the elite, as the beast spread its tentacles establishing secretive organizations and with their fork tongue spread their lies to deceive the people. The primary reason they want to abolish Christian beliefs is to abolish God's greatest gift, free will. Through spreading their lies in evolution has led to millions denouncing their faith in not accepting Jesus as their Savior.

America, I have not heard President Obama express any desires to tax churches, but you also have to realize that we must take this serious. Back in the 1960's we claimed that the talk of Socialists, Communists, and Marxists was just talk and now look where we are at today. It is true that if the churches were taxed they would have less influence on society. They would not be able to give as much food to the needy or pass out as many free Bibles. Personally, I think we need to get rid of all taxes altogether and use a flat sales tax. This would eliminate redistribution of wealth and everyone would pay the same percent in taxes. I do think there needs to be an additional income tax, but that would be for those who make over $250,000 a year as a form of giving back to the community. Not to be given as earned income credit but to be given for governmental improvements such as education, transportation, etc. President Obama as well as the Democrat party would frown on the idea of a flat sales tax. Their belief is that everyone should be equal through society. I believe that we are born equal but you have the right to reap your rewards for your achievement. Only a dictator would believe that you can take the wealth from those who are successful and redistribute it to those less successful. This reminds me of a Bible verse: You reap what you sow, which for me means, if you work hard, you should be rewarded.

The one thing that our forefathers were concerned about was a single power taking over and ruling the country. Even Benjamin Franklin was concerned about the idea of a president for he feared it would be too much power for one to wield. That is one reason presidential terms are limited to two terms and our government is broken down to different branches for checks and balances. This is the very reason why we have a Congress as well as a Senate, to make sure the people are represented. President Obama through his administration has signed in 139 executive orders. America, I call for a great concern for this is far too much power for the President of the United States to have. I ask you to not only review the examples from below but also research them.

-Executive Order 10990 allows the Government to take over all modes of transportation and control of highways and seaports.

-Executive Order 10995 allows the government to seize and control all communication media.

-Executive Order 10997 allows the government to take over all electrical power, gas, petroleum, fuels, and minerals.

-Executive Order 11001 allows the government to take over all health education and welfare functions.

-Executive Order 11003 allows the government to take over all airports and aircraft, including commercial or personal aircraft.

These executive orders concern me greatly. The fact that our president can take over all modes of transportation is alarming; for if they can do this, they have the ability to stop transportation all together. The fact that the government can control the media at will gives them the ability to censor what we hear and allows them to send out false propaganda. Our government can now control all health care, power grid, and even all valuable resources. America this gives the President the ability to turn the power off at will. For an example, if we exercise our right to assemble or even protest the government can easily turn the power grid off in the city we are protesting at. The president can even shut down commercial airlines at will. America, we must wake up! These executive orders were not about preparing for emergencies. When the tragedy of 9/11 happened, George Bush had no problems shutting down airports. FEMA (Federal Emergency Management Act) already has the ability to shut off power grids in case of natural disasters such as earthquakes to prevent fires or accidental electrocutions. I call out to those who truly believe in the Democratic style of government and those who want to restore the freedom we once had. This is far too much power for the executive branch to have. If Martial Law was ever called for, America would never be the same.

Another plan of Obama's was to raise educational standards. He called out for state governors to raise the educational standards in math and science. By raising their standard, they would receive more federal funds. Teachers would also be graded upon students' academic scores. Bad teachers would be removed and good ones would be rewarded with higher pay. I do agree with grading the teachers on how well their students improve academically and by test scores. I do not agree with intensely raising educational standards or their strict behavior policies that is smothering our children. What this has done is put immense pressure on our children. Today the United States educational standards have fallen and we rank 17th in the world. Our graduation ranking has diminished, as we have fallen to seventh in the world. We need to inspire our children to learn through learning programs that are fun and we need to teach our children good Christian principles. It is important for our society to teach our children to have good morals, to have tolerance for one another, to be honest, to have forgiveness, and most important the power of love. America President Obama blamed our education for the reason we have fallen behind in our industrial world and in truth the reason we are behind is because of the decisions of President Barack Obama, Bill Clinton and other crooked politicians. I do believe we need to raise our educational standards but not to the point of putting immense pressure on our children.

We also need to improve the quality of teachers, as well as equipment they use to teach. We must remember that education should be fun and we must inspire our children to learn by giving them more ambition. By creating more courses in English, science and math, we limit courses studied in music, theatre arts, or even physical education. Our physical education program, I believe is the reason why America has received more gold medals than any other nation. I do believe math, science, and English are very important but we must never forget the arts. Two dozen states have continued Race to the Top, while other states have dropped out due to the intense pressure it puts on their students. Credit must be given to those states for they are raising their educational standards but at a reasonable pace.

The first Lady Michelle Obama has imposed her idea for a low-calorie school lunch. First of all, Michelle Obama is no doctor or nutritionist. She was a lawyer until she had to turn in her license for insurance fraud. Kids across America are boycotting her idea of a healthy lunch. I saw one video of a mother who was outraged on what was being served to her child. She held up a 2-ounce piece of chicken that was no bigger than a chicken nugget. I could not validate her claim, but if you go online you will see a lot of complaints from students as well as parents, for what these children are being served. I have three daughters myself and every day they come home starving. My youngest daughter told me one day that she could not eat anything from school. I asked why and she replied that the pizza had green stuff on it. I believe the green stuff she was referring to were either spinach or bell peppers.

I decided one day to attend lunch with one of my daughters, who is in the first grade. I was very surprised at what I saw. The children were served pizza, a side of corn, and a salad. The salad was a few pieces of large lettuce, a few shavings off a carrot, and one cherry tomato, and no salad dressing. The corn was extremely bland, if though it had no butter or salt and surprisingly the pizza was greasy. I used to manage a pizza restaurant and I know that you can cook a healthy pizza on corn meal instead of oil, but I believe the oil came from the low-quality mozzarella cheese. The thing that shocked me the most was the number of children not eating, in fact when I walked to the window with my daughter to give our trays to the dishwasher, I noticed the garbage cans were completely full with food that children did not eat. Parents I urge you to see what's going on in your children's cafeteria. I do think it is important for our children to be served healthy meals but it also important for our children to be served food they will actually eat. There are many dishes that are extremely healthy for children that they will enjoy such as chicken gumbo, spaghetti, or lasagna casseroles. We can even serve our children sandwiches along with a bowl of soup such as chili, chicken noodle soup or vegetable soup. Our government has not only over stepped their boundary with our children but they are attempting to dictate their policies on our restaurants. There have been many attempts to not only ban soft drinks but salt as well as other foods. They have even attempted to impose a soft drink tax. Tell me America, how many freedoms are we willing to surrender to governmental control?

Throughout Obama's administration he has made many cuts in our military. The last three Democratic presidents we have had have followed this pattern. Jimmy Carter, as well as Bill Clinton had cut our military back so severely it had weakened our defense. In fact, shortly after George Bush took office we were attacked on 9/11, where the majority of the troops that were sent to protect our nation were reserves. President Obama's plan was to cut back nearly 490 billion dollars over the next decade. There is no telling how many jobs have been lost due to this massive cut in the military and even private sector. Even Boeing a major military supplier had to make major cutbacks. The cutbacks cannot only be our concern but our security has to be a priority as well. President Obama also cut spending for NASA where he canceled almost all future space shuttle missions. The next rover to Mars will not be built in the United States but will be built and sent from Europe. This too created a major loss in American jobs and for the first time in 50 years America is no longer the leader in spaceflight. In fact, thanks to President Obama NASA's next mission is to reach out to the Muslim world.

America, we were once the proud leaders of the world. Our brave men and women were proud to serve the most powerful military in the world, and we were the most prestigious nation in the world. We were once the land of the free market where dreams come true. We dared to believe, as we ventured into science, space exploration, and we believed we could accomplish anything. We were a nation where the people were free and we were blessed with our indelible rights. These attacks on our own nation has eroded our foundation that our forefathers had established for us all, and they are killing the dream of all Americans. I ask you to take a moment and reflect on those who valiantly gave their lives to establish our great nation. Our great men and women shed their blood not just for honor and duty but for our very freedom. Reflect on what our free market accomplished for our great nation and what inspire those men and women to venture out in science, medicine, and technology. We are the nation of the great inventions such as: the automobile, plane, and electricity. We are also the nation of the brave such as the Wright Brothers who were the first to take flight and Amelia Earhart who dared to fly across the ocean. We were also the first on the moon and when other nations said it was impossible to build the Panama Canal we did it.

The truth is that socialism is smothering our dreams, stealing our wealth and will eventually lead all of America into poverty. We must reevaluate the restrictions. Not just governmental restrictions such as the EPA and OSHA but all restrictions. If we could only lift this burden off our industries, we will once again see them grow. We were once warned that communists, socialist, and Marxists were meeting in America. Yet we did nothing. We were then warned that these radicals were marching to Washington. We simply dismissed it and now you are being warned that these radicals are not only in our government but have infiltrated our White House. Are we to do nothing or simply dismiss it? I tell you America, if we are to do nothing we will hear the sound of boots marching coming from the White House to restrict our freedom and those who resist will be put into bondage.

America this has been a planned attack to destroy America from within. In 1961 the Soviet Union Nikita Khrushchev made this statement in front of United Nations assembly.

"America will fall without a shot being fired. It will fall from within."

Nikita Khrushchev also stated that Soviet Union did not have to destroy America with missiles because they would destroy themselves. Newly released KGB records from the Soviet Union have shown how paid Communist supporters had infiltrated the United States. Their orders were to start Communist Parties or infiltrate colleges where they could pollute the minds of our young. This was nothing less than a brainwashing of America. They would portray capitalist as an evil empire leaving most people in poverty. The truth is that there has never been a nation with a larger middle class. In the former Communist Soviet Union, there was virtually no middle class. Their Social welfare program had bankrupted their nation to the point they could not even pay their soldiers. Today Communist China and North Korea has the largest percentage of those living in poverty. Nations living under a Socialist government are on the verge of collapsing throughout Europe.

America was infiltrated and huge networks sprung forth spreading their venom through society. These networks included SDS, IPS, and CPUSA. They then spread into other organizations and created other networks. Is it not ironic that shortly after Communist sympathizers infiltrated our universities violent riots broke out in universities? These radical organizations called for a revolution and when revolution failed they pledged they would destroy America from within. I have no doubt that President Obama was influenced by his mentor. You also have to come to the conclusion that he was influenced by the radical supporters. When President Obama campaigned in 2008 he promised change. I ask you again: is this the change you wanted; for our nation to be turned into a socialist state? For him to step on our Constitution and create his own laws by overstepping the other branches? Not only has Obama destroyed the fabric of our nation but his and past administrations have slower chipped away at free enterprise. Since he has been in office over 80,000 coal miners have been laid off or half lost their jobs. President Obama's goal was to shut down the coal mines, as he claimed they were not ECO friendly. America, we are on the verge of finding solutions. We already have the ability to clean coal and there has been a lot of progress in creating clean coal fuels.

America, I am sure you remember Bell County, Kentucky, where the people of this county held hands creating a human chain that stretched from one county to the next. Coal mining was this county's lively hood. Shutting down the coal mines would have shut down every business in their county. This is trickle economics; where one major industrial business, even a major coal mine operation would support many local businesses. Obama has also made it impossible to drill oil in America. Since he has been in office oil drilling permits are down by 36%.

I'm sure you have heard President Obama boast about oil production being up, but it is not by his doing. Most of these oil permits were given out before he ever took office. If oil drilling permits are down by 36% is a tremendous loss in jobs that will result to a loss of revenue for our economy. Our government is making it almost impossible for mining companies to operate as well as American oil companies. Yet in 2011, they allowed China to drill oil off the Coast of America in the Gulf of Mexico. America, you have to stop and ask yourself, why is our government not only selling but giving away our future? Don't take my words for all this; I'll give you Obama's words:

"So if somebody wants to build a coal powered plant, they can. It's just that it will bankrupt them because they are going to charge a huge sum for all that greenhouse gas that's being emitted. That will also generate billions of dollars that we can invest in solar, wind, biodiesel, and other alternative energy approaches."

Pres. Obama claimed he was going to change America, but the question should be: what change is he talking about? I will give you the statement of one of his friends, his former green job advisor, Van Jones.

"The United States was built on land that had been stolen from our Native American sisters and brothers, who had been bullied and mistreated and shoved into all the land we didn't want, where it was all hot and windy. But under a renewable energy system, the solar and wind power, Native Americans would now own and control 80 percent of the renewable energy resources. Give them the wealth! We owe

them a debt! He said that the U.S. is willing to exploit immigrants who work out in the fields with poison being sprayed on them, because we have the wrong agricultural system, but we don't want to give them rights, and we don't want to give them dignity, and we don't want to give them respect. our sisters and brothers that are in prison right now or who were formerly incarcerated ought to be among the prime beneficiaries of a green economy, that doesn't have any throw away species, resources, or any throw away people either. A clean energy revolution would merely be the first step toward wholesale societal transformation: We gonna change the whole system! We gonna change the whole thing!"

Van Jones also wanted change, but what he called for was a power shift. If you listen to his speech, there is a contradiction, he clearly states, "Let all the native Americans have the wealth." Then he says: "our sisters and brothers that are in prison right now" or who were "formerly incarcerated" ought to be among the prime beneficiaries of a green economy "This is the kind of talk that comes from the Liberal left that divides our people. Even in the past, if anyone was to disagree with the Democrats they were labeled racist. This kind of language is used to intimidate one group over another or incite racial violence. America when are we to boldly say no more? When are we to become a society that no longer divides the people by their skin color?

In the past, I have read many Liberal articles who blame the Republicans for not allowing illegal immigrants a pathway for citizenship, and its true; there have been Republican politicians who have stood against their opportunity for citizenship. The fact is that the Liberal media, or Liberal press only submit half of the truth because the Democrats share an equal blame. The truth is Republicans have done more for immigrants than the Democrats have ever done. In 1986 Republican Ronald Reagan through his administration, created a pathway for illegal immigrants. In 2007, George Bush attempted to create a pathway for citizenship but was blocked by both Democratic and Republican politicians. During this time, Democratic Senator Barack

Obama voted against this bill. Another fact is more illegals have been deported under President Obama's administration than George Bush's. I do believe that President Obama has all intentions on allowing illegals a pathway for citizenship but he wanted to do it under his administration.

This is an attempt to manipulate the Latino community as well as other immigrants to believe they are supported by the Democrats. This is a tool that the Democratic Party uses well to obtain votes from the minority groups across America. This is another reason why the Liberal left as well as Democrats attempts to divide the public through racial tension. We must not allow history to be forgotten. It was a Republican George Washington that turned down the opportunity to be king of America; instead he laid the foundation to a free America, where American citizens had the opportunity to choose their leaders. It was a Republican Abraham Lincoln who demolished slavery and let us not forget that it was mostly Democratic governors who stood against Martin Luther King Jr. on his pathway to equality. Even before the Civil War it was the Democratic Party who opposed the anti-slavery bill. I will be the first to admit that American history is not perfect, and I am ashamed to know that some of our forefathers not only supported but owned slaves. We must not allow the Liberal left, or anyone else to rewrite our history. I also think it is important to know our history and I will repeat an old cliché, "...*a society who forgets their history is damned to repeat it.*"

President Obama's agenda on change is being done before our eyes. He has enforced more regulations, restricted industry growth, and he is diminishing our freedoms. Today America has more laws written than ever before that are abolishing our freedoms. Tell me America, when there are more laws that restrict us than there are laws that protect us than what form of government are we leaning to? Another thing that bothers me greatly is how everything in our nation is regulated by tax. Our economy is regulated by the government along with our health care. Our government has regulated transportation which includes airports, trains, and even personal transportation. Our auto industry and even the industrial industry are regulated by our government. President Obama has passed stiffer laws that regulate banks and even

Wall Street. Even our personal lives are regulated by the government through taxes and license fees. Tell me America what can you do today without a license or permit, we become a society where we have to ask permission for everything. Even the freedom of speech has been restricted to obtaining a speech permit in order to give a public speech.

Our government has overstepped their boundary's in attempt to tell parents how to raise their children. I ask you once again: is this a free society? These restrictions on our freedoms are not only from the results of President Obama's administration. These changes that have eroded our freedom and restricted industrial growth in America has resulted in supporting our over bloated government thirst for control. The disastrous outcome is a culmination of many administrations before Pres. Obama, but he is guilty as well. We cannot entirely blame the Democratic Party for these problems, for the Republicans are equally guilty in supporting the elite. America, we cannot deny the evil intentions of secret organizations and the influence or power the elite has obtain, as they have bribed and manipulated our politicians for their evil plots. It is time to stand up to Washington and silence the elite for their deceit has poisoned our politicians for far too long. America it is urgent to make our vote count. We need a president as well as Congress and Senate that will uphold our Constitution. When President Obama took office he swore an oath:

"I, Barack Hussein Obama, do solemnly swear to preserve, protect, and defend the constitution of the United States."

This is a very serious oath that every president has been sworn to. To preserve the Constitution, means to keep it in its original form. To protect and defend, means to not allow anyone, domestic or foreign, to distort the meaning of the constitution. For Obama, this oath meant nothing. Pres. Obama statement,

"The original constitution, I think it's an imperfect document and I think it is a document that reflects some deep flaws in American culture, the colonial culture at the time. I think we can say that the constitution reflected an enormous blind spot in the culture and the

framers had that same blind spot. It is also reflected the fundamental flaw of this country that continues to this day."

This statement outraged me, for it is an atrocity to not only America's foundation but the people. I stand up and shout out, this is wrong! It is impeachable, for I know I do not stand alone, I stand with our forefathers. I will bring the words of one of our great forefathers from the past: *"DON'T INTERFERE WITH ANYTHING IN THE CONSTITUTION. IT MUST BE MAINTAINED, FOR IT IS THE ONLY SAFEGUARD OF OUR LIBERTIES." -ABRAHAM LINCOLN*

Our government has stood the test of time for over two centuries and today we have the oldest standing government. The reason was the foundation that our forefathers laid for us, and no president dared to challenge the Constitution until today. America, we must wake up!!! For I will cry out again, and again: America is under siege! What started as communist sympathizers coming from abroad has evolved into a domestic threat from within. President Obama signed in the NDAA (National Defense Authorization Act. In Dec. 31, 2011. On this defense act I will give you the words of Republican Senator Lindsey Graham:

"The homeland is part of the battlefield and people can be held without trial whether an American citizen or not."

I want to roar out; this is not what America stands for! This is a communist regime that is replacing our Democratic government. I ask you: are we to continue to do nothing? If so, then how will our children look at this generation that allowed this great nation to fall? We must take a stance and let our voice be heard as one loud voice. We do not stand alone. Fortunately, we have politicians that are speaking on our behalf that understand that their seats do not belong to them but to the people. I give you the words of Ron Paul who truly spoke out on our behalf in January 2012.

"Mr. Speaker, I rise today to introduce a very simple piece of legislation to repeal the infamous Section 1021 of the National Defense Authorization Act, quietly signed into law by the president on New Year's Day. Section 1021 essentially codifies into law the very dubious claim of presidential authority under the 2001 Authorization for the Use of Military Force to indefinitely detain American citizens without access to legal representation or due process of law. Section 1021 provides for the possibility of the US military acting as a kind of police force on US soil, apprehending terror suspects – including Americans — and whisking them off to an undisclosed location indefinitely. No right to attorney, no right to trial, no day in court. This is precisely the kind of egregious distortion of justice that Americans have always ridiculed in so many dictatorships overseas. A great man named Solzhenitsyn became the hero of so many of us when he exposed the Soviet Union's extensive gulag system. Is this really the kind of United States we want to create in the name of fighting terrorism? Some have argued that nothing in Section 1021 explicitly mandates holding Americans without trial, but it employs vague language radically expanding the detention authority to include anyone who has "substantially supported" certain terrorist groups or "associated forces." No one has defined what those two terms mean. What is an "associated force"? Sadly, too many of my colleagues are too willing to undermine our Constitution to support such outrageous legislation. One senator even said about American citizens picked up under this section of the NDAA, "When they say, 'I want my lawyer,' you tell them, 'Shut up. You don't get a lawyer.'" Is this acceptable in someone one who has taken an oath to uphold the Constitution? Mr. Speaker, of course I recognize how critical it is that we identify and apprehend those who are suspected of plotting attacks against Americans. But why do we have so little faith in our justice system? Have we not tried in civilian court and won convictions of hundreds of individuals for terrorist or related activities? I fully support our continuing to do so, but let us not abandon what is so unique and special about our system of government in the process. I hope my colleagues will join my effort to overturn the shameful Section 1021."

Many of our representatives did speak out against this bill but not enough. I am baffled that not enough of our politicians could see this is a dictator style of government being passed. We the people put our faith into our politicians who we elect, in hope they will represent us all.

We expect that they will uphold our Constitution, safeguard our freedom and preserve our rights. Unfortunately, this is not true. I give you the words of Democratic Senator, Dianne Feinstein: " The indefinite imprisonment of American citizens without charge or trial."

I ask you: what defines a terrorist? If someone were to speak out for the Constitution; or if someone desired to restore the balance of our government would they be considered a terrorist? America, we must realize that this is far too much power for one president to wield. This gives our president or any other future president the opportunity to declare Martial Law. Martial Law did not begin with the NDAA; in fact, it has been around for a long time. What this has done is given immense power to DHS (Department of Homeland Security), as well as our military, and law enforcement. In fact, DHS has purchased and stock piled 1.4 billion rounds of hollow point armor piercing ammunition. Why would a government agency in charge of protecting our homeland need so many rounds of high quality ammunition? Is it not our military's responsibility to secure our safety? But then again Obama is making massive cuts to our military. This bill that was passed was overturned by Federal Judge Katherine B. Forest. Her judgment was that the NDAA was unconstitutional, and it would also infringe on freedom of speech, the first amendment. But once again President Obama ignored a Federal judge, as he did with the Health Care Bill, and restated the NDAA. America, you must recognize that this is an aggressive move by the Executive Branch. To take over and ignore all other branches of government is unconstitutional. This will destroy the check and balances that were established by our forefathers. Once again I give you the words of Abraham Lincoln: **"WE THE PEOPLE ARE THE RIGHTFUL MASTERS OF BOTH CONGRESS AND THE COURTS. NOT TO OVERTHROW THE CONSTITUTION BUT TO OVERTHROW THE MEN WHO PERVERT THE CONSITUTION."**

When the Executive Branch becomes too powerful, we must take notice. Senator Ron Paul continues to speak out for the people and to warn us about the direction of our own government. Ron Paul: "My topic for this evening is assassinations. What have we allowed ourselves to become? Are we no longer a nation of laws? Have we become instead a nation of men who make secret arrests? Are secret prisons now simply another tool of the federal government law enforcement? Is secret rendition of individuals now permitted out of misplaced fear? Have we decided that the writ of habeas corpus is not worth defending? Is torture now an acceptable tool for making us safe? Unfortunately, the single answer to all these questions from the leaders of our country to many of our citizens appears to be yes. And now we are told that assassination of foreigners as well as American citizens is legitimate and necessary to provide security for our people. It is my firm opinion that nothing could be further from the truth. Secret arrests, secret renditions, torture and assassinations are illegal under both domestic and international law. These activities should be anathema to the citizens of a constitutional republic. The real threat doesn't arise from our failure to torture, rather desensitizing our nation to the willful neglect and sacrifice of our civil liberties fought and died for over the centuries, is the threat. The concept of habeas corpus existed even before King John of England was forced in 1215 by his rebellious barons to sign the Magna Carta. This basic principle and expression of individual liberty which has survived 800 years greatly influenced the writing of our Constitution and our common-law heritage. Today, we hardly hear a whimper, either from the American people or a stone-silent US government as our cherished liberties are eradicated. Instead, we have a government that deliberately orchestrates needless fear and makes people insecure enough to ignore the reality of their lost liberties. The latest outrage is the current administration's acknowledgement that we now have a policy that permits assassination not only of foreign suspects but of American citizens as well. Of course, the CIA has used secret assassinations in a limited fashion for decades despite international, domestic, and moral law. When done secretly as in the past, our government at least recognized that assassination was illegal and wrong. Frighteningly and astonishingly, however, the policy is now explicit.

National Intelligence Director Dennis Blair in open testimony before the House Intelligence Committee on February 3rd of this year, acknowledged that American citizens can indeed be assassinated at our government's discretion. The US government attempted to assassinate Anwar al Awlaki, in Yemen without even charging him with the crime. We're told this evidence is secret, that he does not deserve any constitutional rights and that some unknown individual in the administration has the authority to declare him a threat, and therefore a legitimate target for assassination.

"Yes, I know, he's probably a very bad person. Yes, I know that only a few Americans are on the assassination hit list. Yes, I know that artificially generated fear makes a large number of Americans inclined to applaud this effort which supposedly will make us safe. But if this could become standard operating procedure and a permanent precedent is established, let me assure you that this abuse of the law will spread. It's time for Congress and the American people to wake up to the realities of the dangers we face. We must remember as members of Congress that we have taken an oath to protect and defend the Constitution from all enemies foreign and domestic. It should not be that difficult to distinguish the difference between the danger posed by the underwear bomber and the danger posed by a government that endorses secret prisons, torture, and assassinating American citizens."

-Ron Paul

America, we are heading for a socialist style of government and let us not forget Germany was overthrown by the Socialist Nazi Party. In February of 1933, Adolf Hitler burned down the German Parliament, which is similar to America's Congress. He then eradicated the constitution of Germany. Hitler instilled fear in the German people and called out they should protect the German homeland. He sent out false propaganda, claiming that Polish troops were attacking German citizens which helped him attain the support of the people for war. I will not compare Adolf Hitler to George Bush Jr. but during his administration he signed in the Patriot Act. This would establish DHS (Department of Homeland Security). I truly believe that Pres. Bush's Jr. administration had good intentions forming the Patriot Act, especially after the attack on 9/11, still this is a blatant violation against our constitutional rights.

We must realize creating such power can have devastating consequences. I am sure that we all remember the racial profiling, the legalize torture of suspected terrorist, and our government having the authority to listen in to our cell phone conversations. Let us not forget how Pres. Obama attempted to do away with the Constitution, by declaring it is impractical document and don't forget how Hitler destroyed Germans Constitution after he took power. I ask you to listen to reason: how would you judge a nation that allowed torture to others? Or be suspicious of others for the color of their skin? We once again unfortunately repeated our past. During world war II we imprisoned 112,000 Japanese, which over 60% were American citizens.

These Japanese American citizens were forced into labor camps and after the war they were simply released without apology and given a little over twenty dollars. It took America a little over forty years to admit this wrong. During Ronald Reagan's administration, he did just that. He called it mass paranoia on our government's part and racial profiling. The tragedy of 9/11 was trying times for America and it created a feeling of vulnerability. We have allowed these terrorists to profoundly change the political structure of our nation. We must not allow ourselves to live in fear. For fear is the root of all evil. Nor shall we allow terrorists to change who we are as a nation but are we not living in fear? The Patriot Act was nothing more than a luncheon pad for Pres. Obama's NDAA bill.

What he has done is created a militarized police within our own borders that only answers to the Executive Branch. We cannot dismiss this as Pres. Obama's true agenda to weaken our military, while at the same time he creates a powerful militarized police force within our own borders. When the Socialist Nazi Party took power in Germany one of the first things Adolf Hitler did was create SS Troopers which translates into 'Protective Squadron'. The SS Troopers were responsible for homeland security and carrying out Hitler's plans for the horrors of genocide.

During his first term, Obama attempted to create a gun ban which would be delayed due to the Presidential Elections for 2012. Even the U.N postponed their meetings the make a universal gun ban treaty. This indicates that President Obama is hiding his true agenda to ensure he wins his second term. You cannot ignore the fact that President Obama is a deceiver. While President Obama was attending a meeting with Russia's Pres. Medvedev, he did not realize the microphone was still on and was caught commenting, "This is my last election. I will have more flexibility after my election for negotiating on issues like missile defense. On all these issues but particularly missile defense. This can be solved but it is important for him to give me space." Our President has already cut our military to the bone and now he is attempting to negotiate our missile defense? America, it is one thing to sign a treaty with Russia to abolish nuclear missiles but to dismantle our missile defense along with our military leaves us extremely vulnerable. I have a serious question for our president: why would he lean in to what he thought was a private conversation and make such a statement? A better question is: who was he referring to on his comment, "it is important for him to give me space." He was already meeting with the President of Russia so who was he referring to? We all know who he was referring to, Vladimir Putin who works behind the scenes controlling Russia.

Simply what our President has indicated, is the fact he has to keep a low profile on his true agenda until he wins his second term and then he can do whatever he wants. Several things astonished me during this election year. I truly believe the biggest corruption of the 2012 elections was the media. President Obama was portrayed by the media as practically a saint. In fact, a very few would even report on Obama's agenda. For me, I believe Glenn Beck brought more truth out then anyone or any other network but due to the pressure of Media Matters he later resigned from FOX News. In fact, I owe him my awakening and the fact that Media Matters takes pride on forcing his resignation on FOX News gives me a deep unsettling anger.

America, I urge you to no longer support Media Matters and turn your backs on them. Do not even give them financial support or a moment to whisper into your ear because they will only deceive you. This is a deception that runs deep in our country. It has infiltrated all areas of our government and even our media. How can our media praise Pres. Obama as if he could do no wrong? For no other president in our history raised our national deficit so dramatically. During his administration, America's credit standing has been lowered twice, which has never even happened once with any other president. His past is questionable, for he keeps his history tucked away in a dark corner. His executive orders and bills he has passed amounts to one thing, absolute power. His Universal health care and reckless spending will lead to a bankrupt nation. Astonishingly the media still praises this man. I look around puzzled, does anybody else see this?

I know most Americans know what's going on and I've heard many of them say that there is nothing to do, their hands are tied. Well, I'll tell you, the government has not tied knots to you, for we have tied them ourselves. Our forefathers have told us we are the masters of our own government. If we do not take a stance now and boldly speak out while using our powers of voting, we will see our freedoms fade away as we are all shackled to a socialist or communist government. America, I truly believe that our foundation can stand this test in time but we must act now. We must put away our political differences and break down our racial barriers that divide us for there is one thing without doubt. If we do not act now, we will surely share the same fate.

I call for an investigation for all these Communist and Socialist organizations that have infiltrated our government. I ask you: is our government foundation based on the will of the people? Then is it your will for our Constitution to be distorted or removed? These organizations are acting against the will of the people and that is treason? We must also boycott all media stations that spread propaganda or lie, and who neglect to tell the truth or is bias. For I have sounded the alarm like many before me such as Rush Limbaugh and

Glenn Beck. We have even had a few politicians like Ron Paul sound the alarm. Do not let these voices go unheard. Even the Tea Party came out boldly and even though the Liberal media called them racist, Nazis, or even radicals, they continued to boldly stand their ground. America, it is a fact we as a people are not only being manipulated by our government but by the media as well. If one person stands alone they will not be heard, but if we as a people stand together we will be a force. We can no longer allow the media to influence our thinking or allow them to influence our vote. During the Republican primary, I noticed an injustice that troubled me deeply. The media was extremely bias as they favored Mitt Romney. Has our media become so powerful that they can direct our choices for who will win the Republican primary? This answer is yes, if they put their spot light onto this person and criticize other candidates, this could easily persuade a portion of Americans into voting for the candidate they have chosen. This power grab can be no more. For if the media can control who is going to be president it has far too much power. To give more air time to one candidate than another, or give heartfelt stories about their families and to even parade their family on network TV can easily manipulate the American public. Even a Republican candidate Newt Gingrich commented on how the media was biased:

"I think Fox has been for Romney all the way through. In our experience, Callista and I both believe CNN is less biased than Fox this year. We are more likely to get neutral coverage out of CNN than we are of Fox, and we're more likely to get distortion out of Fox. That's just a fact."

I know there are far more bias stations than FOX but Newt Gingrich is right. This is a major problem. America let us suppose that there was no media time given to candidates and we have no choice but to read their policies. Would this not change how we vote? Then you must realize we can be influenced by a bias media. We must create an equal and balanced air time for all candidates. We must demand the media to report the news and not to side with the issues in their own interest. Of course, Mitt Romney would win the Republican Primary but then again he was handpicked by the media. During the presidential elections 2012, our Presidential candidate Mitt Romney attempted to attack Barack Obama on many of his policies, but many of the Liberal networks came out to defend Pres. Obama. America, we must realize that the media is owned by the elite families, which gives the elite a tremendous amount of control over what we hear. I am sure you remember in the elections of 2012 where our Presidential candidate Mitt Romney criticized President Obama on dramatically shrinking our military. Mitt Romney claimed our Navy had not been this small in a hundred years. The liberal networks seemed to make jokes about Mitt Romney's statement by referring to Obama's comeback, "we also have fewer horses and bayonets."

The truth is, this was a major concern for America's security. Pres. Obama along with the Liberal media expected us to believe a smaller Navy was a stronger Navy. This is not the only fact that shows how bias the media was during this time. Obama also received three times more the media coverage than Mitt Romney. In one of the presidential debates Obama accused Mitt Romney of wanting to allow Detroit to fall into bankruptcy. Mitt Romney encouraged Obama and the viewers to research this matter for themselves. This was a false allegation by Pres. Obama and many of the networks had proved this was a false allegation. Pres. Obama continued to spread this false allegation, while also indicating how Mitt Romney lied. President Obama, you are the liar. Surely you knew the facts after the networks came out with them, yet you still continued to spread this false propaganda. Even Bill Clinton came out in support of Pres. Obama. With this TV ad:

"This election to me is about which candidate is most likely to return to us the full employment. This is a clear choice. The Republican plan is to cut more taxes on upper income people and to go back to deregulation. That's what got us in trouble in the first place. President Obama has a plan to rebuild America from the ground up. Investing in innovation, education, and job training. It only works if there is a

strong middle class. That's what happened when I was president. We need to keep going with his plan."

Bill Clinton, are you sure you didn't inhale? Or where you just that delusional? The reason you had a strong middle class was because Reagan economics which you later helped destroy with the NAFTA Treaty. The selling and giving of technology to China gave them a huge competitive edge. Bill Clinton has destroyed our industrial growth was immense EPA regulations and severely weaken our military. I can understand your support for Pres. Obama because you both have the same agenda, to change our nation to a socialist style of government, and to support the elite's goal for a New World Order.

There were also many allegations of voter fraud in 2012 elections where the dead had mysteriously casted their vote and those who were in a vegetative state miraculously did the same. Voter fraud is a very serious problem within our nation and I think it is important to mandate that all states should enforce a State issued ID to vote. The fact that some states have not mandated citizens to have to use a state issued ID is negligent to all American people and must not be allowed anymore. The fact is the dead cannot vote nor can a vote be sold, purchased, or bribed. We cannot allow intimidation like we saw with the Black Panthers in the 2008 elections outside the voting stations screaming out let's kill all the crackers. Once again this is a repeat of history where white voters once intimidated black voters in the South. America two wrongs will never make a right, and will only fuel more anger for future generations. In 2012, the NAACP argued against state laws mandating state issued ID to vote. They took their case to the United Nations and argued that this would suppress minority votes. America, we must wake up. If the NAACP proved that it was unlawful for states to mandate state issued IDs would have corrupted our voting system even further. I would like to know what the NAACP expected after taking the complaint all the way to the UN. Did they truly expect the UN to put pressure on our governmental policies or expect the UN to land soldiers on our soil? I believe the reason that the NAACP pushed this issue was not so much to change the laws on how we vote but to outrage the minority groups to ensure a high turnout vote from the minorities.

Another thing that is illegal but should be enforced is candidates receiving campaign funds from overseas. President Obama received millions of dollars from overseas toward his campaign fund. He is not the first governmental official to receive campaign funds from overseas but this still does not make it right. We must realize that if nations overseas pour money into campaign funds then are they not too trying to manipulate the system? Campaign funds should only come from the people not from American Businesses or American Corporations. This will ensure that not only will the American People's vote count but their voice will be heard too.

America, we must enforce our voter registration laws and mandate all states to require state ID's to cast their votes and banish the electoral system. Every American citizen's vote should count. Not by the vote of the district or state but as the numerical vote of one. This will protect the rights of all and do not listen to those who claim it is unfair for those who cannot get a state issued ID. Instead be bold and ask, why can they not get a state issued ID? We must also ask why we are using the electoral voting system.

President Obama won the 2012 elections by electoral votes for his second term. During the 2012 elections, the American embassy in Benghazi, Libya was attacked. This resulted in the deaths of four Americans. It was not that long ago when President Obama stated that the Al-Qaeda was out of business. The U.S embassy in Libya asked the state department for more security before they were attacked and were denied. They claimed the region was unstable and still our government turned a deaf ear to their request. Other nations had already pulled their embassies and even the International Red Cross had left the area. When the embassy was attacked Tyrone Woods and Glen Doherty employed by the CIA and former Navy Seals could hear the shots being fired from the embassy. They knew the embassy was under attack and were told not once but three separate times to stand down. Tyrone

Woods and Glen Doherty broke orders and went in to protect Americans as well as Ambassador Christopher Steven. This battle raged for over six hours and they were denied assistance even when they called for military support.

You cannot tell me that our politicians in Washington was not aware of what was happening in Benghazi during this attack. There were two drones that flew over the area of Benghazi during this attack. These drones have the ability to send real time video back to Washington D.C. This is negligence on our government's part which resulted in four Americans dying: Christopher Stevens, Tyrone Woods, Glen Doherty, and Sean Smith. Pres. Obama as well as Secretary of State, Hillary Clinton should be investigated for their neglect and a wrongful death of these great men who are serving our nation! This attack was committed by Al-Qaeda terrorists while Sean Smith, who served in the U.S Air Force, had sent out information of what was happening while the embassy was under siege. These brave men not only served our nation but valiantly saved American lives. These brave men had families and children of their own. They stood their ground with faith that the U.S government would send someone to help them. It saddens my heart to know how abandoned they must have felt in those last few moments.

During this attack, another American embassy was attacked in Cairo, Egypt where terrorists had stormed over the wall, took down the American flag, and hoisted their own flag. They then tore the American flag into pieces and set it on fire. Obama attempted to blame this terrorist uprising on an anti-Islamic video, in which I have to admit, was done in poor judgment. But still it does not give the right to Islamic terrorists to act savagely and commit murder. Why do we live in fear of offending or telling the truth about the Islamic terrorist? They have killed people of Christian and Jewish faiths, burned down our churches, and even urinated and defecated on the cross.

In Islamic terrorist faith, they believe they have the right to kill all the infidels in their land, and even when they move to new lands they believe they still have this right. I will admit that there are those who claim they're peaceful, but if you ask most of them if they believe in everything in their Koran, even the part that tells them to cleanse their land of the infidels they will tell you they do. I am not attempting to bash Islam but I must remain true to myself. I did not agree with the horrific crimes of the Catholic Church who forced many cultures to accept their faith by a sword. I also cannot accept a culture that does not allow women rights or for their female population to be educated. America has built schools throughout many Islamic nations, while encouraging these nations to educate their female population. Due to the strength of these people's conviction not to allow their female population to be educated has resulted to many of the schools being destroyed by terrorist. The fact that most Islamic nations will not permit women to receive an education is ridiculous. For many decades, they have been moving into Northern India, and even to this day they have been committing violent attacks against those of the Hindu faith. For Obama to so quickly blame a video was ridiculous. His reaction to this horrible incident shows his incompetence. He claimed he launched an investigation which resulted in four people resigning from the State Department. This was nothing more than an attempt to pacify Americans and the media. Those four who resigned from their post are still on our government pay roll for they were reassigned to new jobs.

I will say it again, this horrible incident must be investigated and we must investigate Secretary of State, Hillary Clinton for her incompetence. Is she not the one in charge of our State Department? Our government is attempting to sweep this under the rug in hopes it will fade away. Our nation failed these brave men who stood their ground. We as a people must not fail them and bring justice to those responsible. Since President Obama has been our president our world has become far more hostile. Revolutions have broken out in places like Libya, Egypt, Syria, and many other countries in Southeast Asia. Violent riots have broken out through countries in Southern Europe. Many Liberals, Democrats, or Liberal media have indicated that President Obama has improved America's relations around the world, yet at this time we are dealing with a hostage crisis in Nigeria along with all this other madness. Hezbollah has continued their missile attacks on Israel while the Muslim brotherhood has grown immensely. Since President Obama has been in office he has presented a much weaker image of our nation. His bowing to other leaders or pleading with Russian President to have more space has changed the world's image of our nation. He has toured the world referring to America as being arrogant, foolish, and uncooperative. How is the world supposed to see us from such statements from our leader? Before President Obama was our president the world looked to us for aid, to solve massive problems, or help secure their borders. I want you to read how Pres. Obama passed the torch to Europe.

"In America, there's a failure to appreciate Europe's leading role in the world. Instead of celebrating your dynamic union and seeking to partner with you to meet common challenges, there have been times where America has shown arrogance and been dismissive, even derisive."

It's bad enough that President Obama has been dismantling our foundation, but he has also distorted how the world sees us today. With the lowering of our credit standing and the dismantling of our military has given America a weak appearance. Tell me, how is the world to view us with this tremendous deficit over our heads and without a strong military? His inabilities to handle the Middle Eastern problems or even stop Hezbollah from firing missiles into Israel shows his incompetence. During his administration, Iran has sponsored many terrorist organizations through the Middle Eastern Region. The Muslim Brotherhood is sponsored by Iran and has spread their ideology around the world. You cannot ignore since President Obama has been our president that the Middle East has become a powder keg ready to explode. Very little has been done to prevent Iran from obtaining nuclear weapons and the tension between Iran and our country has intensified during his administration.

Hezbollah has been firing missiles into Israel before Pres. Obama took office but Pres. Bush did try to bring peace to this region. Pres.

Obama has done very little to ease tension between Hezbollah and Israel. In fact, when he went on one of his Middle Eastern tours, he completely skipped Israel. You have to understand what message this had sent to the Islamic nations. To them it was a sign that America was not going to support Israel. This weakness our president has betrayed, has given Iran the strength to spread their influence and tighten their grip over surrounding nations. Egypt's revolution was instigated by the Muslim brotherhood, which resulted to a tense relationship between Egypt and Israel. While their relationship becomes more intense, President Obama allows Egypt to purchase America's F16 fighters and Abram tanks.

I am sure you remember the three hikers that were captured by Iranian soldiers. These hikers were eventually released but were never on Iranian soil in the first place. Robert Levinson, a former FBI agent has also disappeared in this region in 2007. It is believed he has been held in Iranian prisons while our government has done nothing. President Obama has not only shown how heartless he is but also how unpatriotic he is. America faced a hostage crisis in Iran back in the 70's during the Carter administration and this matter did not get resolved till we elected a strong President like Ronald Reagan. Since President Obama has been our President, he has gone out of his way to please the Islamic people. He has spent 6 million dollars of taxpayers' money building mosques in the United States and overseas. I do give him credit for finding Osama Bin Laden but you also have to give George Bush credit because it was his plan that was still being carried out. I do not believe that President Obama anticipated this outbreak of violence around the Islamic world but this goes to show how ill prepared he was as our president. With his term coming to an end I am sure he was concerned about being elected for his second term. I believe President Obama attempted to sweep this under the rug or minimize these horrific issues to pacify the American public.

President Obama also attempted to postpone many issues till after the election, his gun control bill, EPA's administrator resigning, and he even asked Solyndra to postpone their layoffs. This was a company President Obama invested over 500 million dollars of taxpayers' money in that would eventually file for bankruptcy a year later. There is no doubt he did this to ensure his bid for reelection, even his attempt to downplay Benghazi. I have no doubt that many will attempt to argue this point but tell me is it justice to accept four resignations from the State Department only reward them with new positions? There is no argument for this because four Americans died. Shortly after the election President Obama accepted the resignation of EPA administrator Lisa Jackson. She too was under investigation for creating an alias to continue Obama's war on coal, and other fossil fuels. The alias she created was Richard Windsor. This scandal was uncovered by Chris Homer who achieved a court indictment for the release of 12,000 emails. She created this alias so she could work from behind the scenes and create more regulations.

Pres. Obama promised transparency on his campaign trail and throughout his administration there has been no transparency as he had signed bills behind closed doors. Other government departments had followed suit, with such inappropriate behavior, like the EPA has operated very covertly. Is this really the type of government we voted for? A government that signs bills from behind closed doors or governmental departments creating false aliases? For every law that is passed by Congress there are multiple regulations hidden within them. The EPA received ten billion at taxpayers' expense to act in such an irresponsible manner. America, we must realize the EPA creates hundreds of regulations every year that strangles American industries. This does not just affect the industries; you are paying the bill every time you fill your car up with gas. EPA regulations are also costing you every time you go to the store or even when you pay your utility bills. In fact, the EPA has raised the cost of living across the board. Recently the EPA created a contest for best YouTube video explaining why government regulations are necessary. America, is this something we truly need? More regulations? If you listened to Clinton's commercial where he supported President Obama during the campaign, he claimed the Republicans wanted to deregulate while the Democrats wanted to regulate. Is this what we want? You must realize the two most liberal states, California and New York have the highest deficit due to regulations. In fact, California is near bankruptcy in part to EPA regulations. Another thing that we must all look into, is why it is so important for the EPA to hide the regulations within bills that are passed.

Our nation is supposed to be a nation of the people, by the people. The EPA has not represented the people nor had our interest in a very long time; in fact, Lisa Jackson is a Socialist who believes in redistribution of wealth. This goes to show that President Obama's upbringing and circle of friends has impacted his beliefs in government. He has continued to surround himself with socialist and communist supporters throughout our White House. His policies clearly do not support a democratic style of government and many of those that has been brought into his cabinet are extremely anti-American. Unfortunately, President Obama is not the first to bring such radicals into the White House. If you research Pres. Bill Clinton's administration, field positions throughout the White House with those who supported socialist or communist ideology. Bill Clinton's EPA administrator Carol Browner was a member of the CSWS (Communist for a Sustainable World Society). She was also a former organizer for Socialist International. Toward the end of Bill Clinton's administration, he had illegally helped the EPA pass intense regulations. This corruption eventually surfaced through Pres. Bush's administration, as he launched an investigation where a federal judge ordered the release of all data on EPA regulations and correspondence between the EPA to the Clinton administration.

When George Bush first took office, he attempted to undo the madness of the Clinton administration. The Liberal media as well as the Liberal left were outraged with Pres. Bush, but the regulations the EPA had put in place were crippling America. The rolling blackouts in California were caused by the anti-carbon bills through his administration. Pres. Bill Clinton's mandate for 10 % ethanol per gallon of gasoline had created a tremendous strain on corn crops. This mandate caused the price of corn to sky rocket and many farmers that once only grew hay would abandon this crop for the more lucrative corn crop. This one bill that was passed by the Clinton administration had a domino effect which has severely impacted the price of beef. This is one of the reasons today at your supermarket you will pay double the cost for beef. Americans are now seeing the impact of the EPA regulations and that is why the EPA is using YouTube for a contest to polish their image. In 2003, a Federal judge held the EPA in content of court for destroying computer files at the end of the Clinton Administration. I believe Bill Clinton as well as Carol Browner should be investigated for tampering with evidence. In fact, Carol Browner was brought in by President Obama as his energy and environmental Czar. America this is a good indication that we have totally lost control what goes on in Washington.

America, we must wake up. It is costing America over $350 billion a year, due to intense EPA regulations. In the future EPA regulations are going to cost Americans trillions. The EPA methane permits is another issue that President Obama has put on hold to reassure his bid for reelection. The methane permits will come to a staggering cost, which will only result to destroying our economy. This will have a huge impact on large ranches, poultry farms, farms, and industries which would dramatically raise the price of meats as well as produce. Americans will also see an increase in price of goods made from industries but this is more of an attack on coal and fossil fuels. I want you to recall President Obama's speech when he clearly stated he would bankrupt the coal industry.

He clearly campaigned on change but I ask you again: is this the change we want? I would like for you to recall Van Jones Power shift speech. This was a plan of redistribution of wealth on a massive scale, to take away from those who have and redistribute it through social welfare programs. Van Jones stated "...give them the wealth." America, nothing is given freely; it must come from the working sweat of someone else.

I cry out for you to wake up America, for we are falling under a socialist style of government. There have been many indications through laws our crooked politicians have past and through socialist programs that prove that we have been following a socialist style of government for decades. If we continue this path, we will only have to look toward Europe to know our future. Europe was once on the steps of economic collapse and today it is no longer the question if Europe will fall but when will it fall? Many nations in Europe are facing the same economic collapse such as Spain, Italy, Greece, etc. The pattern clearly shows how America is following France in taxing the rich and passing intense regulations on our industry. More and more Europeans are joining communist parties due to the stress of the economy. The same thing that happened to America through the 1960's was occurring in Europe with the socialist movement. Much of this was brought on by the Communist Soviet Union. They did not only send communist sympathizers to America but worldwide to spread their ideology. Communism bankrupted the Soviet Union which led to their collapse. America, we must realize, a Socialist style government will eventually lead to communism. When the Soviet Union collapsed has stifled the communist movement worldwide. With the fall of communism, the socialist movement begin to flourish as radical groups spread their deception throughout governments around the world.

Today in socialist France, many businesses as well as industries are leaving the country due to high taxation and governmental regulations. What I find shocking is how many people from France are going to Russia to fulfill their business dreams. France too is on the verge of collapse while the unions and communists are gaining strength. Is this America's fate as well: to fall to communism? When communism failed in the old Soviet Union, it almost destroyed the communist movement in America. The Liberal left then began to reeducate, or a better terminology, change our history about communism to make it more acceptable. They started their deception by making Joseph Stalin a hero. They erected a statue of him in Bedford, Virginia. Is it not ironic how the Russians tore down Joseph Stalin's statue for it later to be erected in America?

Joseph Stalin was no great leader, and murdered twenty million; of his own people. He left the majority of the people in poverty and millions were left unemployed. The Soviet Union was facing economic ruin as empty store shelves became normal and the people had to stand in long lines for a loaf of bread or a roll of toilet paper. He was no war hero either. I have recently watched a history documentary praising Joseph Stalin as a war hero during World War II. This shocked me to my core because I know my history especially when it comes to World War II. They praised him because he lost so many men and women in battle. To lose so many in battle does not make someone a great leader, it just shows he/she cares very little about human life.

Carelessly, he sent twenty-six million Russians to their deaths. I do blame Nazi Germany for most of these deaths but you also have to blame Joseph Stalin for most of these men had very little training or no training at all. In his sniper squadrons the men and women had very little training as they were only given a rifle and a handful of bullets and were ordered to kill German officers. Many of the army infantry were sent in unarmed with orders to pick up the guns of fallen soldiers. America has never fought a war like this. We not only value the lives of every American but we attempt to avoid civilian casualties. This documentary claimed the reason we won WWII was because of the Soviet Union however this cannot be further from the truth. When America declared war on Germany we quickly moved our forces to England to prepare for an invasion. America, Britain, and other allies landed their forces on the beach of Normandy. Germany had no alternative but to split their fighting force. Germany pulled tank squadrons, air force, and even infantry out of Russia to defend their western European shores. You have to realize by America's entrance into WWII dramatically weakened Germany due to the fact they had a war on two fronts. Another thing you have to realize is how long the Soviet Union would have lasted if they did not receive America's aid. During WW II, America furnished the Soviet Union with roughly 7,000 tanks, 22,000 armored vehicles, and over 500,000 tactful vehicles such as jeeps and trucks. We also sent 15,000 aircrafts to aide in troop support which included bombers. We furnished their troops with 15,000 artillery guns, and over 130,000 machine guns and submachine guns. This does not even include the trains or railcars, medical supplies, ammunition, boots or even millions of bales of cotton.

I do admit the cold Soviet winter was the biggest factor that weakened the German army. I will conclude if America had never gotten involved in World War II or had never given aide to England, Soviet Union, they would have fallen under German rule. Another thing we must never forget is how Joseph Stalin met with Adolf Hitler to discuss how to divide Poland prior to their invasion. We must no longer allow those to change our history, for any attempt to mislead the people has only evil intentions. We have to set things right, and let the truth be known. Joseph Stalin was a murderer, who had no regards for human life. I have had the opportunity to work with many people from Russia through the exchange student program and they have indicated that he was a murderous dictator. He was a selfish and indulgent man who led his people into poverty. I would like to call out to our politicians to have this statue removed, and if Russia refuses to take the statue, then let us dump it into the ocean. It has no place at a memorial for our fallen veterans. This is a plot that was orchestrated by the socialist and communist movement to de-villainize a dictator by perverting our own history. Another thing that baffles me is how many of the Liberal Democrats have supported dictators or even praised them such as Fidel Castro of Cuba, Kim Jong-II of North Korea, and Hugo Chavez of Venezuela.

The deception of communist or socialist propagandist has deceived billions with false hopes for change and for a better life around the world. In reality, hundreds of millions of people around the world have been slaughtered by their monstrous assault for control. Through their dark agenda to seize control over world governments has left billions in poverty and billions more subjected to a dictatorship. Their Army of propagandists have manipulated world history and polished the image of horrific dictators like Joseph Stalin, Vladimir Lenin, and Mao Zedong as saints fighting for people's rights. They brainwash the masses with their lies as they betray these dictator's as heroes in portraits on banners or flags. Do not be deceived for under their polished image lies the blood stains of the hundreds of millions that were murdered.

When Mao Zedong started the communist revolution in China had resulted to tens of millions being slaughtered in the streets. Mao Zedong became the father of communist China and ruled with an iron fist for 27 years. During his reign of terror, it is estimated that he killed well over a hundred million Chinese. This horrible dictator was delusional under the ideology of communism and his thirst for power was unquenchable as he grasps for total control over China. When the dictator Mao Zedong took control over China he quickly seized control over industry, communication, agriculture, health, and education. This horrific dictator had no mercy as he seized control over farmer's crops that resulted to millions of Chinese dying from starvation. He established over 1000 labor camps where over 40 million were imprisoned and enslaved to grueling labor. His policy ensure that people had no rights and deny them the right to defend themselves by banning all guns in the private sector. Mao Zedong has stated that "political power grows out of the barrel of a gun." Only a dictator would think in such an evil deceitful manner and through his madness had resulted to millions being murdered. We must unveil their dark agendas with truth to destroy their quest for world dominance. Socialism is a direct path for dictatorship, where a socialist government controls all aspects of humanity through their ideology of utopian society. The socialist groups preach their ideology of supporting the working class, but in reality, their ideology smothers the working class with intense taxing to pay for their immense control over humanity, and a corrupted welfare system.

There are different forms of socialism that are all equally destructive to any nation's economy. The aftermath for such ideology will lead the people burden with a tremendous debt. The ideology of socialism is when the population owns and controls production and equally distributes the proportion that was produced back to the people. The illusion, is the fact that the socialist government will control production and the distribution to the people is through a welfare system that will leave the people in poverty. Their ideology is to remove all classes from a society, where everyone has an equal share of the wealth. In reality, socialism destroys the middle class, resulting to only two classes surviving with the majority living in poverty and the very small wealthy class. The two most common practices in socialism is a socialist democracy and Marxism socialism. The ideology of all socialism had derived from the idea of utopian socialism, which was unattainable and unrealistic. The only way they can make this idea work was by removing wealth from the working class through different forms of redistribution of wealth and through a welfare system. The idea of a utopian socialist society is collapsing and a new evil entity is emerging through socialist science. The ideas of socialism have transformed repeatedly in the last century, which is a good indication that the system of government is severely flawed. Socialism produces far less goods while creating a tremendous debt for the people through immense governmental controls and a corrupted welfare system. When socialist forms of governments around the world began to collapse due to their immense debt their welfare system will collapse with it and be replaced by governmentally ran worker programs. Socialist forms of governments have already begun to economically collapse nations around the world and when socialist ideology collapses its evil twin communism will fill the void. There are also different forms of communism and their ideology is very similar to socialism. The idea of a communist society is where the people own all manufacturing or industrial companies, it is a system of government where all property is owned by the community. In reality, a communist controlled government controls everything leaving the people in poverty and without rights. Today's China is controlled by the Communist Party of

China and even though there are other parties in China such as the China Democratic League or Chinese Association for Protecting Democracy they have very little power or control over policies. There is no doubt that China is an authoritarian government bent on absolute control and anyone who challenges their political structure is imprisoned or exiled. The Chinese government is filled with corruption, greed and anyone who challenges their authority or imprisoned. There is no such thing as freedom of speech or press and China has imprisoned more journalists than any other nation around the world. Economically China is very strong with the ability of producing most of the goods sold around the world. The reason for China's economic success is due to a socialist plan for redistribution of wealth on a worldwide scale. Through programs in America like foreign aid or economic relief has transfer wealth from our nation to nations around the world. The world's elite class are also responsible for China's industrial explosion as well as other third world countries. The elite class strategized on how to create a cheap labor force to maximize the profitability by removing their industries to third world countries.

America, throughout my life I have been observant as I have watched our great nation transformed to socialism. I have watched governmental programs for redistribution of wealth come and go such as the government 235 program, which helped low income families afford homes. The welfare program has become a tool of the socialist movement for redistribution of wealth. They have incited the people with their socialist ideology that has fueled violence through rioting. I have seen people protest outside the Food Stamp office, where a lady was yelling "You're going to feed my kids!" Have we truly become a society where people can make their demand for free food, or free housing, and who is responsible for their demands? Social welfare is not free, for it is paid for by the working people. During Pres. Obama's 2012 election, I witnessed on the media a video that went viral of a woman who supported Pres. Obama, because he got her a free phone. Have we become a society where politicians can easily buy our votes? Today I sit back in my chair contemplating our future. The past has been laid out before us and if you would only look you would find the truth. The problems in our past are complex but by breaking them down into separate issues they can be resolved. It is important to right these wrongs of our past, to gives us and our children the ability to have a prosperous future. Before we can right the wrongs of our past we must first end the madness in Washington.

Through over taxation and intense governmental regulations has resulted to industries fleeing America. This will continue into the future if we do not stop this madness! Today our government has passed more intense laws to regulate our industries, banking, and has launched a massive war against our fossil fuel companies. These evil plots have destroyed our economic growth. Our massive increase in taxes has resulted from a big government, and a corrupted welfare system. For the people, by the people has fallen silent as a great beast has risen. The beast that has risen bears many face's, as their evil intent has only one mission, to dismantle America brick by brick. For well over a century they have asserted their monstrous control through programs to spread their corrupted ideology. They have asserted their influence by creating their own political parties. The Communism movement failed in their attempted to overthrow our government, where socialism has succeeded in infiltrated Washington with their evil plots.

America make no mistake, for socialism has taken root within our foundation at the cost of our own prosperity and freedom. Socialist ideology is bent on controlling the economy through controlling industry, which has left millions more Americans in poverty. Their pathway of destruction has led us to an overtax society, and with their intense regulations on our industries has destroyed new opportunities for us all. As these crooked politicians grasp for more power and control has dramatically increased the cost of living for every American. Through their socialist ideology they have established 120 different departments in welfare that is bankrupting our nation. I attempted to add the accumulative spending of our social welfare programs through the decades, which only resulted in my own madness. In the 1970s we spent a little over 500 billion in welfare. Through the 80s we spent 1.5 trillion and through the 90s we spent 3 trillion. Through Pres. Obama's administration we spent almost $10 trillion, America this is ludicrous. If we add the accumulative spending in welfare, we have spent $15 trillion in four decades. This tremendous wealth should have been used for repairing our infrastructure or programs to stimulate job growth within our nation. America, we must use common sense, through their plans to convert us to a socialist country has created immense taxes, and their regulations are smothering our industrial growth. It is not hard to know the plans of the Liberal Democrats and socialist movement, for today they are bold as they openly allow Americans to view their plans. Today there is a movement in Washington to replace the social welfare system with a new plan for basic income guarantee. America, I plead with you to look into this matter for yourself, for if we continue to do nothing will only result to leaving our children with nothing.

The liberal democratic plan to increase taxes on the rich is ridiculous, already the top 50% gross income earners pay well over 90% of all federal income tax. They are also planning on imposing stiffer regulations on our industries, large businesses, and farms. Now there are talks in the liberal as well as the socialist to mandate an employee stock ownership plan known as ESOP. America, we must wake up before all the industries flee America. Our government is leaning towards over taxation, harsh regulations and now they want to force companies to give stocks to their employees? I ask you to use common sense, if you ran a corporation in this challenging worldwide market: would you stay in a nation where the government is draining your income? They have even proposed the idea on putting a cap on what a CEO can make each year. I do agree that CEO in America make far too much money, but by allowing our government to impose such control will only results to more control been placed over the people.

This is socialism America, which will do nothing more than make our CEO's flee across the border. This is already happening on a smaller scale where CEO's or millionaires are fleeing states that have imposed stiff taxes on the wealthy. The majority of these states are Liberal Democratic states that are facing major debt problems through social welfare programs, intensive environmental movement, and excessive pensions that were forced onto our government and industries by the unions. These plans have only resulted in one thing, a massive scale of redistribution of wealth and they are raising the bar on those who can receive earned income credit. They also plan to enhance several benefit programs and there are those who have proposed a plan to give every child born in poverty a thousand dollars in their own bank account while receiving money yearly until they reach the age of five. America, we must realize that in a five-year span, starting in 2009 our federal government spent almost 4 trillion on welfare by 2013. In the same year span our federal government spent close to $700 billion on education and transportation.

Welfare has created a tremendous burden on our nation and is leading to our bankruptcy. The revenue that was used through our welfare system could have been best used for creating jobs, which would stimulate our economy. This would have dramatically lower the number of those receiving welfare benefits. I will say it again, these benefit programs are not free, nor is the money received from earned income credit. It is not fair we live in a society who punishes those who are successful. One of the greatest tools to motivate our young is for them to know they will be rewarded if they are successful. If we destroy this motivation, will it not also destroy innovation? Is it truly fair that we live in a society where a good proportion pays nothing in Federal Income Taxes?

I blame our government for the path we are on, but it is also our fault for not being aware of these massive changes. Because we have not paid attention, our politicians only represent their own agenda or those of big business. Lobbying is one of the biggest corruptions in our government where both Republicans and Democrats are guilty. I blame both parties for supporting the elite. We must vote the politicians out of offices that only support their own agenda or the elite's agenda. The

Democrats and Republicans are equally guilty for supporting the elite, but the Democrats are more responsible for pushing a socialist ideology into law.

America, it is time to turn our backs on the Democrat Party if they do not clean up their party for they have been polluted with ideology that is un-American. I ask you: when was the last time we have had a good Democratic president? I will also be the first to admit the Republican Party has made mistakes but the Democrats have sold our technology, weakened our military, and created so many regulations that industries are fleeing America. Both parties are responsible for bankrupting America but the Democratic Party has pushed more welfare programs which has resulted in the destruction of the middle class. The Democrats are the ones that have put us in a path for a socialist style government, and as they tightened their grip they are squeezing the life out of the middle class. I was shocked to hear Russia's former President Vladimir Putin's speech in Switzerland on economics. He stated that he was going lower taxes on the industry, as well as lowering the governmental demand. What he was calling for was freeing up Russian industries, giving them tax incentives for new growth and less regulations. Tell me is this not what America once stood for? I would like for you to read this Russian newspaper article on how Russia perceives us.

THE PRAVADA

"Putin in 2009, outlined his strategy for economic success. Alas, poor Obama did the opposite but nevertheless was re-elected. Bye, bye Miss American Pie. The Communists have won in America with Obama but failed miserably in Russia with Zyuganov who only received 17% of the vote. Vladimir Putin was re-elected as President keeping the NWO out of Russia while America continues to repeat the Soviet mistake. After Obama was elected in his first term as president the then Prime Minister of Russia, Vladimir Putin gave a speech at the World Economic Forum in Davos, Switzerland in January of 2009. Ignored by the West as usual, Putin gave insightful and helpful advice to help the world economy and saying the world should avoid the Soviet mistake. Recently, Obama has been re-elected for a 2nd term by an illiterate society and he is ready to continue his lies of less taxes while he raises them. He gives speeches of peace and love in the world while he promotes wars as he did in Egypt, Libya and Syria. He plans his next war is with Iran as he fires or demotes his generals who get in the way. Any normal individual understands that as true but liberalism is a psychosis. Obama even keeps the war going along the Mexican border with projects like "fast and furious" and there is still no sign of ending it. He is a Communist without question promoting the Communist Manifesto without calling it so. How shrewd he is in America. His cult of personality mesmerizes those who cannot go beyond their ignorance. They will continue to follow him like those fools who still praise Lenin and Stalin in Russia. Obama's fools and Stalin's fools share the same drink of illusion."

I do not agree with this article entirely, nor do I agree with those calling Putin the next Regan. Anybody in Russia who has disagreed or gotten in the way of Putin have either disappeared or died. Let us not forget it was Russia who invaded Georgia and still occupies the Northern territory. There were two reasons why Russia invaded Georgia: to test the world's response while showcasing Russia's military power and mostly to control the gas lines of Northern Georgia. Today Russia supplies most of the natural gas in Europe. Russia is a socialist nation built on conquest. If they can control Europe's energy sources they then can control Europe.

I will give Vladimir credit because he is very smart. By freeing up industries he gives them the opportunity to grow. This could allow Russia to obtain massive wealth. With Europe falling into mass chaos our generation will probably witness a huge power shift. Eastern European countries as well as some of the southern countries may break away from the European Union and make alliances with Russia. Russia has already made an alliance with Iran and is purchasing a massive amount of oil through other Middle Eastern nations. Another thing to realize is how close the relationship between Russia and China has become. This goes to show how strong Russia's influence has become. The Democrat Party has destroyed growth as well as the image of our once great nation. Russia is predicting America's collapse, and a professor, Igor Panarin has predicted that America will break up into many smaller nations with the Northeastern section joining the European Union.

America, we must wake up! It's not too late. I do not believe Russia can control or tell our future. We must realize the majority of the problems we are facing today resulted from the brainwashing of the old Soviet empire. This brainwashing started with universities, which would eventually lead to organizations such as IPS, SDS, and CPUSA. These organizations became powerful within our own borders and would later infiltrate our own Democratic Party. The past two Democratic Presidents we have had, Bill Clinton and President Barack Obama were no more than puppets to their organization. These organizations would utilize the power of our presidents to pass socialist laws, pass immense regulations and destroy our Constitution. President Obama has also made plans to step on our second amendment right to bear arms. His administration has stated they are for a UN Gun Ban Treaty to prevent the international sale of guns to other nations. He has also indicated he wants to restrict gun sales within our own borders. What I find shocking is that this UN Gun Ban was postponed on two separate occasions. Once in the election of 2012 and the second time was due to Hurricane Sandy. I will be honest. I do not trust our president, for he does not support our Constitution, so how could he possibly support our rights as Americans? During his administration he has bypassed Congress and shows no concern for state rights. He has lied to the American people and signed bills behind closed doors. There is no transparency in his government nor in this man's past. We must realize that if President Obama or Hillary Clinton signs this UN treaty, he can then bypass Congress by passing an executive order and ban all guns in the private sector. The fact is it is very likely we will hear our president has signed in an executive order for all Americans to turn in all their guns. This has already happened to many nations around the world and has been a movement within our nation for a long time. The N.W.O (New World Order) strongly supported by George Soros has been pushing for international gun ban to establish a one world order. George Soros supported Obama's campaign with one million dollars to ensure President Obama would be elected to push through the agenda of N.W.O.

America, I plead for you. Do not make up your mind from what I am telling you until you have done your own research on Bill Ayers, George Soros, and other organizations I have brought up through this book. These organizations understand that there is a deep-rooted pride in Americans and even though there are shameful things in our history we have accomplished and achieved many great things. They have plotted to distort the truth to break the pride of Americans. They have also plotted to bankrupt our nation for Americans will not give up their sovereignty so easily. Their agenda is to destroy our Constitution and corrupt the check and balances of our government. Their next move will be the removal of our arms, so we can no longer protect our Constitution.

The tragic massacre that happened at Sandy Hook Elementary was definitely a dark day for America. My heart truly goes out to those parents of these innocent little victims, the teachers and staff. It truly depresses me to see how violence has escalated in our society but worse of all in our schools. This truly disturbed me for I am the father of three daughters. Each morning I walk my daughters to the school bus stop, as the bus arrives they give me a kiss on the cheek goodbye and to tell you the truth, I cannot even bear the thought it might be the last time I see them. Our schools are supposed to be a safe-haven for our children to learn, grow and not have to worry about such dangers. What I find shocking is how quick President Obama and other Liberal Democrats responded to this issue by promoting gun bans. Even if guns were eliminated in the private sector, would it stop the black market?

During the prohibition, we attempted to outlaw alcohol which failed miserably. Today we have outlawed drugs and have even made massive attempts to keep them out of our schools which have failed miserably as well. Like prohibition, the war on drugs has created violent gangs and made mafia's rich. I do agree with the war to keep drugs out of our schools and off the streets but a gun ban I firmly disagree with. I believe there should be more intensive background checks and screenings on all applications. I also believe anyone who wishes to obtain a firearm must be required to pass a course on gun safety at their own expense.

I also have many questions pertaining to this horrible incident at Sandy Hook Elementary. The biggest question is how Adam Lanzar got his brother's ID and gained entry to the school. His brother indicated he had not seen him in a long time so how could he have possibly obtained his ID? Reports also came out that there were only two guns used in the shootings but as the police later reported there were four guns and the assault rifle that was used was found in Adam's trunk. If Adam never left the school after the massacre, then how did the assault rifle end up in his trunk? Even the coroner clearly stated the assault rifle was used on the victims. The biggest thing that confuses me is the two other men who were apprehended by the police. One of the two men had to be chased by the police before he was apprehended. This incident was heartbreaking but it must be investigated thoroughly. We must find understanding to help prevent this from ever happening again. Psychologically we must look in Adam Lanza's past. If he was mentally ill why was he allowed access to firearms? Also, why did his mother allow him to have shooting practice? His mother was a well-known prepper who believed our society would crumble. Could teachings such as this affected Adam's mental health? Also, where does his father Peter Lanza vice president of taxes and financial services for GE play into this madness? I will not make any excuses for Adam but we must analyze his behavior. We also cannot allow President Obama to use this tragedy to ban guns.

America our biggest problem is not only have we removed God from our society but our schools. There is no doubt that atheism has gained massive momentum in our society. The teachings of Darwinism and the Big Bang theory contradict the book of Genesis. The strong Liberal stance has abolished prayer in school and even a judge in 2010 ruled that prayer day was unconstitutional. Tell me if prayer day is unconstitutional then what happened to "In God We Trust," or "One nation under God?" Our nation was established on the principles of freedom of religion which gave people the opportunity to worship God in their own way. This has been nothing more than an attack on our Christian principles which has resulted to confusion and hopelessness for our young.

How many people today do not believe in the Bible in its entirety? But how can they with such ludicrous theories being taught in our schools? Today there has been much evidence that has come forth to disprove these ridiculous theories but they are continuously being ignored. The removal of God in our society has come with severe consequences. Crime has escalated in our society, along with drug use and teen pregnancies. We have become a society that is corrupt, lustful, and worst of all a "me" society which is based on greed. If our faith diminishes we will then become a society that will not believe we will be held accountable for our decisions. If we distort the reality of our afterlife we will become a society with little hope. They want us to believe that when we die we will simply be turned into dust. It is true, our shell will turn to dust but we have a soul and there is an afterlife. America was once a proud nation by the greatness of God due to our strong Christian principles. This has been an attack on America's true foundation, stone by stone. It began with an attack on our Christian principles and now our Constitution is being attacked. They want to abolish our Constitution along with our rights to bear arms. Their next attack will be on freedom of speech and to silence our Congress. America set your spirit free, let your voice be heard and let President Obama not trample on our Constitution.

America, I call out for you to be weary for very few are at our guard towers. I ask you to come and stand at the wall with me and let us shout in one loud voice "no more!" We must realize President Obama's executive orders result in only one thing: absolute power. The ability to control our transportation, utilities, and even our airports has clearly shown the thirst for power. Today I witnessed President Obama's speech about gun control as he signs his 23 executive orders into law. I have no doubt that Congress will vote against these executive orders. Many state governors and law officials have spoken out against this violation of the second amendment.

I ,myself, do not have a semi-automatic assault rifle but we must preserve the right for those who desire to purchase such a gun for protection. There have been many cases where it has taken several rounds to stop a criminal. I remember one case when I was young where one of my friends had to fire his gun four times to stop a violent attack. Another case that comes to mind was where a woman was home alone with her kids and had no alternative but to fire her gun five times at a violent criminal, and even with being hit five times he had the ability to flee out her door.

President Obama's executive orders are the most intense gun restrictions we have seen in the past decades. We must realize through the years, and even future administrations, there will be attempts to pass more gun restrictions. The UN has made massive attempts for a world-wide band and could later pose gun restrictions on America while violating our constitutional right. America, we must boldly stand up not just for our rights and the second amendment but for all of our rights. Even our fourth amendment has been severely violated by the Supreme Court.

The right of the people to be secure in their persons, houses, papers, and effects, against unreasonable searches and seizures, shall not be violated, and no Warrants shall issue, but upon probable cause, supported by Oath or affirmation, and particularly describing the place to be searched, and the persons or things to be seized.

Today law officials can demand identification without probable cause. They can install cameras on or around your property and even seize your cell phone to review its content without a warrant. Border patrol has even installed roadblocks nowhere near American borders. DHS has been guilty of doing the same; both agencies claim the terminology of "mere suspicion," which gives them the right to search your personal belongings. Mere suspicion is just another term to legalize racial profiling or to judge someone by how they are dressed or what vehicle they are driving. For an example, someone young who is driving an expensive car may be harassed for suspicion of drugs. This can also be used to harass someone who is poor. Without tangible evidence our law officials should have no right to search your vehicle or your personal belongings which include your cell phone without a warrant. I have heard many claims if you have nothing to hide then why does it matter? Well it matters because it is a blatant violation of our Constitutional rights and I as well as many Americans refuse to live our life as suspects. We are Americans, with rights to live our lives without harassment. The infringement on our rights started many decades ago and at first it seemed minor but as you look at it today, you can see we have lost many of our freedoms. Once again I want to quote one of our forefathers: **"ANY SOCIETY THAT WOULD GIVE UP A LITTLE LIBERTY TO GAIN A LITTLE SECURITY WILL DESERVE NEITHER AND LOOSE BOTH."** Benjamin Franklin

America, it is time to take a stand and hold all branches of our government responsible for violations against our Constitutional rights. President Obama has passed laws where Americans can be arrested and held without trial and jury. I ask you, is this the America you want? I have heard many claims they are violating our Constitutional rights with the gun restrictions. America the greatest violation is against our fourth amendment due to corrupted laws that violates our constitutional rights. This concerns me greatly for a rage burns with in me for many of you are still asleep. This onslaught against our Constitutional rights has been going on for many decades. President Obama is destroying our Constitution but to only lay the blame on his administration is foolish for this attack has been going on for many years. Our government has the power to listen to our phone conversations and even track our mail. They have the ability to know your complete medical history and for what reason should they have all these rights? The people once lived in the land of the free but this land is no longer free as it is fences and great walls are erected. We must take a stand and a stand we must to ensure our rights. We must banish those in Washington by removing them from their seat of power and restoring their seat to the people. Let Abram Lincoln words echo across America "we the people are the masters of our government and the courts."

I was proud to see so many Democrats had taken a stand against President Obama's plan for gun restrictions. This gave me a ray of hope until I heard the words from Democratic Congressman Hank Johnson and Democratic Representative Charlie Rangel claim that anyone who did not support President Obama on gun laws was racist. I am sick and tired of this race card being continuously used. Tell me can you not have an intelligent debate without using this race issue? Our nation was established by check and balances to ensure American voices were heard. The very design of Congress or even our Senate was established by debate, for debate. The establishment of our government was debated by our forefathers and we must encourage debate today to ensure we take the right path without violating the people's rights. Our forefathers divided the Legislative Branch into two separate entities, the Congress and the Senate to ensure stronger debate for a stronger check and balance system.

The reason why politicians use the race card is to intimidate the opposition so their voice will be silent. Tell me, do we really want our government to be controlled by one party through intimidation, manipulation, or this ridiculous propaganda that is being spread out through their Liberal media? Recently, I have heard those from the Liberal media compare the NRA to the Nazi party. There is no denying it, the Democratic Party is now a socialist party and what were the Nazi's? A socialist party. The Democratic Party has filled their ranks with socialist and communist ideology. They have passed more governmental regulations and restrictions than any other party. The Democratic Party has also passed more socialist reform than any other party. Today nearly everything in our country is regulated by our government and with the destruction of our Constitution we will be no more than subjects to a dictator.

America the subject I am about to get into shook me to my core. I wanted to cry out "no more!' for the realization that our once great nation may not be here for our children. This is a red alert for the threat is real. Our government is moving into a direction for total dominance. In 2010, President Obama signed in an executive order establishing a panel for Council of Governors. This is a panel of ten that will be hand-picked by our presidents in case of an emergency or if martial law is ever declared. The plan is to divide America into ten zones, in which each governor would be responsible for their own zone. President Obama has signed this executive order for two reasons. The first is to obtain optimal control and the second reason is to eventually dissolve all state rights along with their Constitutions. The Federal government has continuously through the years violated state rights. The federal Government has also passed laws that have weakened state rights and its thirst is power. The Federal government is violating the tenth amendment and if we the people do not stop this grasp for power then who will? The Tenth Amendment clearly states: ***"The powers not delegated to the United States by the Constitution, nor prohibited by it to the states, are reserved to the states respectively, or the people."***

This clearly states that the Federal government's power is limited and nor can it exercise its right over state issues. Our Federal government has plans to put into action an international ID which would give DHS the power to eye scan and fingerprint every American. There are even plans to insert a chip into the international identification card. I have no doubt this plan will fail. What I am insinuating is they will later claim to prevent identity theft; they have no alternative but to insert the chip under our flesh. This is a severe threat to our privacy.

This international identity card would give our Federal government instant access to our private records. There has also been talk of inserting a microchip through the Universal Health Care Act. They can also establish scanners which would give them the ability to track our movement. America, you must wake up! You will not even be able to work without this international ID card or microchip nor will you be able to purchase goods.

America, you must wake up for already today you cannot work without a state issued ID nor can you have your utilities turned on without identification. My concern is not so much about the state issued ID but the international ID is nothing more than a course for dominance. The N.W.O or One World Order is behind this push in the international ID card. They also want to push for a one world currency or a cashless society. A cashless society is where cash has no value. As you go to work you will be paid through your bank in credits or debits. Do we really want to give up our sovereignty and who will control this one world order? For me to imagine that one person could attempt to rule the world is horrifying. I do not want to believe this is the direction that the government is pushing us into but there is evidence that cannot be ignored. The super elite has orchestrated their control over the world's economy and have adopted socialism as a form of government for a New World Order. George Soros is a strong supporter of the N.W.O and is very close to our president. Throughout my life I have heard and even read many conspiracy theories which I will be the first to admit most hold no validity but there are some conspiracy theories that are no longer theories but are facts. For years, we heard the Illuminati were just a myth, but Rockefeller admitted in his biography he was an Illuminati and he helped establish the United Nations to launch their plan to usher in the New World Order.

There are many powerful leaders or those who have powerful influences manipulating our government such as David Rockefeller, George Soros, and the Rothschild family. These powerful elites have put us on the course for a one world order. I have read articles explaining this one world order or this new world order and found their definition varies. One idea is to dissolve all governments and create a one world government supported by a one world military. It seems most lean to nations keeping their sovereignty while relinquishing their governmental powers to a one world governmental panel. This panel reminds me of the UN as they attempt to increase their power over nations. They support the international ID while attempting to pass an international gun ban. It frightens me to know this may occur in our lifetime and we must realize how much power this would give China. With China's massive population you can easily conclude they will carry one-third of the world's vote. That is if we are even allowed to vote. Another thing we must realize is how corrupt this one world panel would become. By allowing communist countries like China on the board they can easily rig these elections to ensure they have the balance of power. I do hope this new world order is not a threat to our nation but if it is not a threat then why have Russian leaders vigorously fought to keep the NWO movement out of their country? Another thing that concerns me immensely is the Georgia Guide stones which many have referred to as the new Ten Commandments.

The Ten Guides

1. Maintain humanity under 500,000,000 in perpetual balance with nature.
2. Guide reproduction wisely, improving fitness and diversity.
3. Unite humanity with a living new language.
4. Rule passion, faith, tradition, and all things with tempered reason.
5. Protect people and nations with fair laws and just courts.
6. Let all nations rule internally resolving external disputes in a world court.
7. Avoid petty laws and useless officials.
8. Balance personal rights with social duties.
9. Prize truth, beauty, love, seeking harmony with the infinite.
10. Be not a cancer on the earth, leave room for nature.

Let me end this talk now about these "new ten commandments," for there are only ONE set of Commandments and they are found in our Bible. The very first so called commandment concerns me greatly and that is to keep the human population under 500,000,000. Many have indicated this means nothing but if it means nothing why would anyone go to the expense to erect such a monument? This subject of controlling human population has been discussed through many circles around the world in the past and present. In China, they are limited to one child per family. What worries me is we can eventually become a society where you must obtain a governmental permission before you can have a child. I am not indicating this will occur in our future, but I will state human society has a tendency to repeat the past.

In the 1940's, Socialist Nazi Germany laid out a plan to increase the number of blonde hair with blue eyes in their population as they called it purifying their race. They created breeding facilities to accomplish this goal and raised the children in makeshift orphanages so the mothers could continue to have babies. These poor German children grew up never knowing who their parents where was a blatant violation against human rights. The Nazis also discussed the matter of only allow those who are the most intelligent and fittest to be allowed to have children. This ideology from the Nazi Party along with the very meaning of the Georgia Guide stones is a violation to humanity. Another Law in the Georgia Guide stones that troubles me is we must balance personal freedom with civic duty. This so-called commandment or law will lead humankind to a corrupted dictatorship that will lead us all to enslavement. We must never become a society where the people are forced to give up a portion of their freedom to governmental control. America, we must see the dangers that are lurking in the darkness and how many of these organizations have infiltrated our government to fulfill their evil plots. Many of these evil organizations have merged their armies of deceivers to bring forth their plans for world dominance. Even our own politicians have become sickened from their wine of deception for the New World Order. We must never allow America to fall into a one world order or the N.W.O. for this monster will only result in one thing: a communist style dictator. The old Soviet Union once believed in a world that was controlled by communism. For me the old Soviet Flag could indicate what type of world we would have to endure. The blood-soaked flag represents the millions that were murdered and the hammer represents the forced labor. The scythe, the very instrument that the fictional Grim Reaper carried shows how communism has the control of life and death. I have faith in the American people and many of our politicians will not allow this atrocity to happen in America. The thing that baffles me is the fact that we fought against Socialist Nazi Germany in World War II, and today I see many nations has adopted socialism or at the beginning stages of socialism. World governments are being overran by dictators that are influenced by the powerful elites of The World.

America the abuse of the executive power within our nation concerns me greatly. For most of the history of our nation the executive branch was kept fair and balanced by the Constitution. The executive branch was kept in check by the Legislative or Judicial Branch and Capitalism remained free. Today the Executive branch overpowers everything, as they have become the masters over our health care, education and our economy through controlling industry. Our politicians step on our Constitution like its yesterday's trash. The Federal branch blatantly ignores state rights and proceeds as if though the states have no Constitutional rights. The Executive branch attempts to control the Congress and the Senate or bypasses them with executive orders. Even the Judicial Branch is under the control or is bypassed by the executive branch. The Executive branch has become America's monster and its next move is to exert its power over the people. We must not forget how Pres. Obama stated the Constitution was an impractical document, and how many other presidential administrations have passed laws that were unconstitutional. I truly believe the Executive branch understands this will cause civil unrest by the removing of our Constitutional rights. This is the very reason they are attempting to pass more gun laws to disarm America. If they can disarm the private sector and abolish the first amendment to keep us silent they will then move to abolish the Constitution.

In America, we once had the right to assemble but today we must have a permit or license to assemble. Is this not asking our government for permission? In the Constitution, it clearly states in the first amendment there shall be no laws restricting the freedom of speech. America, we must wake up, the first, second, and fourth amendment have severely been trampled over by our government. We must not allow the International Gun Ban to be passed by any administration. Nor shall we allow the executive branch to have the power to bypass the legislative or judicial branch. Before us lies a grueling task, for we cannot allow the executive branch or Congress to disarm America. There is no doubt our Executive branch has prepared for martial law. DHS has become an extremely powerful militarized federal police force. They have become so powerful that many governmental departments have fallen under their jurisdictions. These powers give them the ability to stretch their tentacles across America. These departments that fall under their jurisdictions are the NSA, U. S. Coast Guard, FEMA, U.S. Border Patrol, U.S. Custom Officers, Immigration officers, and many more departments that gives this agency tremendous power. They have recently purchased another two hundred million rounds of ammunition to add to their already accumulated 1.4 billion rounds of .40 cal. ammunition. There are those who claim this abundant stock pile of ammunition is being used for target practice, but I tell you this is nothing but a lie. The ammunition they have ordered is a high power .40 cal. hallow point rounds designed for maximum damage. They have also ordered 9 million rounds of sniper ammunition along with stock piling immense riot gear. It's not just the question of why they are stock piling ammunition but why are they ordering powerful .40 cal. ammunition?

DHS has established a plan to set checkpoints across our nation in cooperation with other agencies. They have purchased armored vehicles, armored pillboxes; does this not remind you of the old Soviet Union or Nazi Germany? Our military has orchestrated live training exercises in cities across America for preparation of civil unrest. America, you must wake up and see the power that could bear down on us by the executive branch or our own military, DHS, Border Patrol, and your local law enforcement. They are already tightening their grip upon us all. DHS has already arrested Americans for exercising their Constitutional Rights.

It wasn't that long ago, in New York, a network was filming a peaceful march where a police officer ordered a cameraman to stop filming. They were not on private property and as the reporter expressed his rights to be there the police officer ordered the man to quit filming again. The police officer then became enraged and placed the camera man under arrest. The reporter then tried to indicate to the police officer he could not do this in which the police officer responded boldly, "I can do whatever I want." He then threatened to arrest the reporter. If we allow this corruption to continue we will no longer have rights. It is most urgent for us to stand up for our rights today for if we wait the chance of deviating from this horrible course will be too late. If martial law falls on us the Executive branch would then have the power to execute their plan for complete control. The Executive branch will control our media through President Obama's executive orders. Military and DHS could then halt all traveling which would isolate cities and towns across our nation. If civil unrest was to break out in our cities the executive branch could use another executive order passed by Pres. Obama and shut off the utilities for those cities.

America, you must realize this is a serious matter, the DHS has armed their department with militarize weapons. They have purchased armored vehicles, drones and even biometric surveillance to spy on us all. It truly worries me that one day we may live in such a society where the people have no privacy or rights. How impossible would it be to live without the international identification card or chip implant? You will not be able to work or even purchase goods. Imagine how it would feel as you're coming to a checkpoint and you have to pull over to the side because you do not have the international card or the chip implant. They would then demand to see your papers as you are no longer treated as a citizen. By then your name is probably already put in on a list as anti-American or potential terrorist. There already is a governmental watch list established and many have indicated the DHS has their own watch list. If you are Pro-Constitutional, pro-life or even a member of the NRA your name may be on the list. I have recently heard of a campaign manager finding out her name was on a list. Tell me is this the America our forefathers laid out for us? I have read an article where there were plans to use the media to encourage Americans to turn in their neighbors or even family members who could be suspected as terrorists. This may not be a plan of the Executive branch as of yet but you have to realize the socialist ideology of the Liberal left will seep in like a sickness into the Democratic Party then this infection will spread through the Executive branch. The socialist movement in Germany utilize fear to structure a new form of government for the Nazi Party after Germany's Parliament was burned down. It was evident that the Nazis party were responsible for this fire but they quickly use false propaganda to blame the German Communist Party to silence their adversary. The Nazis also use false propaganda to commit their nation to war against Poland and other nations by falsely indicating that these nations were attacking German settlements. We are becoming a nation that is being ruled by fear as our politician's pass laws to give us a false sense of security. I would like to remind you of the words of one of our presidents. *"WE HAVE NOTHING TO FEAR BUT FEAR IT SELF."* *-FRANKLIN D. ROOSEVELT*

Are we to become a society who lives in fear? This has been a tactic perpetrated by our own government to create a fearful society, in order to politically corrupt our system and to dissolve our constitutional rights. In fear, we have held our heads low to the ground for far too long. I call out America, for there is a master that has risen and is about to assert its power over us all. Today our Military in cooperation with the DHS has the power to arrest without charge and detain without trial any supposedly suspected terrorist. Even Americans!!! This is an outrage; our Constitution has been completely thrown out the window with the NDAA Act Pres. Obama signed in and the Patriot Act Pres. Bush signed in to law. America, we must realize how our past two presidents have infringed on our rights and we are all without true representation.

The executive orders that Pres. Bush and Pres. Obama have signed into law or un-American. These laws have corrupted our system of government and have infringed on our personal freedoms. We must rip these corrupted pages from our law books, so we may restore Americas true foundation. The Patriot Act, Directive 51, and the NDAA Act must be removed, for they are abomination to America. I was shocked that Pres. Obama could pass such a law, considering he was once a civil rights lawyer. His executive order is a violation against our Constitution, and a violation against human rights. He is a great deceiver, as he not only destroys our dreams he brings forth the demise of our freedom. These executive orders by our past two presidents will send a shockwave of fear and panic across our nation when activated to their full intent if martial law is declared. Their intent is to shock fear into all of Americans in order to pass more laws to make us all obedient. It truly shocked me to see so many politicians supported Pres. Obama's and President Bush's executive orders that threatens our rights. Many republicans in few Democrats argued against their executive orders, but unfortunately it was not enough. I would like to give you the words of Republican Ron Paul: *"It puts every American citizen at risk."*

Clearly you can see, this massive militarized police force that is controlled by the Executive branch. The Executive has also prepared the military as well as the police force in case of civil unrest is called. They are using the terminology "civil unrest" to minimize the reality of martial law. If martial law was declared the harsh and cold reality that we are no longer a free society will be realized. Our children will go to school seeing armed soldiers standing in street corners. As we attempt to travel we will have no choice but to suffer the long lines at check points. America will then be divided into ten districts were ten Council of Governors will enforce the executive laws. There may even come a time where you have to carry papers like a passport to travel from one district to the other. In the future if martial law was declared the Executive branch has become so powerful they can shut down Congress, Senate, and even dissolve the state Constitutions. This horrific assault on our foundation had derived from many administrations such as Pres. Bush's Directive 51 Act. These deceitful executive orders give unbelievable presidential powers to dissolve the legislative and judicial branch. No longer would state laws be recognized and even state borders could be easily erased. The Executive branch will establish a new government and the council of governors would be responsible for carrying out these orders. America, I will be the first to indicate this is far reaching but we must realize our government is definitely preparing for martial law. The Executive branch is destroying not only our Constitution but the very establishment that our forefathers have set for us. You also have to admit that democracy has been brought to her knees by the crushing blows of socialism. A better question would be, what would be the groundwork to bring forth martial law? I can indicate many things such as a natural disaster or the collapse of our economy.

I believe the preparation for martial law is to bring forth a massive change from the Executive branch that would result to civil unrest. The Executive branch is well aware that civil unrest will occur by the removal of the Constitution or making guns illegal in the private sector. There evil plots that has unfolded before us is to ensure our nation's compliance with the United Nations International Gun Ban and there is no place for our Constitution in their plans for a New World government. This is the reason they have been preparing a militarized police force and organizing FEMA for martial law. FEMA has established a plan to install over 200 concentration camps across America. They have also purchased old prisons and have gone through the process of refurbishing them with modern equipment. They have also made plans for reeducation facilities which would only result to brainwashing. There is even a plan to utilize these facilities into forced labor camps. America does this not remind you of Nazi Germany? They have even made plans to transport these suspected terrorists by utilizing the railroad as transportation.

In recent years, FEMA has purchased well over 100,000 boxcars and have allegedly purchased shackles. This is the same way the Socialist Nazi Germans transported the Jews to their concentration camps which would later lead to horrible crimes of Genocide. FEMA has also stockpiled millions of suspicious plastic rectangle boxes that can be easily used for coffins around our country.

America make no mistake, for we have been infiltrated by socialist ideology for well over a half a century. The powers of their organizations are far-reaching and very influential, as they insert their puppets in governments around the world. This infestation had gained momentum in our nation shortly after World War II through Project Paperclip. This was a top-secret plot that was initiated by our own government that allowed nearly 2000 German Nazis safe refuge in America. The fact that we gave war criminals immunity was a criminal act on our government's part. These were German engineers, scientists, and other high-ranking SS members, that would receive safe refuge in America. In fact, we absorbed a Nazi Spy Network to aid in spying on the Soviet Union, along with employing a little over 1000 Nazi Spy's into the CIA, FBI, and other governmental departments is disturbing. We must realize the socialist movement infiltrated our political branches through corrupt political organizations and their own socialist parties. They have infiltrated our state Department and many other departments in our government. These are departments like NASA, where Werner von Brown was director, and how many of these Nazi spies had worked their way up through the FBI or CIA. This has created a monster, for they have not only gained power through our political structure, that have also infiltrated our agency's that are responsible for our nation's security. Let us not forget how Director Hoover of the FBI warned America of the threat of communism and the Joseph McCarthy hearings had accused 205 members of the State Department of being communist or connected to communism. Even Pres. Kennedy warned America about secret organizations working from behind the scenes before he was assassinated. The monster of communism had lost momentum and was absorbed by the monster of socialism, but then again, they are both about absolute control.

This atrocity has fallen upon our shoulders for we have allowed it to happen. What is shameful is that we as taxpayers have paid for this monstrous act to take over which may lead to our demise. America, I call out for those who have awaken for now you have seen the beast. Now it is your duty to awaken your family, neighbors, and all those around you. Awaken them so they may see the horrible nightmare that is bearing down on us. I warn do not call out for arms for this monstrous government has prepared for you to do such a thing. Remember how Martin Luther King Jr. and all other great leaders called out for a peaceful march. I have indicated before that I am a strategist and I am telling you, you will be a fool to fight a war on their terms. America our greatest power is to know the truth in our power to vote. We must break through the walls of division and come together as one people. Let us shed this dark cloak of deception so truth and justice may be served. We must utilize our powers not to transform our government but to restore it to its original foundation. We must then abolish all laws that are unconstitutional and restore the balance of power in Washington for the Executive Branch has become too powerful, so we must set laws to restrict these powers. We must not allow our military to police our people on American soil for it is illegal. This law Posse Comitatus Act was established to prevent our military from ever violating our rights. We the people must never forget we are the masters of our government and our courts. In one loud voice, we must cry out that you cannot tamper with the Constitution nor shall it fade out into the darkness. Nor shall we allow their evil deception to entangle our minds with their lies, we must shatter their illusion with truth.

Pres. Obama accuses America of being colonialist, which sounds a lot like the rhetoric we hear from the socialist and communist parties. We must not listen to this rhetoric. The very foundation of America was built on anti-colonialism. The thirteen colonies suffered greatly under the British rule. The people had no rights and were treated as mere subjects to the king without a voice. This tyranny our forefathers suffered set the fires that brought forth Democracy. We were a nation of ideas, a people that desired freedom and demanded their voice to be heard. President Obama sees America through his father's eyes which influenced him greatly as a child. His intent is not just to redistribute wealth through America but through the world. This is the wealth that has been accumulated by not just from the sweat of your parents or grandparents but many generations back. He has attempted to halt coal mining and has made it difficult to obtain permits to drill oil in America, yet he allows China to drill off the Coast of America. He has also given South American countries billions of dollars to drill oil. Is this not redistribution at taxpayers' expense? His mission as our president is to sustain our economy and to create jobs in America yet he delayed or halted the Keystone pipeline and even invested in countries abroad. This destroys the opportunity for thousands of jobs in America. Tell me does this sound like the actions of someone who is pro-America? This onslaught against our nation's economy has continued for well over a half a century through many administrations. America, we have given trillions of our taxpayer dollars for economic relief to foreign nations for decades. We helped turn Third World countries into economic super powers by giving billions to industrialize their nation. Today South Korea is the seventh largest exporter in the world and has become the sixth largest military in the world. The United States transferred billions of taxpayers' dollars throughout the 1960s and in in 1965 we sent $600 million in economic relief to South Korea. The president of South Korean utilized this tremendous revenue to build power plants, water treatment facilities, and had industrialize their nation.

Today South Korea is one of the largest auto exporters and builds over 40% of the world ships. This is how America's wealth has been transferred to other nations throughout the world. For decades, our politicians have squandered our wealth by giving billions in appeasement for alliances. This atrocity to the American people has got to stop, our politicians have been careless and incompetent. Our politicians foolishly give our wealth away that has brought forth our nation's demise. These foreign nations utilize this tremendous revenue in economic relief to industrialize their nation which has resulted to more Americans losing their jobs as industries flee overseas. These Third World nations had industrialized overnight with a cheap labor force and when the NAFTA treaty was signed in by Pres. Clinton the stage was set for America's downfall.

Pres. Obama is attempting to bankrupt America through overspending and is destroying American industries by passing intense regulations. Our president has increased taxes on the rich that has resulted to slowing down of our economy and the rising of prices of goods sold. Even his universal health care is going to put a tremendous burden on America and how are we to pay for such a cause while managing our deficit? The Federal Reserve has reported since 2007 Americans have lost nearly 40% of their wealth. This could be easily indicated with the loss in value in real estate across America. Six million more Americans are now living in poverty and today half of America subsidizes their income with some form of government assistance. His plan to redistribute America's wealth worldwide has had a horrendous effect on America's wealth.

Pres. Obama has weakened America's ability to defend our nation with massive cuts in our military, as he secretly pledges with Russia to dismantle our missile defense system. He has planned to reduce the number of nuclear missiles we have in our arsenal. While not encouraging countries like North Korea, China, and even Russia to follow suit. I do not agree with nuclear weapons like many of you. We to realize our nuclear weapons or our missile defense is a deterrent preventing other nations from using their nuclear weapons on us. I do believe we must reduce the number of nuclear weapons around the world and even one day eliminate them altogether. First we must learn to work together to ensure everyone's safety. What Pres. Obama fails to realize is we live in a much more volatile world than ever before. Since his administration tension around the world has increased dramatically, especially in northern Africa or the Middle East. In fact, there has been a movement to unify the Islamic nations, which is a massive threat to America's and Israel's security. Pres. Obama has done nothing to stop the Islamic Brotherhood from spreading, nor has he attempted to stop Iran from obtaining Nuclear weapons. Instead present Obama has released $150 billion to Iran and has given billions more at taxpayer's expense. America this is appeasement! Pres. Reagan warned us in his speech, "we must fight" about giving into dictators demands, as he boldly stated "there is a line that must not be crossed."

There are many organizations through the Islamic movement strategizing on creating a caliphate and to usher in sharia law through the New World Order. America, it is urgent for us to wake up, for there is a movement through the globalist community to usher in worldwide sharia law. In France Pres. Obama stated, we need to educate ourselves on Islam, and if we add the Muslim population in America, we will be the largest Muslim nation in the world. Pres. Obama is spreading his deception, for we are a Christian-based nation, and the Muslim population is a little over 1%. Why has Pres. Obama attempted to deceive America, and what is his objective? A better question is; why would he indicate that America is an Islamic nation? If we had a president that indicated we were a Christian nation, the liberal left would be outraged. America, we are a Christian nation and we were founded on Christian principles.

Pres. Obama has praised Islamic nations and reached out to Islamic communities around the world. He has spent a fortune building mosques in Islamic nations at taxpayer's expense, while millions of Americans are left in poverty. America, I call out for you to do your own research for there are multiple dark agendas being committed on the political world stage today. The socialist and communist movement is fulfilling their evil plots to profoundly change America's structure to their style of government. Their beastly tentacles intertangle with other un-American movements to fulfill their evil agenda. The liberal movement, the illuminati, corporate elite, and the Islamic movement have all worked together through socialist or communist organizations to destroy democracy in America. Let us make no mistake for their agenda has been laid out before us, and the first mission was to destroy our faith. They infiltrated our educational system to pollute the minds of our young with their lies in evolution and have manipulated our history to destroy patriotism. Why has Islam or the Muslim faith been accepted as a standard subject to be taught in many schools across America? While Prayer, The Commandments, and even the Pledge of Allegiance was removed from public schools. This onslaught of false propaganda has destroyed faith by the millions and have silence millions more. A federal judge has declared prayer day unconstitutional, while businesses across our nation demand employees to hide any Christian symbols. We Christians need to unify and be proud to announce our faith proudly once again. We shall no longer be persecuted or kept silent, for our strength is our faith in God and our faith in humankind. America, we must unify to stomp out the madness that has enveloped all people and rip the pages of deception from our society. Let a great voice speak from the past:

"If I could conceive that the general government might ever be so administered as to render the liberty of conscience insecure, I beg you will be persuaded, that no one would be more zealous than myself to establish effectual barriers against the horrors of spiritual tyranny, and every species of religious persecution."

-Founding Father George Washington

There are multitudes of Islamic nations that desires to see the destruction of America, Israel, and our allies. I have no doubt Pres. Obama is anti-Semitic through his policies as our president, and his inability to defend Israel. Through his administration he has had a dramatic effect in the Middle Eastern nations and terrorism has continued to spread. The fact, he skipped Israel on one of his Middle Eastern tour's and has shown very little support for Israel has strengthened anti-Semitism in the Islamic world. He has toured the Islamic world giving great speeches of motivation while villainizing America. Pres. Obama has spent well over $1 billion of taxpayer's money in repairing mosque around the world. The State Department declares it is to strengthen relationships throughout the Islamic nations, well I call it appeasement. Throughout Pres. Obama's life he has sought out mentors like Prof. Edward Said where he has studied anti-colonial beliefs. According to their beliefs, they believe Israel is a small colonial power that must be removed from the face of the Earth. America, we must support Israel. President Obama has dramatically changed how the world perceives us today. He is accused America of being arrogant, lazy, and a colonial power. Throughout his tour in Europe he stated "in America there is a failure to recognize Europe's leading role in the world. There is been times when America has shown arrogance, been dismissive, and even derisive."

During Pres. Obama's administration, Russia and China has become a major influence around the world, while Europe crumbles under the weight of socialism. We must realize European nations has been our strongest allies, and if Europe falls, where would that leave America or Israel for tomorrow? There is no doubt Pres. Obama has strong connections to the Islamic world, and has appointed many people of Islamic faith to his cabinet with strong connections to Islamic nations. Pres. Obama has appointed Rashad Hussein as his Deputy Associated Counsel, which he has been linked to known terrorist groups. Rashad Hussein has also publicly defended a known terrorist. Pres. Obama has also pointed Valerie Jarrett as Senior Advisor, she was born in Iran and through her family has strong communist connections. Valerie Jarrett faith does not concern me, what does concern me is her close ties to her native-born country Iran and her communist connections. America there are great masters of deceivers in Washington orchestrating their evil plots. The Democratic Party has been infiltrated by socialism communism and both major parties are infested with crooked politicians that are in league with the corporate elites. These corrupted politicians will ally themselves with any political organization to fulfill their agenda. This is a severe threat to democracy, our freedom and we must no longer listen to their lies or their false propaganda. America this is a serious problem, as truth has been trampled over by political correctness. Truth must never be compromised through appeasement for political correctness. We must become a society with a firm foundation in truth. Without truth, we will become a society enslaved to the liars who deceived us all.

I find it very destructive how Pres. Obama has spent us into the trillions through his administration. He has increased our debt well over one trillion through each year of his administration and we cannot sustain such a debt. Before Reagan's administration our deficit was a little under 1 trillion and through five separate administrations our deficit is approaching 20 trillion. America, we have become a dismissal society, we dismiss corrupted politicians, corrupted laws that violate our constitutional rights and the debt crisis our nation is facing. There is no greater danger than to dismiss our debt crisis, for this will lead to the collapse of the U.S. Dollar. The world's economy is based on the American dollar; never before has any currency has such power. The U.S. dollar is used in petrodollars for purchasing oil and support the world economy by establishing the foundation for world trade. The corporate elite has manipulated the world economy for their own selfish interests. The evil plots of the world elite have hoarded the wealth of the world and controls the majority of all natural resources. The corporate elite sustains themselves by pouring more money into governments allowing the political arena to become larger and more powerful. These large governments pass more laws controlling their own people as they strive to control other nations with an imposing military force.

America, we must awaken, for there is a dark force that is about to envelop us all into enslavement. The final nail is being driven to establish a one world government as their evil plots unfold before us all. They have raised war on our Christian beliefs, by establishing laws that prohibits biblical teachings in our public schools. They destroy our faith with their false propaganda in teachings of evolution. Our educational system has been infiltrated with a corrupt ideology in socialism, and they have manipulated our history to destroy patriotism. The elite have seized control over world governments through there manipulative ways through bribing political leaders to fulfill their evil plots. This has resulted to them obtaining a tremendous amount of wealth as they form monopolies, leaving the people of the world in poverty. They concealed their evil agenda by controlling the media networks they own. In their pathway of deception, they utilize these media networks to control what politicians serve us in Washington. Through their army of propagandists has turn brother against brother, inciting violence in our society and around the world. This has resulted to a police states forming that has violate personal privacy and constitutional rights. They have imposed their unfair taxing system for their plots for worldwide redistribution of wealth that is bankrupting our nation and nation's abroad. America socialism is a severe threat to our nation and their strong influence manipulates our politicians to write unfair laws. Through their propagandists they manipulate the masses with the illusion of fairness and equality. A society where everyone has the same and no one lives in poverty. They teach that capitalism [a free market] is based on a selfish society. America, we must come to our senses, socialism is a system of government that believes in absolute control. It is a dictatorship where the government controls and regulates businesses. It is an unfair taxing system to support their policies in redistribution of wealth and their controls over media networks. There is no freedom of speech, freedom of press, and personal freedoms are constantly violated. America, this atrocity is occurring today in our nation with governmental controls over businesses, an unfair taxing system, and our personal freedoms are being violated.

A socialist government absorbs the control over industry, corporations, education and healthcare. This creates the need for a large government for so much control, which dramatically increases governmental spending. This form of socialist control has resulted to intense regulations on our industries and over taxation's that has destroyed the middle class. The aftermath of socialism has stifled our economy and increases the numbers of those on welfare dramatically. This indicates that socialism creates a selfish society where people demand for their benefits will increase. America our own welfare system has bankrupt our nation and today the Democrats support a worldwide distribution of wealth will leave us in ruins. Through over taxation to support an over bloated government and their corrupted welfare system will lead our nation into financial ruins. We have got to start using common sense, with our deficit approaching 20 trillion in the lowering of our nation's credit standing is a good indication that we are on the wrong path. Socialism has put our nation on his pathway of destruction and has devalued the worth of the US dollar. This pathway of socialism will eventually lead to the collapse of our economy that will profoundly change our governmental structure. Our constitutional rights will be no more and freedom Bell will never ring again. The

American people will be forced to their knees as the weight of a dictatorship will smother our dreams. Under a dictator style government there will be no form of social welfare, as it will be replaced with worker programs that will lead us all to our enslavement. This path of destruction has been brought on by the wicked elite and other corrupt organizations to bring forth the New World Order. The grand puppet master has chosen socialism is the law of the land and they are plotting to destroy our nation's currency. Their next step is to impose a one world currency through a one world banking system for their plans for optimal control.

For centuries, there has been a secret war on who controls the New World Order through religion and other secretive organizations. The illuminati were founded by Adam Weishaupt and strongly supported by the Rothschild family. They filled their ranks with powerful elites of the world and their goal was to create a one world government without religion. We must not be deceived for it is evident the illuminati conceal a secret faith in the worship of Lucifer the fallen Angel. Their goal was to create a one world government through the United Nations. The Catholic Church is equally guilty of supporting a one world government with their religion as the center of the New World Order. In 2015 Pope Francis call for a New World order through a global government. The Catholic Church for centuries has attempted to spread their influence around the world covertly. For centuries, the Pope utilized a secret organization called the Jesuit order to infiltrate governments around the world. In 1864 Pres. Lincoln stated at the end of the Civil War "this war would've never been possible without the sinister influence of the Jesuits. We owe it to Popery that we now see our land reddened with the blood of our noblest sons." The Jesuits goal was to overthrow our political structure and replace it with a papa's centralized government under the control of the Vatican. Throughout the history of the Catholic Church have believed the Pope has the authority to rule over the world spiritually and materially. They believed that everyone should be subject to the spiritual powers of the Pope and they believe there is no spiritual salvation outside the Catholic Church. The Pope also believes he has the power over all governments as a supreme ruler of the world. The triple crown the Pope wears refers to his power through lordship over heaven, earth, and hell. This is one of the reasons so many people have fractured away from the Catholic Church to start their own religion. These churches that broke out on their own had strong beliefs that God gave mankind free will and the pathway to salvation was accepting Jesus Christ as their Lord and Savior.

Another powerful force for a New World Order is in the Islamic movement and today they are moving quickly toward creating a caliphate. This movement in the Islamic nations is to unify all Muslim nations under one government and to usher in sharia law. There has also been a strong Islamic movement throughout Europe and even cities in the United States. Pres. Obama has allowed millions of Islamic refugees into our nation and many of these people are calling out for sharia law. In Dearborn Michigan four Christians were attacked for passing out their brochures by Muslims throwing rocks and bottles as they chanted for the Christians to get out. America, I ask you to look into this matter for yourself, these four Christians were arrested and their constitutional rights were violated. In Sharia law, there is no such thing as freedom of speech, and the women have no rights. In Islamic nations throughout the world that have accepted sharia law women have been brutally beat and even beheaded. Children have had their hands and feet cut off for stealing and women have been stoned to death for committing adultery. Sharia law erases all expressions from women as they are forbidden to show any flesh, excluding the hands our eyes. Women are forbidden to receive an education and must always remain servient to their husband. I am not attempting to bash Islam, nor will I conceal the truth in fear of offending. America, we must see the danger that is looming, the Islamic movement has already established compounds for training in guerrilla warfare in Hancock New York and many other states throughout our country. These bases are in rural areas with small police departments and the Muslim compounds are well armed. We must see the dangers in allowing Islamic refugees into our nation, many of these people do not support our Constitution or America's sovereignty. There is a strong Islamic movement for a worldwide caliphate and sharia law. There are several powerful Islamic leaders in our nation proclaiming that Europe and America will fall under Islamic control by the year 2050. America, we have allowed safe refuge for millions of Islamic refugees and in return they established facilities for false propaganda and training facilities for guerrilla warfare. They strategize how to take over our nation through Islamic control and celebrate those who commit terroristic attacks against our own nation. When the tragedy of 9/11 occurred untold numbers of those of Islamic faith gathered in the streets celebrating and cheering. The European nations have allowed millions more Islamic refugees into their nation and they are facing massive problems in terroristic attacks today. I will be the first to indicate that there are millions of Islamic people who have rejected radical Islam and those who have spoken out against radicalism have been threatened or rejected from their own Islamic community.

The Islamic movement has established a department in the United Nations for Organization for Islamic Cooperation or better known as the OIC. The goal for this organization is to create a third caliphate, the first caliphate began in the seventh century and had erupted from Arabia and the second was in the fourteenth century the Ottoman Empire. Today the OIC's plan for caliphate is supported by 57 Islamic nations and they are working through other organizations throughout the world. The OIC is based in Astana the capital city of Kazakhstan, where they have established the capital of the Islamic New World Order. The OIC is supported by the Arab League, the Gulf Cooperation Council, the Council of Arab economic unity, West Africa Economic and Monetary Union and many more organizations. The Dictator Nazarbayev has poured a tremendous amount of revenue they have received from petrodollars to build a complex state-of-the-art capital city for the New World Order in Kazakhstan. The Dictator Nazarbayev is a known human rights violator and has bribed U.S. politicians to fulfill his evil plots.

The International Socialist Organization and the International Communist Organizations both support the New World Order. We have also had presidents and even politicians that support the new world order in speeches or addresses to the American people. I have no doubt there has been conflicts between these different fanatical groups who support a one world government. When Dictator Saddam Hussein stated that he was going to remove the petrodollar and replace it with the euro, the United States quickly mobilize their force to remove a dictator. I am not indicating that the United States went to war with Iraq to prevent the currency change for purchasing oil, but I do find it very suspicious. Especially when Dictator Qaddafi stated that he was going to remove the petrodollar for purchasing oil and replace it with his plan to purchase oil with gold, the United States once again quickly mobilize our military against Libya to remove a dictator. If these dictator's plan had succeeded it would have destroyed our nation's currency and the elite class would have lost a tremendous amount of wealth. America, we are facing many conspiracies and many more plots to destroy democracy. Eventually these radical ideas for a New World Order will lead to a horrific World War III. The Pope would not stand for a one world government based on Islam, nor wood Islam accept a one world government based on Christianity. The New World Order movement is about control and who or what religion will control this one world government.

America, it is time to stop this madness and make our vote count in the 2016 presidential elections. For too many years our government has worked covertly behind enemy lines sponsoring terrorist organizations to bring forth political change. Pres. Obama has supported Isis and other terrorist organizations. We have a tendency to repeat our history with other past administrations supporting other terrorist organizations such as Al Qaeda or the Taliban. Pres. Obama has also supported selling weapons to known drug cartels in Mexico, through his project Fast and Furious. These weapons that were sold to the cartel had no tracking devices, which made it impossible for our agencies to track these weapons. These weapons that were sold to drug cartels have already resulted to the loss of an American life with the murder of one of our border agents, and how many Mexican civilians or law officials have been murdered from these weapons. For decades, there has been a war between the Mexican government and the drug cartel that has resulted to thousands of people losing their lives. Why would our government sell weapons to known criminal organizations? America, we must come together and retake Washington by the power of our vote and eliminate these crooked politicians from office! Once we reestablish the foundation of our nation we must set up a panel to investigate unlawful activity in our government. America, it is time to bring justice to those who denied so many justices and we must make an example out of these crooked politicians by making them survey mandatory sentence for their crimes. The 2016 presidential election is just the start, for it will take years to undo the madness and criminal activity in Washington. America, it is time for the truth, how many millions have died through governmental programs in giving or selling weapons to known terrorist or criminal organizations. For well over a half a century our government has worked covertly undermining or disabling governments around the world and violating other nations sovereignty through infiltration. The CIA or the Secret Service has been involved in training terrorist organizations that has resulted to the death of thousands. These agencies have no mercy or compassion for humanity and have no respect for foreign nations sovereignty. Their only desire is to have control over the world and will commit to the evilest of deeds in assassinations to fulfill their agenda. There has been a tremendous amount of evidence that the CIA has allegedly purchased drugs and smuggle them into the United States. I ask, what is the purpose for such criminal activity in our government?

The 2016 presidential election is between Democratic Hillary Clinton and Republican Donald Trump, and I believe this will turn into the biggest smear campaign ever for Pres. nominee Donald Trump. I fear the media networks will be extremely bias, as our past history has dictated how the media networks has ignored or paid very little attention to many of the Clinton scandals. In fact, many of the media networks have come out and defended the Clintons, especially when Pres. Bush called for an investigation into these scandals. The Clinton power is beyond belief as they continue to escape justice. Many of these scandals had come forth under the Clinton administration where files mysteriously disappeared or were shredded during the investigations. Several Clinton family members, friends, and business partners were found guilty and the key witnesses refuse to testify against the Clintons. Rumors of alleged bribery's and shady deals made behind closed doors kept the Clintons out of prison. I do find suspicious that many of the key witnesses refuse to testify against the Clintons, and were later pardoned by Pres. Clinton. We must not forget how the Clinton's were investigated by the FBI, Department of Justice, the Oversight Committee, and the Whitewater Independent Counsel for criminal activity. The Clinton's have been investigated for the Travel Gate Scandal, the Whitewater Scandal, the Clinton's Swedish Slush Fund, the Asian Hedge Fund Scandal and many other scandals. The Clinton's have repeatedly lied and lost files that mysteriously reappeared after their acquittal. I am truly shocked that Hillary Clinton could be a possible candidate for presidency. Well over 20% of America believes that Hillary Clinton is a liar, and the FBI had indicated a Hillary Clinton was incompetent. There are also allegations that indicate the Hillary Clinton's lawyers had erased multitudes of emails. The IRS is also investigating the Clinton foundation and 60 members of Congress has demanded an investigation for bribery and other scandalous activities.

There has been tremendous amount of evidence that proves Hillary Clinton did not win the Democratic primary. There is been cases of voter fraud, or voter tampering across our nation and all Bernie Sanders votes were not counted. In polling stations for the Democratic primary were instructed to give non- party preference voters provisional ballots that resulted of those votes not being counted. There are also many allegations in flipping the electronic voting machines, where the numbers were turned to Hillary Clinton's favor. WikiLeaks released emails that proved the Democratic primary was rigged from the beginning. America this is no longer a Democratic society when the voting system can be corrupted by crooked politicians, un-American political organizations or controlled by the media. On Hillary's Clinton's campaign trail, she promised to increase social welfare and create new programs to raise the standard of living. America, we cannot afford another huge increase in our welfare system; our current welfare system has never benefited our society as a whole. In fact, the current welfare system has contributed to millions more living in poverty and a declining middle class. Our government cannot give a dollar away without taking a dollar from someone else, we must realize welfare is not free. She has also stated that she was to raise minimum wage to combat the problem with lower wages, the reason our nation has a problem with lower wages has resulted from the NAFTA treaty Pres. Bill Clinton signed in. The other contributing problems with lower wages has resulted from an unfair taxing system and governmental controls that has caused industries to flee our nation. Raising minimum wage is not the solution to the problem we are facing with lower wages and will result to companies raising the cost of their goods to offset the extra labor costs. We need to create industrial jobs in America by making amendments to the NAFTA treaty for fair trade and create a fair taxing system that will encourage new industry growth. Hillary Clinton pledged to make healthcare more affordable by making adjustments to Obama care, let's not be deceived Hillary Clinton failed miserably in passing Her Hillary Care Package and it cost taxpayers $32 million. In the Democratic primary, she stated her biggest enemy were the NRA, health care companies and pharmaceutical companies. The reason Hillary Clinton stated the NRA as her biggest enemy is because she does not support the constitutional rights to bear arms. Presidential nominee Hillary Clinton has received more campaign contributions from health care lobbyist and pharmaceutical companies than any other candidate. The reason why these companies support Hillary Clinton is because she was set laws in motion that will increase the profitability of their companies. Even major media networks like Time Warner has contributed $500,000 to the Clinton's. You will not hear about this news on major news networks like CNN, because CNN is owned by Time Warner. These donations from big corporations are given to the Clinton foundation where a small percentage goes to charitable donations. Hillary Clinton has received well over $1 million in giving speeches at major pharmaceutical companies and other healthcare companies. America make no mistake, Hillary Clinton is in league with the elites of the world and her mind is corrupt with socialist ideology. I do not believe in Hillary Clinton deserves to run for president of the United States and she should be investigated for her criminal activity. I also believe we need to reopen the Benghazi case where four Americans were murdered. Hillary Clinton as head of the State Department failed miserably and neglected her responsibilities. Hillary must be investigated for her negligence and other criminal activity from the Clinton family! America is time for the truth and those witnesses that refuse to testify against the Clintons in past investigations should be re-summons. I find it very suspicious that the witnesses that refuse to testify against the Clintons in pass investigations were pardoned by Pres. Bill Clinton.

Hillary Clinton has already started with her smear campaign against Donald Trump and she has pointed out some issues that raises concerns for me as well. It is true Donald Trump has a bad temper, but let's be honest America we should all be angry in the way our country has been ran in past administrations. It is clear Hillary Clinton's campaign strategy is to betray Donald Trump as a racist, con artist, phony, a bully, religious bigot and many other slanderous comments. Hillary Clinton has the audacity to betray Donald Trump as incompetent for presidency when, in reality, Hillary Clinton has proved repeatedly that she is incompetent in the way she handled her affairs in the State Department, and let us not forget the horrible tragedy of Benghazi. She has betrayed Donald Trump as a crook in one of her campaign messages, come on America who's the biggest crook here. Hillary Clinton's campaign strategy is to twist Donald Trump's words or take them out of contents to manipulate the people into believing that he is a villain. Donald Trump has made some horrendous statements about women as well as immigrants and his plan to deport millions of immigrants is wrong. There is only one issue I agree with Hillary Clinton on, and that is immigration reform. America, I pray for you to have heart, these immigrants came from faraway lands or crossed deserts to break away from tyranny. The flight was for freedom, the right to dream, and their ability to make their dreams come true. These poor immigrants have held onto their hopes with prayer to one day becoming an American. They dream of giving their children the opportunities they never received in getting an education and living in a safe neighborhood. America these are not just immigrants they are humans with children and they have sacrificed everything to come to our nation of dreams and opportunity. Our nation is a nation of immigrants, and centuries ago our ancestors made the same journey for the same reasons. Denying the immigrants citizenship and deporting them back to their country as Donald Trump had indicated is a sinister act.

America, I plead with you to open your hearts and see how so many immigrants have become Americanized over the years. They have married into American families and many of them have American kids. These immigrants have married other immigrants and if we were to send all the illegal immigrants back home where will we send the children who have parents from two different countries. What are we to do with the American kids that were born from immigrant parents, are we to deny their birthright to be citizens or will we become a society willing to tear families apart. I will tell you now, I want no part of any society that has no conscience or a heartless society that shows no mercy as they result to a horrific action of ripping the hearts out of families across our nation. These people are our friends, coworkers, and strong pillars of the community. They are people who love their children the same as us. We need to create a pathway for citizenship for the immigrants who obey the laws of our nation and pay their taxes. These people who have lived in our nation for years or have American children should have the opportunity for citizenship and we must realize that many these children do not speak or write their native language fluently. This will only result to hardship for these children if they were to be sent back to their native country. The fact that these children have been Americanized could result to cruel treatment from other children in foreign schools. I call out to the American people to unite and let our politicians now this atrocity can never happen. We must set a pathway for citizenship for those immigrants who meet the requirements. I believe that all recent immigrants should be sent back home, and I support Donald Trump's plan to build a wall to halt the immigration problem.

I also support Donald Trump on his economic plan and I believe he can create a tremendous amount of jobs for our nation. Donald Trump is a brilliant strategist and has the ability to bring people together. He is a problem solver, has a tremendous inner strength, and I believe him when he said we can make America great. He showed great strength when he stood up to the elites of the world when he pledged "we will no longer surrender the people or our country to the false song of globalism." Presidential nominee Donald Trump has the ability to accomplish great achievements for our country economically and I agree with his plan to repair our infrastructure. He pledged to strengthen our military, which I find very important for America's security. He pledged to restructure our educational system and create a fair-trade system with other nations. Donald Trump talks about many the issues that are important to get America back to financial stability. Donald Trump is a great businessman and many these issues can be resolved because of his talent in his field. Donald Trump could accomplish great things as our president, but America is not a business or an industry, we are a nation for the people by the people. We need a Pres. that will protect our Constitution and restore America to her true glory. We need a Pres. that will vanquish lobbying to ensure the American voice will always be heard and to restore our true foundation as a nation under God.

We must put our faith in God and assemble in a peaceful manner. We must retake Washington not by force but with our votes. We must call out those who do not speak the truth and once again make honesty one of our virtues. It is important for us to elect a politician to establish truth and transparency to our government. We need someone who would not only shrink our governmental spending but shrink the size of our government as well. We need a politician who would throw out unjust laws and demand laws to stand on truth, principle, and morals. We must rebalance the Scales of Justice as we bind one law to protect everyone. We must also restore freedom and make sure justice prevails. We must cut the shackles that restrict our free market through government regulations and high taxes. The only engine that can save America's prosperity is the economy. Lifting the burden off of free enterprise would result to a new growth in America. We must better utilize our government by combining governmental departments and shutting down departments that are unnecessary. This would allow better monitoring of governmental spending. We must stop governmental borrowing and mandate they not only follow but create a responsible budget.

For peace and prosperity, we must put away our differences and work together to save our nation. I remind you, we must organize in a peaceful manner because civil unrest will only bring forth Martial Law. If Martial Law was declared, it would not only be a loss of freedom but the consequences could trigger a depression in America as we would plunge our country into darkness. If Martial Law is declared, I call out to law enforcement and military to remember your oath. You swore to protect the Constitution and serve the American people. Do not forget Americans have Constitutional rights that you swore to protect. This does concern me greatly and I hope our military and our law enforcement will not turn their guns on the American people. We are not just citizens; we are your parents, your spouses, and your children. Remember the American people support you and we have faith you will protect the Constitution. We must believe that our system still works and put our faith in God. Let Liberty Bell ring once again and let our churches unify for the good of the country. We must once again establish Christian principles for our foundation. Rise up; you must, for I call for a change. With the Constitution as my shield and my pen as my sword, I will bring light to this darkness. Do not let me stand alone, for there is strength in numbers. Gather your courage America and commit yourselves for the love of our children. Our nation is in disarray and our government is corrupted but the strength of our bond is our faith in God and it is our duty as Americans to resurrect our great nation. We must believe if we all unite with peace and love for one another. I truly believe we can save our great nation and never forget for God and country.

Believe

I truly believe our nation can stand proud once again if we unite, not under some party banner but the American flag. We must merge as patriots with faith in God to undo the wrongs of our past. I have set aside twelve topics that I believe can restore balance to our government. There are also several issues I decided to break down into chapters that includes education which I believe can bring light to this darkness that has polluted our children. There are also chapters in restoring our Christian principles and family bond. Let us come together and vanquish this evil intent once and for all.

"For we wrestle not against flesh and blood, but against principalities, against powers, against the rulers of the darkness of this world, against spiritual wickedness in high places. Wherefore take unto you the whole armor of God, that ye may be able to withstand in the evil day, and having done all, to stand. Stand therefore, having your loins girt about with truth, and having on the breastplate of righteousness; And your feet shod with the preparation of the gospel of peace; Above all, taking the shield of faith, wherewith ye shall be able to quench all the fiery darts of the wicked."

-Ephesians 6 13:16

Limit Executive Powers

The abuse of executive powers has gone on for far too long. We must limit executive orders for only in cases of national emergencies. Which should never be permanent and should only remain in effect through the duration of the emergency. The legislative branch is responsible for passing laws and the president's duty is to sign the bill into law or veto the bill. From our past, to our present, we have had presidents write their own laws as executive orders. These Executive Powers violates our constitutional rights and they are dismantling the framework of democracy. The powers of the elite have exercised there might through manipulation and bribery to insert their dark ideology upon our politicians. Politicians proclaim that there is nothing in our Constitution that prohibits executive orders, but I will tell you the language is in the framework. Our forefathers had established a system of checks and balances to ensure that no unjust laws that violated personal freedoms were ever signed in. Our system of government was broken up into three branches in order to bring forth true democracy. These three branches were the Executive, Legislative, and the Judicial and they were given their own responsibility. The Executive Branch has abused their authority through executive orders that has overstepped boundaries and has controlled state issues. Our Constitutional rights have been violated as the Executive Branch has grown immensely. Our personal privacy has been violated through domestic surveillance and phone monitoring. This is not freedom this is paranoia. This is about the abuse of an out of control big government. Let us rise to reestablish a true people's government, so we may once again have a president that speaks for the people. The power that is granted by the people to the president should no longer be abused. As our representative, he or she must ensure that no unjust laws are signed. The laws of our Constitution must be upheld and should be admired for it is the blueprint of Democracy.

Limit Terms for Congress and Senate

This good old boy, country club scene in Washington has gone on for far too long. Most of the Senate and Congressmen and women have failed miserably in representing the people yet they spend their life and careers in office forging friends and partners. The legislative branch was not designed to forge careers; it is a service to the people. We the people are not represented in such a manner when our politicians receive bribes for political favors. They make friends with lobbyist who in turn give them the life of luxury as they pour cash into their campaign funds. This marriage between government and corporate elite has got to stop. Let our voices be heard and we will shatter this unfavorable bond between lobbyists and politicians. Our first move is to limit terms for the Senate as well as the Congress. This will end the private club scene and will allow new and true representation. Our second phase for true representation is to mandate the legislative branch to be bounded to the Constitution to ensure no unfair laws are passed. Our Congress should be responsible for upholding just laws and never bring laws to the floor that would conflict with the Constitution. It is our politicians' job to serve the people and assure our government stays within a system of checks and balances. The Congress and Senate have failed miserably in keeping the balance for the Executive Branch's power has grown immensely. It is Congress's job to stop this madness. They have the power to veto and even block presidential abuse of power through impeachment. I call out to the Senators, Congressmen and women to represent the people or else you will lose your seat. America, it is up to us to restore the balance in Washington, but we the people must come together to vote all crooked politicians out of office. To truly bring change starts here in our legislative branch. I have often heard people cry out to restore our grassroots, for this to be possible we must first restore our Christian principles. We must elect politicians with strong Christian faith and good morals. I am calling for the largest Christian movement ever in our nation, for it will be impossible to pull our nation from the abyss without faith in God. Let the people's movement start here America, let us rise from the wake of destruction. Let our rise inspire the people around the world to rise, for the world belongs to us the people.

The Judicial Branch must be bound to the Constitution

For far too long the executive branch has attempted to control or ignored the Supreme Court. The Supreme Court justices are selected by the executive branch and for years there has been a battle in Washington for who controls the Judicial Branch. The Republicans attempt to appoint conservative justices while the Democrats attempt to appoint liberal justices is to attempt to control the outcome of a verdict. America this battle is about control and if the executive branch can control the Supreme Court then the checks and balances of our system has failed. Our forefathers established the judicial branch to ensure we remain a Republic. This idea of a Republic style government did not originate from our forefathers; it was based on the Greek author that was never adopted as a system of government for Greece. The Greek empire was more of a Democratic style of government, later this idea would be adopted by another nation known as the Roman Republic. The idea of a Republic style government prevents the government or Senate from over stepping their boundaries by establishing laws through the judicial branch that protect the citizens. For well over two centuries the Roman Republic thrived but around 130 BC Rome had become a democracy. The Roman system of government had become corrupted for wealth and power that would eventually to their demise. In 0027 BC Rome, would become an empire, which would lead to their citizens losing their rights. Rome had become a tyrant, bent on conquering other nations. Their economy was based on the riches they stole from other nations and the people they had enslaved. Many historians have indicated that the fall of the Roman Empire was due to over taxation and a welfare system.

I also believe the reason Rome fell was a loss of a check and balance system. The fact that the Roman economy was based on war worries me greatly, for if you look at the super elites of today have profited immensely from wars of our past. I find it shameful that so many elite families profited so immensely from wars, from corporate elite bankers loaning government's money in order for nations to pay for war supplies. Other elite families profited immensely during past wars, such as the steel industry and oil industry. America the super elite has set the world stage and we have paid for their evil deeds with our blood and tears. We need to become a society that strives for peace and let us tear down the walls of hate. We need to become a moral society that realizes how precious human life is, and to restore our true foundation to ensure our freedom. We must realize if America loses our check and balance system would lead to a collapse within our own government, which would lead to a socialist form of government. Benjamin Franklin was asked what style of government was being established he then replied. "A Republic, if you can keep it." The reason our government established three branches of government was to ensure the citizens of America would keep their indelible rights.

Through the past decades our Supreme Court has become more liberal than ever before and has profoundly change America. I do not believe that our forefathers would have ever believed our judicial system would become so corrupted. America, we must reestablish these three primary pillars of our foundation to ensure the longevity of our nation. The idea that our Supreme Court Justice can serve for life is ludicrous and this is too much power to will by any branch of government. We can no longer allow the executive branch to select our Supreme Court justices due to their attempt to control the judgment of this High Court. This battle for how many Liberal or Conservative Supreme Court Justices there are is ridiculous. They are not voted in by the people but selected by our president and voted in by the Senate which is not true representation. I do believe it is important for America to have a Supreme Court; it was part of our original foundation. Once again this is too much power for one group of people or branch of government to wield. I believe to bring balance to this system; we should no longer allow our president to appoint Supreme Justices to serve us in the Supreme Court. In fact, I believe we should no longer allow one group of justices to rule in the Supreme Court. When cases do appear in the Supreme Court, we need to have a system that will randomly select nine federal judges to rule over these cases. This is the same principle as you or I can serve as a juror, the only difference is we will be randomly selecting nine federal judges which would be an honor to any federal judge. This will limit the control that Washington has over the Supreme Court and bring forth true justice for all.

Vanquish Lobbying in America

We were once a nation of true freedom, and we were blessed in the signing of the Constitution they gave us our indelible rights. Our great forefathers were free to pursue their dreams; may it be in business, law, farming or digging for treasures in the earth. In those days, there were no such thing as giant corporations or monopolies attempting to control Washington. America was mostly made up of small businesses and the majority of the population worked for themselves. They were free to worship and family unity was a priority. From the birth for nation and onto the next century we were a nation of dreams. We dream to connecting America from East to West with roads, railroads, interstates, telegraph lines, and other great feats of engineering. It was a time when someone who is small could accomplish great feats. They were a society that truly understood what it was to be free and out of the clutches of a dictator. Unfortunately, this age of prosperity throughout the 1800s had given birth to super elites. Today the great puppet master has asserted itself over the people as we have become enslaved to our debt. This master of deception parades monsters upon the world stage while hiding its own true evil agenda. We the people sell away our rights for the illusion of temporary security. We allow corporations, banking industries, and other in the elite class to have control over Washington with bribes and promises of new career opportunity for our politicians. The lobbyists twist and manipulates our Constitution to their favor so they may assert their power. We the people can never be truly represented when our politicians' pockets are filled with corporate cash. The people cry out for justice but unfortunately our cries fall upon deaf ears. There was a study done at Princeton University that asked a simple question on whether the government represented the people or big business? They found that the people have very little representation while the elite or big business have true representation from our politicians. What I find more disturbing is the fact that they are special interest groups and lobbyists writing laws that are being passed through Congress. America if we do not wake up we will be bounded to a Dictator Style Government that will not be favorable to the people. When corporations have the power to write laws, along with a strong arm of big government to enforce the laws we the people have lost. In the past we have had politicians try to outlaw lobbying in Washington, but lobbyists through Corporation control have purposely misinterpreted the first amendment in our Constitution. The first amendment gives the people the right to petition the government for a redress of grievances. This constitutional right was not for Corporation or the elite, it was written for the people. We must no longer allow lobbyists to have power over Washington. No longer can they bribe our politicians with campaign money or job offers. This unfavorable system where special interest groups hires lobbyists, who then bribes our politicians with campaign contributions has not, and never will be favorable to the people. Today we have the highest health care costs in the world and we have a taxing system that is not only complicated but it is unfavorable for the American people. Corporations in America spend billions of dollars to not only control Washington but to write our laws as well. Our government was divided into three branches to ensure no unjust laws were written, and with our forefather's great wisdom had divided the legislative branch to ensure we keep our indelible rights.

America, I call out for all, to cry out in one loud voice no more. Let us end this partnership between government and corporate elite so we must once again have true representation. We must establish a law that prohibits corporations from bribing our politicians through campaign funds or job promises. America this is our country, and for too many years' corporations have profited into the trillions due to their control in Washington. This union has created unfair taxing system for governmental control that has led to the destruction of our constitutional rights. The government along with super elite have bended and manipulated a new system of government for their own benefits. We must realize before we can truly reestablish the foundation of our nation we must first draw out the poison that has sickened our government. This corruption of the corporate elite must be extinguished for if goes unnoticed then future generations will pay for this criminal act. We must reestablish the three pillars of our government and establish laws that prohibits bribery or benefits to anyone who serves us in Washington. We must ensure the anti-bribery law is enforced in any politician in violation shall have the survey mandatory sentence for their crime. America, we must take this serious, for any bribery of our politician will only lead to a lost in our personal rights. Let a great voice speak from the past: **"Once a republic is corrupted, there is no possibility of remedying any of the growing evils but by removing the corruption and restoring its lost principles; every other correction is either useless or a new evil."** -Thomas Jefferson

Shutdown the Federal Reserve

The concept of establishing a central bank in the United States is unconstitutional. Our forefathers warned America, like Thomas Jefferson as he stated "I believe that banking institutions are more dangerous than standing armies. If the American people ever allow a private bank to control the issue of currency, the bank in the corporations that will grow up around them will deprive the people of their property until their children wake up homeless on the continent their forefathers conquered." Many other forefathers denounced the central bank idea such as Benjamin Franklin who referred to this concept of the system of money manipulators whose greed runs so deep that it will deprive the wealth from the people. This concept of the central bank controlling and producing a nation's currency is far too much power for any Institute to have. This power to produce our nation's currency belongs to Congress. For well over a century the American people would not stand for the idea of a central bank. Although this idea would not simply fade away as prominent banking families continue to push this idea. In the early 1900s the banking system was controlled by four prominent families JD Rockefeller, J.P. Morgan, Paul Warburg, and Baron Rothschild. These four men were ruthless in attempting to control the market and the banking Institute. The prominent banking leaders realized the only way to establish a central bank for America was to create a panic in the financial system. Later they created the panic of 1907 where New Yorkers lined up outside the banks to collect their savings. Let us not forget the article was written in Life Magazine, by Frederick Allen who accused Mortgage Interest of taking advantage and precipitating the panic of 1907. As their evil plot continued to play out Sen. Nelson Aldrich recommended that a central bank should be established so we may prevent another panic in our financial system. Sen. Aldrich had close ties to the banking Institute and later married into the Rockefeller family. In 1910 a secret meeting was held on Jackal Island off the coast of Georgia by the elite bankers to establish a central bank in America by writing the Federal Reserve Act. The fact that this bill was written by the elite class of bankers is atrocious. This bill was then giving to Sen. Aldrich, as he pushed it through Congress. In 1913 Woodrow Wilson, would become president through tremendous sponsoring from corporations and the banking industry. Pres. Woodrow Wilson pledged on his campaign trail that he would sign in the Federal Reserve Act for campaign support. Congressman Lewis McFarland stated it was a carefully contrived occurrence, international bankers sought to bring about a condition of despair so that they might emerge the rulers of us all. This was a tremendous amount of power that was given to the Federal Reserve. The Federal Reserve have the power to control interest rates and inflation, by controlling the production of money. The Federal Reserve works on a debt system where every dollar that is created is loaned to the government with interest. If the Federal Reserve created the dollar and loan it to our government, then how can the government pay back the interest? The federal government has no alternative but to borrow more money from the Federal Reserve to pay back the interest on the previous loan. This will only create a debt cycle that will continue to increase our debt. Pres. Woodrow Wilson regretted supporting the Federal Reserve act and I would like for you to remember what he had stated, "I am a most unhappy man. I have unwittingly ruined my country. A great industrial nation is controlled by its system of credit. Our system of credit is concentrated. The growth of the nation, therefore, and all our activities are in the hands of a few men. We have come to be one of the worst ruled, one of the most completely controlled and dominated Governments in the civilized world — no longer a Government by free opinion, no longer a Government by conviction and the vote of the majority, but a Government by the opinion and duress of a small group of dominant men". America, we must wake up before we are totally enslaved to our debt. The fact that 1% of the world's population the elite controls well over 50% of the world's wealth is an indication of the corruption in our system. Even in 1933 there was an executive order that force all Americans to turn in their gold coins, gold bullion on and gold certificates with the threat of imprisonment. In the same year, they also abolish the gold standard which is what gave our currency value. America, we must wake up, for this power of the Federal Reserve to regulate our money supply and to regulate its worth is the power to control us all. I plead with you to look around and take notice for the same elite families that controlled the financial market or banking industry a century ago are still in power today. Today the Rockefeller family is still in control of the Federal Reserve and the Rothschild family controls the World Central Bank. Even J.P. Morgan is still a major player in the financial banking systems. A century has passed since the elite grasp for world dominance over the economy has resulted to enslavement around the world. The corporate elite families are harvesting the human race for their cheap manual labor, and their true dark agenda is unraveling before us. America, we must be alert for a world banking system has already been established through the World Central Bank, which is controlled by the Rothschild family. They have stolen the wealth of the world and through their greed has left Billions destitute to a life in poverty. Well over three billion people around the world severely struggles on a little more than two dollars a day, due to the greed of the elite. The aftermath of their thirst for gold and other riches of the world has left billions with severe health issues due to malnutrition. While they delight themselves with their riches and fine dining there are hundreds of millions of little children starving. America is time for us to come together, and rise we must, for this dark entity carries no compassion for humanity. They have become sicken by greed for their thirst for wealth and they are filled with dark ideology. It is time for us to shut down the Federal Reserve and demand the Rockefellers the payback all the interest they have stolen from the American people by applying it to our deficit. Let the movement start here America and let us bring forth justice in the world court for their crimes against humanity. Our forefathers warned us about the central bank concept and if our forefathers were here they would help us root out this evil that has entangled itself and our fabric of life. By freeing up the wealth they have accumulated through there manipulative deeds would enrich every society around the world and raise the standard of living for every family on our planet. We could create projects for clean water around the world which would aid in preventing starvation, diseases, and the purified water would help prevent many illnesses that is contributed to dirty water. These projects could help stimulate the economy worldwide and bring forth food to the family tables around the world. I call out for you America, do not give into to disparity because they are evil has deceived you and thinking you are powerless. To the elite money is power, but I tell you it is just paper, for only man can move mountains. We the people is what gives money power, so let us come together and take control of our own destiny.

Shutdown The IRS. For a Flat Tax

The Federal Income Tax was established in 1862 by Pres. Lincoln, to help control inflation and pay for the Civil War. He did not intend for the income tax to remain permanent, the extra revenue was intended for repairing our rebuilding America's infrastructure after the war. Many politicians combated the federal income tax for decades, and many times they proved the federal tax was unconstitutional. This argument would continue for decades as the federal Income Tax was removed and restored. Congress would settle this issue by passing legislation to amend the Constitution with the 16th Amendment in the year 1913. It is ironic how they deceived America with two evil plots within the same year, with the Federal Reserve act and the Internal Revenue Service. America, we have been deceived, for there is no law in the 16th Amendment that requires the people to pay a Federal Income Tax. I have researched the 16th Amendment as well as several books on tax laws, and I have never found a law that requires the people to pay an income tax. In fact, if you research the IRS own handbook it clearly states the federal Income Tax is a voluntary compliance. Tell me

America how many of you have voluntarily signed up to pay your federal taxes. The 16th Amendment clearly states that we are responsible for all lawful taxes, lawful taxes are tobacco, oil, firearms, etc. Which were legally voted into law by Congress and signed in by the executive branch. What I find shocking is how the IRS is exempt from abiding by constitutional laws. They have seized people's property, garnished wages without due process, which is illegal according to our Constitution. America, we have all been deceived by our own politicians and this has contributed to the crippling of America's growth. The Democrats would like for you to believe otherwise as they believe in immense taxing for their plans to extend welfare. Use common sense! If tremendous tax burdens are placed on the people will only lead to the slowing down of our economy. These tax burdens that have been placed on the people has stifled our own economy. We must restore common sense in Washington, by eliminating the federal income tax would result to increasing the income for families across America. This would result to more goods being purchased, which would boost our economy immensely. The Democrats uses false propaganda in their attempts to deceive the people in believing the Republicans only support the rich, but that is not entirely true. The truth America, both parties support the elite, the extreme wealthy of the world. These tax burdens have destroyed the middle class and has stifled industrial growth. America, I ask you to look around and see how many industries, and technological jobs have left due to over taxation or immense governmental regulations. The Republicans have argued for a lower tax and deregulation, while the Democrats have had their ways for decades in creating immense taxes to support their corrupted social welfare programs. They call it redistribution of wealth; however, I call it stealing. Tell me how can something be gained when something is given away freely? The Democrats continuously indicate how the wealthy do not pay their fair share in Federal Taxes, but I tell you this is another lie from this party. The top 20% of gross earners in our country pays nearly 85% of all Federal Income Tax and nearly 50% of the people pay no Federal Income Tax. The massive increase in over taxation compounded with intense regulations has crippled our industrial growth and destroyed the middle class. All this destruction to our economy, to broken families, and loss of property has resulted from their madness. While the super elite tends to escape over taxation by hiding their money in foreign accounts, has placed a tremendous strained on the true working class of America. The Democrats are now supporting another form of redistribution of wealth by supporting the United Nations global taxes. This tax would accumulate up to $400 billion for third world countries, which would leave our nation in ruins. When do we stop this madness, when our debt collapses our nation and we become a third world country? If we continue to take from those who are successful and give to those who have little we will destroy ambition, motivation, and creativity. This redistribution of wealth has to end to release this great tax burden off our industries; all this is in the name of social welfare. We must realize that too many people would rather live a meager life that is free, than to live a good life they had to work for. The biggest corruption in our welfare system is the fact it keeps people in poverty, I do believe in a welfare system. We need to reconstruct a new welfare system as a tool to advance the standard of living for all. The cost of our current welfare system is astronomical; we have spent trillions of taxpayer's dollars over the decades. This has resulted to crippling our economy and has left millions abandoned to poverty. This tremendous revenue could have created millions of jobs for our nation, by creating projects for repairing our infrastructure. We must cut welfare spending to reduce the tremendous tax burden that is destroying our economy and has destroyed new job opportunities. In order to do this, we must limit the duration of a person can receive welfare benefits, by encouraging them to improve their opportunities for employment. We must make it mandatory for those who are receiving or applying for welfare to fill out an action form that will help them get off these benefits. This could encourage people to get their GED, attend a trade school, or even a college degree. We must come to the realization that our current welfare system has failed miserably and has dramatically increased those living in poverty in our nation. We must undo this political madness and bring forth a structure to raise the standards of living for everyone.

America, it is time to take heed, for our destiny is no longer in our hands. In the past decades, we have been overwhelmed with corrupted politician's field with socialist ideology that sold away the people's rights, so they may obtain their own wealth from the corporate elite. We have been deceived by our own government and the greatest deception is those in the elite circle that control our government. The IRS is not even a governmental Department, in fact it is owned by IMF the International Monetary Fund, which also has control over our treasury. The IMF works very closely with the United Nations in preparation for a New World Order, and they have made plans to extend the IRS globally to increase their own profitability for their devious agenda.

These wicked agendas are not a coincidence, they have a true purpose, and that is to empower the elite class. America, it is time for us to shut down the IRS along with the Federal Reserve, for they have never serve the people. By shutting down the federal income tax would enrich every family across America. This would increase the average family's income dramatically which would increase the spending in our economy. For well over two centuries the elite class has manipulated world governments for their own interest. Today the Rothschild Families accumulated wealth is estimated far into the trillions. America the whole world needs to awaken to this madness. The elite class controls over 50% of the world's wealth, and they have achieved this evil plot for greed through manipulation of world governments. America think about that seriously for one minute, less than 1% controls 50% of the world's wealth. The top and 10% of the wealthiest people in the world controls 80% of the world's wealth. This leaves 90% of the world's population fighting over 20% of the world's wealth. This is the reason the elite class keeps the people divided by raising their walls of hate to prevent people from uniting.

This is the reason I say no more, are you truly prepared to surrender your will to there might. Are you prepared to give up your sovereignty for their plans for a New World Order? America, it is time to vanquish this monstrous control that has burden of the people and left so many in despair. Let us come together to establish true economic balance that will be fair for everybody. It is time for us to establish a flat tax that would be fair and this goal could be achieved by consolidation of governmental departments that would reduce federal spending dramatically. I truly believe for a flat tax to work we must first downsize our government and demand our politicians to follow a budget. I believe the flat sales tax must be set at 18%, and today the average American spends around 30% of their earnings paying taxes.

I do believe we need to install a federal income tax for those who are making 250,000 a year or more through the United States Treasury Department. I also believe we should establish tax credits for those companies that are expanding or upgrading machinery. For every dollar that is spent for improvements or upgrading will receive .50 cents off the dollar owed in taxes. Many Democrats will call this a tax break and I call it stimulating our economy. America, we can achieve great things if we could unite in faith and together we can vanquish their dark agendas from our nation. In the past, many politicians have called for the dismantling of the Internal Revenue Service for a flat tax. America, we must come together and stand with those politicians who have fought for our rights. We must come together to assert our rights as the true Masters of our government and never forget for the people by the people.

"I want the people of America to be able to work less for the government and more for themselves."

-Pres. Calvin Coolidge

Application for Politicians

To be a politician is one of the greatest jobs in America. It gives one the opportunity to serve the people which is a great responsibility. We must realize with great responsibility comes with great power. Too many times people vote for candidates they know very little about. We vote for people who stand on one or more particular issues that we agree on while knowing very little about where they stand on other political issues. Many times, we do not even know our politician's past or what other organizations they were affiliated with. To represent the people, it is a job and like any other job you apply for you must fill out an application. It must be required before anyone announces their candidacy for whatever office they are running for. Candidate must fill out an application. This political application will serve all branches of government and can be easily reviewed by the American public. We must not allow this application to become complex and should be no longer than a few pages. This application should be like any other application with segments of education and employment history. We must reserve a segment of the application for a questionnaire that must be filled out by the politicians. The questionnaire will help the people understand where this politician stance on important issues. They should also be required to fill out a section on which organizations or political groups have supported them and their campaign. This application should exclude personal information such as their address, phone number and social security number. Today there are too many politicians in office who are members of socialist or communist organizations. I do not believe they would have won their bid for office if the people in their district knew about their communist or socialist ties. An application would give us a better opportunity to better understand the candidate and his/her principles. It would give us the ability to cast a well-informed vote not solely on their speeches and debates but knowing their educational background and employment history as well. They shall be judged by their merit, and it is important for us to know if they have communist or socialist ties. It is time for a call of duty. We must know who we are electing so we are better served in Washington!

End Electoral Voting System

The electoral voting system started in the 1780's. This was passed for several reasons. They thought too many were uneducated or did not have enough knowledge about the candidates. This resulted in our president being elected by electors not our personal vote. America, we must rise above this. Everyone's vote should count as the numerical value of one. If our votes cannot be counted truthfully or fairly then who is choosing our politicians for us? There are other reasons I disagree with this system. The fact that the state will carry all electoral votes for one candidate is wrong. For example, if the state only carried 51% of the vote for one candidate, it would result to all votes going for that candidate. What happens to all the other 49% who voted for the other candidate? Does their vote not count? I have heard many people claim they did not vote because their vote would not be counted or they claim their candidate would not win. I have also heard those indicate they did not care to vote because their candidate was winning and as long as their candidate could carry their state, it was all that mattered. It is time for us to change our voting system so that everyone's vote counts. No longer shall we divide states into districts for the Electoral College for this is a vote for all of America. I think it is important to maintain a Federal Panel to protect voters' rights and laws. This panel's responsibility would be to establish a new voting system where every American's vote counts. The panel must also prevent voter fraud or voter tampering by making it mandatory for a state issued ID to vote. We must once again become a society of the people. No longer shall we allow big industry or foreign nations to pour money into campaign funds. If candidates receive money from overseas it results other nations manipulating our voting system. The money that pours in from big industry lobbyist is stomping out our voices. This Electoral College may have started from the generation of our forefathers but it is past time to right this wrong. We need to create a fair and equal voting system where everyone's vote is counted. Let us bring forth a new dawn for America where everyone believes their vote is counted. Today we are more intelligent than ever before. Today in some cases we get the news faster on the internet than news stations can release it. Today I call out, let us know our politicians so we can cast our vote with intelligence and goodwill.

Consolidating Governmental Departments

Today billions of dollars are wasted every year from the overload of government departments and wasteful spending. In the past century, governmental departments have sprung up everywhere across the nation. Many of these departments were helpful such as the FDA and Health Department as well as the Labor and Social Security departments. Through the decades they have brought many other departments such as the FBI, DEA, ATF, DHS, and many more. America, it is time for us to end this madness. This has all resulted in infringements on our freedom and is bankrupting our nation. We have become a paranoid society, where the seeds of fear were planted into our subconscious by our own government, so they may continue their quest for dominance. It is time for us to consolidate departments in our government that would truly work for today's society. We can save billions by combining governmental departments or shutting down departments that are unnecessary. Have we become a society that needs so many law departments to secure our safety? Multiple departments only create confusion, which leads to the breakdown of communication between law enforcement. Today we can save billions by combining departments; this will also aid in American security. We can place under the umbrella of the FBI, departments such as ATF and DEA which would save billions. The FBI's responsibility is to uphold federal law. They have stood the test of time with mafias and even communists. Combining these three departments would not only save money but make it easier for them to share information and evidence collected.

We should also combine departments under the umbrella of the NSA (National Security of America). These are departments such as Coast Guard and Border Patrol that would not only save taxpayers' expense but make it safer for America. I feel that DHS (Department of Homeland Security) should be shut down for such a young department its power has grown immensely. In fact, it carries many departments such as FEMA and many law enforcement agencies under its umbrella.

It is far too powerful for any government department to wield. This department needs to be shut down and their responsibility needs to be shifted to other departments such as the FBI or NSA. Allowing the FBI to focus on domestic protection and the NSA to focus on national security issues would be beneficial to everyone. We can also save a tremendous amount of revenue by combining welfare programs under one program. It is ludicrous that our government funds over 100 different welfare programs and has made it impossible for them to monitor fraudulent claims. There are also many programs through the EPA and many other departments that costing taxpayers a tremendous amount of revenue and must be shut down. America, I truly believe we can change our direction but we must elect politicians that will bring common sense to the White House. They must evaluate these departments and find better ways to utilize them or shut them down. By combining departments, it would not only save money and resources but time as well. We would have to increase the budget for the FBI or NSA but in the long run we would not have to cover many other expanses. We can slash government spending by half by combining or cutting back on these departments. This would save tax payers' by cutting back on building expenses, building maintenance, governmental employee cars and office workers. Our goal should be a small government doing big things, not a large government draining us dry. This is our nation; let's tell them in one voice, they work for us.

Unifying Healthcare

To be a moral society we must ensure health care is available to everyone. Today our country spends well over 1 trillion dollars in multiple departments such as Medicaid, Medicare, Veterans Care, and Obama care. Through the years many different administrations have brought forth many different departments at the total cost of 1.5 trillion for 2016. The fact that there are so many different healthcare departments has made it impossible for our government to monitor fraudulent cases. Healthcare fraud is costing taxpayers billions of dollars each year. I call out for the shutdown of all governmental health care plans. If we appeal to common sense we only need one comprehensive healthcare plan for everyone, young and old. This universal healthcare plan will cover seniors at the age of 63, the brave men and women who serve our country, and for those living in poverty will be covered. For those who are working or have families, the deductions for personal or family insurance should come out of their check. Employees should have the right to choose their own coverage through a governmental or private insurance company. People have the right to choose what insurance plan they desire for themselves or their family. I know this is a bold move but you must realize governmental health care is out of control and is bankrupting our society.

Our government spends well over a trillion dollars in health care yearly, which is more than enough to cover every American with health care insurance. This is another form of combining multiple departments that would cut back on expenses and give everyone better health care. We will also benefit with lower health care premiums from government competition with other private insurance companies. We must become a moral society that understands the health care needs for everyone but we must also use common sense. We must structure a health care plan that is not only easy to follow but easy to monitor. This is our country and for far too long we have allowed health care lobbyist and an incompetent government to corrupt our health care. Let us make a stand today, for a better healthcare for America.

Change the Way We Handle Foreign Affairs

America, we are traveling down a road that has been paved for us by an out of control and irresponsible government. I fear for our future and what desolate life we are leaving for our children. We were once a great nation of honor and prestige; there was a strength that pulsed within our land. We were the great builders of the world; with strength and ingenuity we accomplish great feats. Today we are still the great bread basket of the world but sadly we are no longer the great builders. We give our wealth away and give technology to other countries which is dooming our children's future. America, we are to blame for this foolish path, as our money flies from our pockets through over taxation, and our brave soldiers shed their blood on foreign soil. President Obama called for a change but I ask you is this the change you wanted? For decades, Democrats have had their way by creating intense taxes and regulations on our industries. They call for more social welfare for a brighter America. They even call for more laws to restrict our freedoms and violate our constitutional rights, while claiming it is for our safety. The Democrats have spun their web of deceit, while their social ideology has crippled America. Today our deficit is well into the trillions of dollars while we live in a land that is threatened more than ever. Through the decades America has made many enemies around the world and several of these nations are in the Middle East. Many are plotting our destruction. There are also powerful nations such as China and Russia who manipulate markets in an attempt to lead America into financial ruin. The inability for our leaders to handle foreign affairs is atrocious. America, we must wake up and bring forth a politician who will make America first.

I find that the Democrats are at fault for many of America's problems we are facing today but you cannot exclude the Republicans. Both of these parties have declared war or attempted to police the world in order to bring democracy to other lands. Around the world America's image has been distorted and turned villainous. President Obama has even indicated that America was once colonialist which sounds a lot like propaganda from other nations. We are accused of being tyrants, warmongers and occupiers for bringing peace to other regions. Our brave men and women are called to duty to not only protect the sovereignty of other nations but to prevent tyrants or rogue regimes from committing mass murder. We have stormed the borders of nations to dethrone dictators who oppress their own people or commit murder on their own soil. Our leaders send our brave men and women into harm's way and for what? So, their people can chant for our troops to get out while they burn our flag?

Our leaders claim it is for democracy but I say otherwise, it is for diplomacy, so more shady deals can be made behind closed doors. America, we must realize that many the wars that have been fought around the world was inspired by the dark agendas of the elite. The grand puppet master has pulled their strings of manipulation to make politicians and world leaders dance to their bitter music as they become drunken off their wine of deceit. This unjustifiable act has caused brave men and women from nations around the world to commit themselves to war. Our government as well as our corporations have gotten rich on foreign resources especially oil. America has greatly shifted their power around the world, especially in South Western Asia to ensure an adequate supply of oil. In Asia, there are two superpowers and several Islamic nations grasping for power in this region. The idea is that whoever can control the South-Western corner of Asia will have dominance over the markets. For thousands of years' goods were sold throughout the known world by crossing this region. They were known for shipping precious metals, valuable silks, and spices on trade routes that crisscrossed Asia and led into Europe and Africa. Since ancient times, kingdoms and nations such as Babylon, Persia, Greeks, Romans, Ottoman Empire, Germany, and England have fought over this precious region and trade routes.

Today it is oil that makes this land volatile as nations grasp for power over who will control these resources. America this is foolish, for no longer do we need this route for transporting goods. Today most goods are sent by shipping or air. The only true valuable resource in this area is oil but I believe we can obtain our own oil or even purchase oil from other nations. This struggle for power in this region with Russia, China, and rogue Islamic nations is bankrupting America. It is urgent for America to get out of this fight and use our energy and ingenuity to create a new fuel source. By creating an abundant, reliable, new energy source we could dramatically change the world. No longer will black gold be a commodity that countries will fight over.

While we have focused our attention on the continent of Asia for well over a half a century, we have ignored or paid very little attention to other regions around the world. America, it is time for us to no longer purchase oil from Middle Eastern countries because of this mass wealth has led to the corruption in their own government. Through the year's trillions of dollars have been poured into this region while the majority of their people are left in poverty. The Islamic leaders tell their people that their suffering is due to Western Nations; while we try to ease the suffering of these people through foreign aid. The problem is the Islamic Nations have irresponsibly handled their finances. Instead of boosting their economy they have poured their wealth into the creation of massive armies while their leaders or kings live luxurious lives in palaces. What is even worse is how many leaders in Islamic Nations such as Mahmoud Ahmadinejad have financially sponsored terrorist groups. Many of the nations in the Middle East have allowed terrorists groups to live within their borders. These nations have betrayed the whole world by allowing these terrorist groups have safe refuge. We have helped build water treatment facilities, power plants, schools for their children and in return they teach their children to have hate for the Western Nations by teaching Jihad. America, our path here is reckless. You cannot purchase allies nor can you spread Democracy by the force of military. This strategy has failed in Vietnam, Cuba, Afghanistan, Iraq, and many other nations. It is time for us to pull our military and resources from this region; and utilize our own resources to strengthen America.

China's explosion of growth in the past decades has come from the expense of every American. With free trade, they have manipulated the markets with cheap labor, child labor, and no employee rights. China has stolen our technology through cyber warfare, or allowed those to counterfeit the American dollar in their country. All this has dramatically weakened our nation through economic distress and brought our once proud nation to her knees. America, we need to dramatically change the way we handle our foreign affairs, for no longer can we police the world nor can our soldiers bring democracy to other nations. You cannot bring Democracy by force for in the past it has only made us look like oppressors or occupiers. If people truly want freedom and Democracy, then let them fight for it like we once did. Let us restore our birthright and allow democracy to once again flourish within our lands so the world can see what true democracy is like. America, you must realize that people around the world envy the freedom that has been bestowed upon us by our forefathers. This is the very reason so many nations have turned against us. Even China and North Korea will not allow an uncensored worldwide internet in their country because they fear that democracy or the call for freedom will spread.

For many years, people around the world have called out for freedom by protesting in the streets or even rioting. In China, college students protested while one even stood in front of tanks even with the threat of being ran over to answer the call of freedom. America, we began with the precious gift of democracy and freedom but I fear we are taking this great gift for granted. Though we travel the wrong path for prosperity I believe we have the power to change our course. We must first establish the foundation of our government and elect leaders who will truly represent America. We must re-engineer America, for it is urgent to once again see products made in America.

America was once the industrial might of the world and today we have become a nation of consumers. When I was a child I was taught to be proud of the term, "Made in America," and I remember how people called out to buy more American made goods. Goods made in our country were highly sought after because of their quality but today we have replaced them with cheap manufactured goods from around the world. The voice from our past to buy American made goods has been silenced to a whisper. I say no more, be bold and proud, to call out loud, "Buy American made goods!" If we continue this path in purchasing foreign goods will lead to more American industries relocating their business overseas, which will only result to a loss of more American jobs. Today America is facing a tremendous trade deficit with China. We have a $300 billion trade deficit. This indicates that China is exporting $300 billion more in goods to our country then we export to theirs.

Around the world our trade deficit is well over $500 billion yet our leaders seem contempt to leave this deficit in the red. We once had laws to protect American industries so they could compete with nations with lower wages. Now, American industries are being attacked on three fronts through high taxes, regulations, and the NAFTA Treaty. The North American Free Trade Agreement was a massive blow to our economy. Time is of the essence and we must support American industries for they are the backbone of America. American industries are the strength of our country. They stimulate the economy which strengthens our job market and creates high paying jobs. I call out for all Americans to dramatically cut back from purchasing foreign made goods. Let us live by a slogan, for every American made product purchased, it is an American job saved. We must elect a leader that will undo the madness from past administrations and rebalance foreign trade. Unfortunately, we cannot remove the NAFTA Treaty, due to the fact that it was also signed in by other countries, which would create a trade war.

We can forge strong allies and strong economic partners with other nations. Today our relationship with Europe and many other nations around the world has diminished. Today America appears to be weak and on the verge of economic collapse. I believe we can change and change we must for our children's sake. No longer shall we be divided by rich or poor, young or old, or black or white, FOR WE ARE AMERICANS. We must come together, for our future counts on what we do today. Together let us change Washington for a government for the people, as we roll up our sleeves to prepare to work. I believe there are three steps that we can take to bring prosperity and honor back to America. For far too long we have allowed our leaders to make the same mistakes year after year.

First step to secure America's role in foreign affairs we must maintain a powerful military to ensure America's security. Our military needs to play more of a defensive role than an offensive role. For many decades, our leaders have been too quick to interfere with other governments' affairs. These actions have done very little to bring security around the world. We must realize that most nations today are ruled by socialism, communism, or dictatorship. Many nations around the world fear the idea of democracy for it gives people the power to control their government. Today what few allies we have left around the world are threatened more than ever before. I believe it is critical for our military to have a strong capability to quickly deploy our forces, so we can protect our allies. In the future, it is important for America to know who our true allies are.

In the past we have allied ourselves with nations that care very little about American interest. Even nations in Northern Africa such as Algeria, Morocco, Libya and Egypt have allowed hateful propaganda to spread against America throughout the region. Many of these nations we have given foreign aid to or have made them rich by purchasing their oil and for what, so they can allow Islamic terrorists to plot our destruction? Even Pakistan has portrayed themselves as one of America's allies yet they have done very little to combat the terrorists that have hidden within their mountain regions. In fact, Pakistan allowed China to examine one of our military Stealth helicopters that crash landed in their country. The truth is that most Islamic nations do not consider America as an ally; today they see us as nothing more than infidels. They portray Western nations as evil empires, filled with lustful and sinful people.

We must realize that most religions around the world can coincide with one another. These are religions like Christianity, Hinduism, Buddhism, and Judaism that can work together for a common good. The fundamentals of these religions are to have acceptance or tolerance for other religions, forgiveness, and not to be judgmental. In Christianity and Judaism, we believe that God gave mankind free will, but in radical Islam they believe they must cleanse their land of all the infidels. They are killing Christians in Africa and throughout the Middle East. In Israel, they are attacking Jewish settlements and are even moving into territories in Northern India where they are attacking those of Hindu faith. America, we must wake up! Most of the Islamic nations in the Middle East or Northern Africa are not our allies.

In George W Bush's administration, we spent trillions of dollars on a war on terrorism in the Middle East. A tremendous amount of these funds went to building schools, power grids, water treatment facilities, and even mosques. This has done little to change America's image in the eyes of these people. In fact, our troops are still being attacked in the Middle East and two American embassies were attacked in Northern Africa. Let us not forget the hostage crises in Algeria or the fact Iran has held American hostages and still allegedly has one in their custody. For far too long we have poured our wealth into these regions and I say no more. We must stop purchasing oil from all these regions all together and no longer send foreign aid. There are regions in Central Africa where millions are dying from starvation every year. Let's put our foreign aid to a better use in these areas where our aid could fundamentally change people's way of life. In the past decades America, has opened very few diplomatic channels in areas of Central Africa and South America.

We must change the way we handle our foreign affairs for our future and security depend on what we do today. I do believe we must protect our allies in Asia for they too live in a volatile region. These are allies like Israel who have been our friends for far too long for us to turn our backs on them. We must also protect nations like India, Kuwait, and South Korea who depend on us for their security. In the future, we must choose our allies well by basing our decision on the principles and morals of their nation. They must support humanitarian laws for their people. They must have a system that is fair and balanced for their people where women have the opportunity to achieve an education or pursue a career. These nations must swear to protect America's interest as we swear to protect theirs. No longer should we allow our president to deploy American forces on foreign soil without the approval of Congress. This is a system of checks and balance that must be kept.

The second step is to make amendments to the NAFTA Treaty. The NAFTA Treaty was signed in without conditions which was not only foolish but irresponsible. This has only rewarded nations that have low wages, no employee rights, and where child labor thrives. Many nations around the world have allowed slavery to continue, even the Chinese used slave labor to prepare for the 2008 Olympics. The merchandize that was sold at the Olympics was produced by child labor work force. When I read or hear of the news of what was happening with the global workforce, especially the crimes of slavery, I was left in a state of disbelief. It was as if the whole world was losing their morals. I also lay blame on the Olympic committee for allowing such an atrocity to occur.

We can no longer allow the world to ignore humanitarian laws, for it would only lead to the breakdown of societies around the world. When the NAFTA Treaty was signed in, Americans had no alternative but to sacrifice their morals. Today millions of Americans are living in poverty and more Americans are working for lower wages. I do support the NAFTA Treaty but with conditions. For a nation to trade with America they must enforce humanitarian laws. They must enforce a minimum wage that does not have to be equivalent to America's minimum wage, but it should still remain close. Employee rights and benefits should be required as well for free trade. It is urgent for the NAFTA Treaty to be used as a tool to raise the standard of living around the world and not the opposite.

The third step is to dramatically change the way we do business around the world. For too many years China had dictated our trade policy. This has created a tremendous trade deficit that is costing America nearly $300 billion per year. China will remain the great builders of the world as long as we allow them. We can create a more prosperous America by opening up trade negotiations with our neighbors in North America, South America and African nations. These negotiations should also include European countries, Japan, Australia and many others to create a fair and balanced trade.

To ensure fair trade we must also mandate that these nations establish employee rights and an equivalent minimum wage. This will raise the living standard around the world and will create a fair and equal trade system. It has baffled me for years why our governmental officials have poured so much attention and resources into Asia while ignoring our closest neighbors. America is so well protected by two oceans; imagine how much more protected we would be if we strengthened our relationship with Canada, Mexico and South American countries. We can call this the America First Plan, where North and South America ally themselves as trade partners. This will not only strengthen the economy in America, but in Mexico and countries all through South America. If we purchased fewer goods from China and more goods from Mexico or South American countries would stimulate their economy, which would result in a better living standard for their people. I have no doubt that if we continue the path we are on today; China will become a monstrous power. We must realize we can no longer pour our resources into a nation halfway around the world while our neighbors are left in poverty.

We must also utilize our resources to deliver more natural gases to Europe so they may no longer be dependent on Asia. Europe has been America's ally for many years but in the past decades our relationship has severely weakened. During the Cold War, America swore to protect Europe from any invasion including the Soviet Union. During this time America appeared strong on the global platform but today our image has severely diminished. Too many in the world today are predicting America's downfall, so let us rise and show them that we will not fall. We must realize by creating a fair and equal trade with other nations, especially our neighbors, would only result in the strengthening of America's industries. America's might is our workforce, our ingenuity to solve problems, and our creativity. We must stand together to show strength and solidarity. The world will once again know we are not to be pushed around. I am not calling for an embargo against Asian nations but for far too long they have dictated our trade policies; what I am calling for is common sense. We no longer can support countries that does not support humanitarian laws and forces their people to work grueling hours and low wages. Due to China's low wages, it has forced American industries to move overseas or face bankruptcy. America, I call out to end this madness now. For if we continue to ignore these issues then our children will pay for our neglect.

Panel to Investigate Unjust Laws and Un-American Conduct in Office

For too many years our politicians have ignored the voice of the people. They have met behind closed doors to sign in laws that were unfavorable for the American people. They have made alliances with corporate elites, social organizations, and political parties that were un-American. Together many have plotted to change America from a democratic style of government to a socialist style of government. For decades, they feared their actions would be seen so they hid their laws within bills. Today they are bold; you can easily go to any website and find their true agenda. Many of our politicians have indicated that we now live under a socialist style of government. Their idea of redistributing the wealth has bankrupted our nation and now there are Democrats who support a worldwide distribution of wealth.

Today we have administrators of governmental departments who are creating false aliases to rage a cloak and dagger war on fossil fuel industries. These actions were unprofessional and are illegal. For far too long our voices have been unheard; our politicians no longer see the people as citizens but as subjects. We must draw out this poison that has infiltrated our government. They do not see the pain of hunger or the millions of homeless. The millions who are living in poverty is a direct result of the unjust laws, an increasing taxing system, and a corrupted welfare system that is strangling America. Tell me, if the social welfare program that has been created over the past century is benefitting our society then why are there more people living in poverty than ever before? In fact, the numbers of those in poverty have increased dramatically. Tell me, if taxing the rich and passing intense regulations on our industries was such a good idea, then why have so many factories moved to faraway lands? In fact, President Obama has given money to other nations so they may drill for oil or stimulate their own economy by building new industries. This is another democratic plan to redistribute money worldwide. Our government has been reckless and to tell you the truth it's hard to tell who they have been serving. At a political meeting with Russia our president whispered into the ear of the Russian president "Tell him I need more space." I ask once again, Space for what Mr. President? So you can weaken our military and our missile defenses? You are nothing more than a deceiver because you would have never made that comment if you knew the microphone was still on. This is a good indication that there is deception in our government. Believe me America, for I will tell you this deception did not start with Pres. Obama.

This deception was to ensure Pres. Obama would win his second bid for president, which meant he was deceiving the American people. His rage war on fossil fuel industries and claims that you will bankrupt the coal mine industries are a plague upon our land. You have taken credit from the increase of oil production in America, which you had very little to do with. The increase in oil had derived from the oil permits signed in by the Bush administration. The reason Pres. Obama took credit for the increase in oil was due to the pressure he was receiving; the American people were outraged about his war on fossil fuels companies. Our president has stepped on our rights and declared our Constitution unconstitutional. Our president has passed laws with intense regulations that restrict industrial growth and personal freedoms. He claims it is to better serve us but six million more Americans are now living in poverty since his administration began. Pres. Obama's NDAA bill and Obama care were both unconstitutional. Federal judges declared in a court of law these bills were unconstitutional but our president ignored their verdict. Many people have questioned if our president is American by birth but I question if our president is American by heart.

America our nation has been under siege for decades, tell me where does it say in our Constitution that we can sell away America or give up our sovereignty. Tell me where does it say in our Constitution that laws can be created that violates the people's rights or freedoms. The NAFTA treaty has devastated our nation's economy and halted industrial growth. President Bush Sr. Paved the way for this bill, as the next president the Clinton administration was signed this bill into law. This one bill proves that the Republicans and Democrats are both working together to bring forth the New World Order. In fact, in the past several presidents have promoted this devious plan for a one world government. Pres. Bush Jr. signed in the Patriot Act and directive 51 which is a severe violation to our constitutional rights. The executive order directive 51 will lead to the destruction of our nation that will leave us under a dictator style of government. The executive order directive 51 gives executive branch the power to consolidate the legislative and judicial branch under presidential authority. America this is the move to dismantle the framework our forefathers had created to ensure we keep our personal freedoms.

America times are desperate and for far too long our vote has not counted. We must abolish the electoral voting system so every vote counts. Let our voices be heard as we retake the seats in Washington. We must elect politicians who will serve the people and make America a priority. The Executive Branch has become too powerful over the past decades and we must limit these powers. Congress and Senate must be limited to no more than three terms to ensure true representation. Once our voices are heard in Washington we must demand a panel to be established undo the madness from our past. This panel's responsibility will be to restore America's true foundation and once again bring balance back to Washington. The Executive Branch has become too powerful over the past decades and we must limit these powers. Congress and Senate must be limited to no more than three terms to ensure true representation. This panel's responsibility will be to aid in undoing the unjust laws that were signed in from our past. The laws that are declared by the panel to be unjust or violate constitutional rights must be resubmitted to the legislative branch so they may be voted out and remove from the law books. They must also investigate how much our politicians are influenced by socialist, communist parties or organizations. This is especially needed in the Democratic Party, where many of the Democratic politicians who are serving us today have ties to these radical groups. The panel's responsibility will be to investigate presidential abuse of authority. This would also include Pres. Bill Clinton giving or selling our advance technology to other nations that has led to the weakening of our defense and has diminished of our competitiveness in the world market. I also believe the Benghazi case must be reopened, where Pres. Obama and Hillary Clinton should be investigated for their negligence.

I also believe this panel's responsibility is to organize a world movement to bring justice to the elite families of the world. I am calling for the largest lawsuit in world history for their evil agendas has left billions in poverty. America, they have manipulated governments into war and while brave soldiers gave their lives, the elite families profited immensely. They corrupted our politicians through their wicked bribes to do there evil bidding. The corporate elite orchestrated the NAFTA treaty, and once again the elite prophets immensely from a worldwide cheap labor force. A century ago the elite bankers created the great panic through their evil deception to usher in their money manipulating machine. The Federal Reserve act has created tremendous debt for our government, which is led to increased taxes for the working class. Today the elite families control the economy and have corner the gold market. I believe the wealth they have obtained through the centuries must be seized and returned to the people of the world through projects for new schools, water treatment facilities, and farming equipment. I do not believe in redistribution of wealth but these families have manipulated governments around the world and have created wars for their own benefits. The elite families also own and control many of the media networks and they have used these networks to control what we hear. These networks must be seized and sold back to the public, because we can no longer allow such deception.

This is un-American and I believe all information that is gathered through this investigation should be released to the public. I am also asking for the Nixon files and tapes to be released to the public so they may be reviewed. There is no doubt that the Democratic agenda is pushing our nation into a socialist style of government. Through redistribution of wealth they are trying to create a utopian society where everyone is cared for. This has not worked and will not work, even evidence has shown this. Yet the Democrats push for more laws, regulations, restrictions and more social welfare that is tearing our country apart. Many of the Democrats have pushed for worldwide redistribution of wealth as they strategize for the New World Order. I am calling out for the Democratic Party to denounce members that are tied with communist or socialist ideology. If politicians do not take this step, then we the American people must vote them out of office for they cannot serve the people with such an un-American agenda.

In the future, our politicians must serve us with prestige honor and good morals. We must never forget the power to be is within the people. Let us not become discouraged because these problems are too massive; if we break them down one by one we can find simple solutions. I have laid before you what I truly believe our forefathers intended for our nation. We must come together as one people and no longer be divided by race or religion. Let us come together, young or old and cry out in one loud voice: "no more!"

Make Your Vote Count

We live in such a privileged society today. The very right that was bestowed upon us by our forefathers gives us the opportunity to cast our votes to elect those suited to represent us all. King George was shocked when he realized George Washington refused to be America's first king. Hearing this news, still shocked, he stated that George Washington would go down in history as a great man.

Indeed, George Washington did go down in history as a great man who helped establish a system of government with checks and balances. He desired the government to be for the people by the people. Today I have seen so many people neglect or refuse to partake in their very right to vote. How can we possibly elect those best fitted to represent us if so many are carelessly voting or not casting their vote at all? On many different occasions, I have met those who have proudly shared who they've voted for in past elections. When I asked what their motivation was for voting for their candidate, I was shocked to hear that so many knew very little about their candidate or their policies. How can they possibly choose a candidate whose policies they know very little about or where they stand on important issues? I have had people tell me their reason for voting for their candidate was because they were the most popular choice. I have also heard of people who vote straight Republican or Democrat without even knowing the candidate.

How can we successfully put the best candidate in office if we do not pay attention to their principles or their ideology? How do we know if bringing prestige back to our great country is their number one priority? What I find even more alarming is how many people don't know who their state senators or congressmen are. I don't know if people feel that helpless or just don't care. So many people in America feel that they have lost control on what goes on in Washington DC. I have heard many say that Washington DC has become its own world and its thirst for power will never be quenched. America, we must wake up and come to our senses, for Washington may be its own world but it reaches out through our nation and controls us all like a grand puppet master.

We must research each of our candidates and find out where they stand on their policies on domestic or foreign issues. It is important to judge our candidates character and morals. We must be willing to vote for someone new and who has not been tainted by Washington DC. Do not depend solely on the media, by doing your own research and paying attention to what your candidate believes in, you will be better informed and less brainwashed by the media. I find that the media plays a great role on manipulating people. How can they possibly consider it fair if they give more air time to one candidate than they give to any other? I have also watched the media ridicule the policies of one candidate while praising another candidate's. Whatever happened to an unbiased media? Let the people decide for themselves! I find our media extremely bias. I have watched them ridicule or even mock conservative candidates while praising the liberal candidates. How can we possibly stand by and allow the media to manipulate the people in such a manner? Have they forgotten how to report simple facts or are they satisfying their own political desires? America, we must wake up for we are being led like sheep to the wolf's lair. The fact that the elite class controls the media and it pours a tremendous amount of campaign funds to the candidates of their choosing is controlling the outcome of all branches of our government. This control of the elite class in our country is abolishing our rights and destroying our opportunity for a prosperous future. America, we must shatter this unfavorable bond to reestablish our constitutional rights and to give every American a chance for a more prosperous future. We must also abolish the electoral voting system. We must make every vote count equally and create a new electronic voting system. We must also enforce laws to prevent voter tampering or fraud.

America, I urgently call out to you to cast your vote in a responsible manner. The very future of our children and grandchildren depend on what we do today. I have heard many people say they feel as if their voice is silent. Silence your voice no more and cast your vote! Do not trust the media do your own research. We must choose a politician that is best to serve us all, man or woman but who is willing to stand up for our nation and its Constitution. We need someone who will not allow another country to force their policies on us. We must realize that America is strong. We have one of the richest countries and resources and we help feed over a hundred nations. We must act now to preserve our very freedom and democracy. We cannot allow another politician to spend us into the trillions. Today I only see two outcomes for our great nation because our deficit is running into the trillions. How will our kids pay off this massive loan not to mention the tremendous interest? Our politicians are selling our technology and are making it impossible for big businesses to remain in this country. How are we possibly creating a future for our children? Even our politicians are not utilizing our resources and they are selling the very rights to our resources to other countries. If we do not stop this path of self-destruction, how can we possibly answer the question that our children will ask us in the future, why did we not fight?

We do not have to continue this path but we can go down in history as the people who said, "No more," and take a stand. We must no longer turn a blind eye to our politicians' carelessness. We must hold them accountable. We must become one people that right the wrongs to our past. We have to fight to bring prestige back to our country for the generations to come. The voice of the people is our great power. America, I call out for you to assemble and let the truth be known. The 2016: presidential election is upon us and we must be prepared for the biggest smear campaign ever. Do not let your hearts be deceived for the powers of the elite and those who support the New World Order are fearful of Donald Trump. Do not allow the media networks to deceive you, nor shall we allow the Democratic politicians to spread their deception. I call out for every American to empower yourself with wisdom, for the pathway for freedom is truth.

Deception of Health Care

Today in America, we have one of the best health care facilities in the world. We are capable of giving patients artificial hearts and organ transplants. We are also capable of curing many strands of cancer and with medication we can fight back viral infections and diseases. Through ultrasounds and CAT Scans we can peer into the human body and diagnose serious illnesses. As a result, people are living longer lives, but all this has come at a tremendous cost. The cost of health insurance is unattainable for so many Americans, and millions do not have the funds to seek medical attention.

It saddens my heart to see that so many people cannot afford medical treatment, nor can they afford the high cost of insurance. America is ranked 37th in health care in the world. I believe the reason why is because so many are denied the health care they desperately need. Today, insurance companies manipulate their policies on what is covered and not covered for their best interest. I ask, "What has happened to the best interest for the people?" Insurance companies have even refused to cover certain tests that would help doctors diagnose more serious illnesses that could save lives. Have we become a society that has no conscience and denies care for all? Is this not legalized murder? Can you imagine a society with the technology we have today, and the care we can give, along with the morals of yesterday?

It wasn't too many decades ago when doctors would come to your home and provide medical treatment. If the patient or the family could not afford to pay for the doctor's service, the doctor would accept some form of trade. At that time doctors, did not choose their profession for wealth. Their true desire was to give care to the sick, heal the wounds, mend broken bones, and bring new life into this world. To them the greatest reward was to serve the people. This is a practice that has gone on since the beginning of mankind. Archeologists have found ancient skeletons where broken bones have been mended. They have even found medical instruments, such as a scalpel, that dates back thousands of years into our past from Egypt.

One of the best attributes of being human is the fact that we care for one another. I would hate for us to become a society where humans are treated like machines or are used for spare parts. Today, I wonder if we are becoming such a society. For if a person dies due to lack of funds or insurance, does our society still not want him/her to donate their organs? I think it is noble and great to extend someone else's life by donating your organs, but everyone deserves the best treatment that can be provided. We are living in a hypocritical society.

Today our health care is completely overrun with fraudulent claims. It shows the incompetence of our government. Not only for the fact there are so many fraudulent claims but also for the outrageous spending in our health care system. Our government spends well over a trillion in Medicare, Medicaid, Veteran Care, and other programs each year. I find this outrageously criminal that so much revenue is poured into healthcare, and especially the fact that so many Americans have been abandoned.

If you ask my opinion, I call this embezzlement. They are stealing from the working class and giving proceeds to the poor. Then they have the audacity to tell Americans, if they do not have insurance or the appropriate funds to take care of their medical needs, it is their own fault. This is already having a huge impact on middle class. It is us, Americans, who are flipping this multi-trillion-dollar bill. Our society is becoming an inverted pyramid, where government and CEO's and other massive corporations are riding the top, and we the people are only receiving the short end of the proceeds while carrying the load.

There are three entities that are causing the destruction in our country. I use to think government and big business are the worst in destroying the foundation of our country but now I find that healthcare is just as evil. They collaborate together to drain the wealth from America. They are all bent on absolute power and they are molding our country for their own personal gain. Healthcare and big business are lobbying our government for the most beneficial gains and tax breaks. Is this not bribery? If big business and healthcare are pulling the strings in our government, then who is representing the people?

There are those who want to make dramatic cuts in Medicare or Medicaid funding. Medicare and Medicaid is not the problem. The problem lies with the government and those who are running these programs. There are so many greedy hands that are taking from this wealth that the people have invested in. Is this not fraud and why is the FBI not investigating this matter? Has the FBI lost its power or ability to investigate or bring charges against those in government or corporations for embezzlement? America, I call for you to make your own investigations especially for those who work in these departments. It seems that the truth has been distorted and it may be difficult to uncover the facts but do not allow this to deter you. Once you see the truth, contact your senator. Turn your evidence over to the proper authorities and demand an investigation. America, we must wake up! A little over 25% of Americans are on Medicaid and Medicare and for our government to have such massive problems with the amount of money they are receiving is ridiculous.

After President Obama was elected into office, there was a stimulus package created from 2009 until 2011 that was over $100 billion funneled into health care. America once again, we are looking at an outlandish amount of tax payers' dollars. We must realize how scandalous this is. I find it intrusive that Obama arrogantly creates a Universal Health Care bill without consulting or having the will of the people. I not only find it arrogant, but ignorant for our politicians to bring such a bill into action without reviewing its content. The Universal Health Care bill would have a drastic change not only in our economy but it will devastate American families. Small businesses will not be able to contend with such a bill and the increasing taxes only bring hardship to all Americans. Even today major corporations and even small businesses are cutting back on full-time employees, while creating more part-time positions. This is the result of big and small businesses attempting to avoid the high cost of Obama care.

America, we must use common sense and realize that these major policy changes are hurting the working class. For well over a century politicians had attempted to glorify their name by creating their own department in healthcare and other departments. These are departments such as Hillary Care that fortunately did not succeed or Obama Care, which was signed in without proper review by the Senate or Congress. This bill not only unconstitutional it will also aid in bankrupting our nation.

The fact that Obama Care will cost us well into the trillions within its first decade is piling a tremendous amount of debt upon us all. I have no doubt that our government truly desires absolute power. By creating such a bill will intrude on our private medical history but it also allows our government to decide on what form of healthcare we will receive. Another issue I find equally disturbing is the fact that our government is utilizing the Internal Revenue Service to police every American to ensure each Americans has insurance. This is a deliberate attempt to ensure the success of Obama Care which has stepped all over our constitutional rights.

Many nations have carried Universal Healthcare for years, and today there are many countries going bankrupt due to out-of-control spending. The bigger issue today is the quality of healthcare they are providing for their people has declined. Also, several nations have created a panel that declares what type of healthcare they will receive. For these people to have to go before a panel to plead their case is horrifying. Many people wait months just for the panel to review their case. Thousands have died in waiting. There is no humanity in such inaction. We must support those who have taken legal action and taken a stand against this bill.

America, do we truly want to put health care in our government's hands in such a manner? Imagine a poor child having to wait for a panel's decision for the type of healthcare she or he will receive. There is coldness and represents a heartless society, to know their very lives depend on such a panel. We must rip the pages of this bill from the very foundation that it has entangled itself within, for such a law only destroys prosperity and hope. This power that this government seeks will only create tyranny.

I can understand why Obama would want to create such a healthcare bill, due to the fact that there are a little over 14% of Americans uninsured. By resolving this problem, allowing the government to take over in this manner is not the answer. I find that there are many contributing problems in our private healthcare sector. The very fact that there are health care insurance companies profiting with profit margins into the billions is part of this problem. We must realize that billions in profit is preposterous especially when there are over 40 million Americans who cannot afford Health insurance. There are CEOs in the private health insurance sector that are making nearly 20 million per year. Is this not greed? This would be equivalent to these CEOs making over $380,000 per week. The consequential fact is our healthcare is corrupt from the inside through government healthcare and private insured companies.

Unfortunately, the greed and corruption does not end here. Even pharmaceutical companies profit well into the billions of dollars while the price of prescription medication seems to continue to rise. There are many Americans who cannot afford their medication as they go without their life saving medication or skip every other day on taking their medicine. You have to wonder how many deaths has this contributed to because of this horrendous problem. This a greed that runs deep within our government, private insurance companies, and pharmaceutical companies yet the problem does stop there. Even pharmaceutical companies lobby our doctors to only write prescriptions for their variety of medications. The fact they give them bonus checks or other incentives is bribery. There are doctors receiving a tremendous amount of revenue every year from these bribes.

Over the years there has been no attempts to end the corruption in our health care. The healthcare industry along with pharmaceutical companies continue to raise their prices without consideration of the hardship this puts on every American family. The major problem is the fact that Washington, our politicians have become corrupted by the healthcare industry. Most of the CEOs will make more money in one year than most Americans will make in their lifetime. Their greed has run out of control. They have abused the very freedom our forefathers have constructed. The healthcare industry along with the pharmaceutical companies brag about their profit margins while thousands of Americans die every year. They have thrown outlandish parties or taken lavish vacations around the world while so many have suffered.

I cry out today, where are the voices of the people and what has silenced our leaders? The very root of this problem is we are all being deceived. Our politicians do not have our best interest at heart, for they are being bribed. The healthcare industry and pharmaceutical companies have all hired lobbyist to lobby Washington in their best interest. How can our politicians have our best interest if they are being bribed? Their greed has deafened their ears for they can no longer hear the people.

Many Americans are struggling today. The extreme cost of dentistry or the high costs of ophthalmologists are posing tremendous hardships on Americans. Those who do not have insurance are struggling far worse. One trip to the emergency room could easily turn to five or more separate bills. For example, you would be charged for the emergency room visit as well as a technician fee and if you had any blood work done, that would create a lab bill as well. This does not include a doctor bill or any other test that could be required such as an EKG, X-ray or CAT scan. Within one month you would receive bills from all departments demanding payment immediately. To be billed in this manner along with other bills creates intense stress upon families.

Hospitals have divided their business through departments, which has created several businesses in one. Each department is responsible for their own billing to increase the profitable revenue the hospital can receive. There could be over 30 separate departments in a hospital. We must realize by establishing so many multiple departments have no interest in actually serving people, it's to serve their own personal greed. I have no doubt that greed is their driving force and too many has commit fraudulent claims as

Even if you're hospitalized, it could come with outlandish bills. If you were required to stay the night at the hospital, it could cost you well over a thousand dollars a night just for a room. If you were to ask for Tylenol or Aspirin, you would be billed for that as well. Come on America, thousands are dying because of these horrendous and barbaric actions. With outrageous costs for insurance and the out of control billing from hospitals or doctors, it is no wonder so many live without insurance. Where is the care and humanitarian code that we should all live by? Have doctors forgotten their Oath or was it just meaningless? This is part the classical version oath that many doctors around the world had sworn by till the early 1900s.

Classical Version Oath

"I swear by Apollo the healer, by Aesculapius, by Health and all the powers of healing, and call to witness all the gods and goddesses that I may keep this Oath and Promise to the best of my ability and judgment. I will pay the same respect to my master in the Science as to my parents and share my life with him and pay all my debts to him. I will regard his sons as my brothers and teach them the Science, if they desire to learn it, without fee or contract. I will hand on precepts, lectures and all other learning to my sons, to those of my master and to those pupils duly apprenticed and sworn, and to none other."

Modern Day Oath

"I swear to fulfill, to the best of my ability and judgment, this covenant: I will respect the hard-won scientific gains of those physicians in whose steps I walk, and gladly share such knowledge as is mine with those who are to follow. I will apply, for the benefit of the sick, all measures which are required, avoiding those twin traps of overtreatment and therapeutic nihilism. I will remember that there is art to medicine as well as science, that warmth, sympathy, and understanding may outweigh the surgeon's knife or the chemist's drug. I will not be ashamed to say "I know not," nor will I fail to call in my colleagues when the skills of another are needed for a patient's recovery. I will respect the privacy of my patients, for their problems are not disclosed to me that the world may know. Most especially must I tread with care in matters of life and death. If it is given me to save a life, all thanks. But it may also be within my power to take a life; this awesome responsibility must be faced with great humbleness and awareness of my own frailty. Above all, I must not play at God. I will remember that I do not treat a fever chart, a cancerous growth, but a sick human being, whose illness may affect the person's family and economic stability. My responsibility includes these related problems, if I am to care adequately for the sick. I will prevent disease whenever I can, for prevention is preferable to cure. I will remember that I remain a member of society, with special obligations to all my fellow human beings, those sound of mind and body as well as the infirm. If I do not violate this oath, may I enjoy life and art, respected while I live and remembered with affection thereafter. May I always act so as to preserve the finest traditions of my calling and may I long experience the joy of healing those who seek my help."

The classical version of the Hippocratic Oath set a poor foundation for the medical field. I understand this oath was written 400 BC, but respectfully I think this oath should be part of the history books because it is outdated and never should've been used. The majority of our medical universities has abandoned the classical version oath, but many universities continue to swear to this oath into the 1950s. Even today there are still universities that are teaching the classical version oath and even encouraging the medical field to swear to the original Hippocratic Oath. I can see why our medical field has lost its morals. Not only for greed but the very fact that they pledge an oath to Apollo and Asclepius, then they call upon Gods and Goddesses as witnesses is without belief and impractical. If they do not believe in their oath, then how can their pledge have merit? The new oath was written in 1964 by Louis Lasagna. The modern oath is lacking compassion, patience, and understanding. Nor do I agree with the phrase in the modern oath "my power to take a life". I find that we must rewrite a new oath, for the best interest of the people. The new oath should uphold kindness, and must bring truth and honor to our medical field, where healthcare of the people is their first priority, not wealth. They must proclaim an oath to do all they can do to preserve human life and have compassion for all.

America once again I call for us to end lobbying. The billions of dollars our politicians have received have drowned out our voices for too long. If we can end lobbying it would create a better opportunity for smaller healthcare and pharmaceutical businesses to grow in this intense market which could also help lower healthcare cost. If the politicians do not hear our voice, we must remove them from office. They must realize that their seat of power does not belong to them but to the people. Our politicians must once again become our voice. They must no longer represent big business as their priority. We must elect politicians who are willing to take on big corporations and dramatically scale back their wealth. I understand this is a free country and free market but large corporations have abused their freedom for far too long. This is the very reason why we must not accept President Obama's universal healthcare plan. For not only is it full of bureaucracy, it serves more of an interest to corporations in the medical field than to the people.

The fact this is going to cost taxpayers well over a trillion dollars is ludicrous and the burden on businesses across America will be tremendous. I have no doubt that many will judge me for criticizing

President Obama's healthcare plan, but I will tell you that I have looked into his plan, and if you follow suit, you will see the madness. This is the reason we must end lobbying but that is not the only problem. We must stop these corporations from dumping a tremendous amount of their wealth into political campaign funds and prevent them from throwing lavish parties for them as well. This is why your voice is not heard America, for they are not only being wined and dined but their pockets are being filled with cash.

America, I want you to seriously think about my plan. Establishing one health care plan for all Americans is the way to go. Our government has many health care plans such as Medicare, Medicaid and now even "Obama Care" which creates a tremendous overhead at taxpayers' expense. You must realize by having so many separate governmental healthcare departments only result to corruption. Our government has done a poor job monitoring this wasteful spending and even the oversight committee has failed miserably.

By creating a one governmental health care plan would save taxpayers billions of dollars every year and it would be much easier to monitor and control healthcare spending. This is common sense America, by eliminating the overhead cost of multiple departments and preventing billions in fraud every year would allow millions of Americans to be insured. The senior citizens would lose no health care benefits for the benefits will stay the same and it should be free. Those who are in poverty will receive free healthcare but this must be monitored to ensure it is not abused. For us to be considered a civilized society we must be humanitarian at heart. We cannot turn a blind eye to the people in poverty. Our goal should be to bring them out of despair.

For those who are in the middle to upper class, the insurance fee should be deducted from their paycheck like any other insurance company. This would create competition between the governmental health care insurance and the private healthcare insurance which would dramatically lower our cost. What I am indicating is, if a company or big business wanted to upgrade their insurance, they could easily go to the private sector. Ensuring all Americans are ensured would also lower healthcare cost because it would do away with medical bankruptcy and unpaid medical bills. America, I am asking you to use common sense, do you honestly think it costs well over a trillion dollars per year or Obama's plan which is projected to cost more than a trillion dollars within the next decade to provide health care for America? I ask you to do the math. How much do you think it would cost to cover every American? We must make sure all Americans are insured, so they may be provided with health care.

Even the power company today cannot cut someone's power off if the temperature is below freezing or someone is on life support. These are humanitarian laws. Before these laws many have died by freezing to death. Today are there not thousands dying because of the impossibility of obtaining health insurance? As you read this book there are thousands suffering tremendous pain, is this not unnecessary?

It was not long ago I heard of a 27-year-old mother dying of cancer because she could not receive care because she did not have health insurance. Let me ask you, who wants to be the one to tell her children when they grow up that their mother died in vain because there were no regulations set upon health care nor were there any laws to sustain her life. How would you explain the greed of big corporations or the corruption of our government? How would you describe the fact that our politicians received bribes to submit to the will of these corporations? We must remember freedom belongs to the people, not corporations. For far too long corporations and CEO's have abused their freedom bought with their money. As I have said before I do not believe in governmental regulations but I believe everyone has the right for health care.

Let us make a stand; we must correct the wrongs of our past. Let us not leave this corruption for our children to fix. It is our duty, for we are on the watch tower. We must not give into despair. Our civilization is crumbling before our eyes while our government absorbs more power.

While corporations and CEO's obtain more wealth the number of those in poverty expands. For this is our watch, let us not fail. Let us regroup and show the power of the people. We must make this stand today before it is too late. We shall not be a people that are governed, we must reassert our power. For the thousands who have died before us, for the families who have cried out in agony for lost loved ones, let their voices be heard!

Education

The meaning of education is the passing down of knowledge from our past to inspire our young for a brighter future. Before schools, we educated our children to read and write at home, so they too could pass down the gift of knowledge. So, the beginning of education started with family. It was the very thing that strengthened the family bond between parents and their children. It was not just the knowledge that was passed down, it was the morals, respect, honor, and Christian values. As generations passed, parents understood the values of passing down these lessons to their children. Not only did they control what was taught to their children they understood the importance. Today I look around and wonder who truly is in control of our children's destiny. Who decides on the textbooks or the lessons our children are forced to learn? Have the lessons that were once taught by the family become meaningless or obsolete?

America, while we have slept we have lost total control of what has been taught to our children through public education. Our right to dispute the lesson plans has been taken away and the few in charge of education refuse to listen to the people. Today, I find that many parents are lost and confused about what is being taught to our children. Hitler had once indicated "Give me control of the textbooks and I will control the state." Controlling textbooks was a tool the socialists Nazi used to brainwash their own people. Even communist nations use propaganda to spread their ideology to poison the minds of their own people. America has been affected as well through communist and socialist ideology that has infiltrated our government and our children's education. These groups with dark agendas have assaulted our Christian principles and have manipulated our history to destroy patriotism.

Today in public schools across America children learn very little about the great deeds of our forefathers or the true meaning of their wisdom. Instead they villainize our forefathers through their own interpretation of history or portray them all as slave owners. I do not condone any form of slavery past or present, but this does not give reasoning to allow our government or other groups with their sinister agenda to villainize our once great leaders through the manipulation of their legacy. Unfortunately, the horrible crimes of slavery are part of American history, as well as the horrible crimes against the Native Americans. These horrible crimes of racism or enslavement must be a required course for our schools, to ensure our children never repeat these horrible deeds in their future. There were other horrific crimes in American history that is kept silent from our history books, such as the whites that were sold into slavery like the Irish. There are other issues such as the cruel treatment of the Japanese, Chinese, and the lack of equal rights for women. We must always learn from our past mistakes to ensure our children have a better future.

Our forefathers were not perfect, nor did they come from a world that was perfect. They come from a world where the people did not have rights and they were subjects to dictators or monarchs. They came from a world that was filled with the ideology of the naturalist movement, these delusional ideas are what inspired the master race concept. Those patriots who dared to stand for a new idea of freedom, liberty, and a Constitution composed of our indelible rights set in stone must always be admired. We must never forget their sacrifices and how bravely they stood against the mightiest army in the world. We can no longer allow those in the Department of Education to pick and choose what history is taught to our children. Our nation was not perfect from his foundation but with time we became the freest society on earth.

Education is tremendously vital for the future of America. It is not just essential for economic growth but it is crucial for stability. Education is the building block for our future. For the generation that is being taught today will be the generation that will lead our country tomorrow. What I find shocking is that our children are being taught very little about the procedures and the principles of our political government. In fact, our children today know very little of the politicians who are serving us in Congress or even in Senate. If you were to ask most teenagers in high school today who their politicians or state governor is, most of them would not know. The majority of our children knows very little or as no understanding of the constitutional rights nor can they recite the Pledge of Allegiance. I speak out today, for I believe that the government is blinding our children for the future. In fact, they teach our children very little about our forefathers who established the very pillars of our great nation. They even distort the truth about our history or deny them the opportunity to understand the freedom our forefathers bestowed upon us all. I will prove this with one fact, our forefathers strongly opposed the central bank concept. When King George order the colonists to stop producing their own currency and demanded them to receive their currency from the Central Bank of England was one of the contributing factors for the Revolutionary War. The elite bankers have manipulated or utilize their own wealth to impose their dark agenda upon us all. If our children were to learn the truth about our forefathers and how they strongly disagree with the central bank concept, then they would not agree with the Federal Reserve Act. This is the reason those in the elite circle are attempting to control what is taught to our children. I have watched several documentaries on the Revolutionary War, and never have I heard how our forefathers strongly opposed the central bank concept or how this was a contributing factor for the war for our independence. You have to wonder if their agenda is to weaken the minds of our young and to destroy patriotism.

"Education makes a people easy to lead, but difficult to drive; easy to govern, but impossible to enslave"

-Henry Peter Brougham British political leader

The assumption of slavery might be far reaching, but as our leaders grasp for more power while tightening their grip upon our land has laid to waste the meaning of our constitutional rights. There is a true evil, I call out for the people to not be deceived, for their evil deeds have gone unnoticed for far too long as they plot to control us evermore. We must wake up America, for our children need to understand the true meaning of democracy. They must understand the meaning of liberty and freedom that has been bestowed upon them. It should be a requirement that all students study the Declaration of Independence and The Constitution. It is important for our children to understand what it was like to live in a system that was overtaxed and without a voice or representation. I believe this course should be taught in high school and middle school as well. I also believe that social studies need to be expanded, it should be required that our children should follow and be tested on the political decisions that are being made in Washington by their politicians.

Even the morals that sustain the very fabric of life have been distorted. If we do not teach our children good morals, then how will they treat us in the future? They will be our caregivers! The Department of Education has removed prayer as well as the Commandments from our schools. They have defiled the book of Genesis by teaching Darwin's Theory and polluted our young children's minds with the teaching of sex education. Do they no longer have respect for family values or Christian beliefs? We must realize the damage this has caused to our society through the generations. The Ten Commandments set a standard for honorable behavior and since the removal of the Commandments our schools have fallen into disarray. Schools have become more violent and so many children seem lost and confused. This leaves our children vulnerable as so many reach for drugs and alcohol to fill the void in their life.

The Department of Education claim they have many of these issues under control by teaching alcohol and drug abuse courses yet addictions continue to increase. We have to ask ourselves if our society is better today than it was decades ago. By the 1950s, evolutionists had a firm grip over America, and is it not ironic how much crime had increased by the 1980s. Several people claim the crime has declined in America in the past decades, but I would say that is not true. Since the teachings of evolution, along with the removal of the Ten Commandments has profoundly changed America. Today our law enforcement departments have almost quadrupled. Our school systems, especially inner city schools are fenced in like prisons and many have installed a guard shack at the entrance of their schools. Most schools across our nation have installed metal detectors and have armed police officers patrolling the hallways. Over the past decades our society has changed dramatically especially when it calls for this much security in our public schools to ensure the safety of our children.

The fact that the government removed religion from our schools to serve the few, left the majority questioning their faith or morals. We were once taught that our spirit, our conscience, controlled our mind which controlled our body. Now, I find so many people think like animals. They listen more to their bodies' than their mind and so many believe they don't have a soul. It is easy to go through life and believe we don't have a higher power to answer to. If we become a society that only listens to our own desires or passions, then are we not living like animals? Could this be the very reason crime has intensified throughout our nation?

We today are becoming a society without a conscience and few morals. Our leaders seem confused and do not know how to respond to the predicaments we are facing today. Their manner of resolving the crises we are facing is creating more laws so they can tighten their grip on our society. If we are treated like humans, we will act like humans, but if we are treated as animals, then we will be animals. We must once again inspire our young to not only believe in a higher power but to listen to their conscience. It is crucial that we start to teach our young once again that they have a soul and God has a divine plan. We must break down these diseases that have infiltrated our schools and poisoned our children's minds, one by one. This corruption has infiltrated the Department of Education through a corrupt and immoral government. For decades, Socialism has concealed its intentions within the Liberal movement. Today socialism has bounded itself in the fabric of our society.

"The American people will never knowingly adopt Socialism. But under the name of 'liberalism' they will adopt every fragment of the Socialist program, until one day America will be a Socialist nation, without knowing how it happened."

-Norman Thomas

They have distorted our history and attacked Christian principles. I truly believe that the attack on Christian beliefs was the first assault on our nation's morals and principles. By the removal of prayer from school and the pledge of allegiance has severely weakened the moral fabric of our society. They have made prayer day unconstitutional while attempting to remove "In God We Trust," from our society. If we continue to allow our society to be corrupt and allow this movement to continue to poison the minds of our children, where will that leave our society in the future?

We must realize the damage that has been caused to our society by Darwin's Theory of Evolution as well as the Big Bang Theory. If our children believe we came from apes, then how can they possibly believe that there is a God? Does it not say in the Bible that God created Adam and Eve, the first man and woman? If they are taught that the universe was created from the Big Bang Theory, then the story of creation, in Genesis, is just a story. Before we can debate Darwin's Theory of evolution we must first establish his credibility and research his standards of gathering information. It is crucial to not only understand his mental state but his educational background as well. His theory has been debated for far too long.

Charles Darwin was born in 1809, in Shrewsbury, England. His father, Robert Darwin was a doctor and his mother Susannah Darwin was a financier. At the age of eight, his mother passed away, which must have been a traumatic experience. Charles attended Shrewsbury school, where he was known for making up wild stories, being very rambunctious and mischievous. He also loved being the center of attention. Later on, he was removed from his school due to his poor grades. Charles would eventually attend Edinburgh University where he would study the medical field. He could not tolerate medical procedures, therefore he dropped out. Due to pressure from his father, he was forced to enroll in Christ's College at Cambridge University. Charles's father had put tremendous amount of pressure on his son to finish his education. His father was worried that his son, Charles would be an embarrassment to the family. Many during this time thought Charles was unstable. He had a passion for hunting birds so he could examine them and he would also examine other animals as well as insects.

In 1831, Charles Darwin began his journey on the HMS Beagle. His quest lasted five years. In that time, he had the opportunity to explore the Galapagos Islands as well as other islands off the coast of South America. He observed species he had never seen before, such as the sea iguana. He claimed that the species on these islands had either evolved or adapted. He indicated the sea iguana had evolved because it had developed web-feet but I disagree with his assumption because this is adaptability. When the Iguana swims, it stretches its clawed feet, which stretches the skin membrane and gives it the appearance of web feet. There also breeds of dogs and even cats that have web feet, which does not indicate evolution. This is where he came up with his theories such as survival of the fittest, adaptability and his theory of evolution. He theorized that all life forms on Earth were related and had evolved from simple life forms within the ocean. After his voyage Darwin returned to England where he held back on publishing his research. For years, he battled with his ideas of Christianity and evolution. He was afraid of how the Catholic Church would review his findings.

At the age of thirty, Darwin married his first cousin, Emma Darwin. Years later, Darwin's first daughter died from tuberculosis. Losing his daughter had a profound effect on Darwin, which caused him to turn against Christian beliefs. I can only imagine the pain of losing a child, for I am a father myself and the fact he lost two more children later on must have devastated him. At the age of fifty, Darwin published his book "The Origin of Species." The theory of evolution did not take well with the public but throughout the decades it gained acceptance little by little. The Naturalist movement quickly accepted Darwin's theory as fact. This organization believes that there are superior races, or stronger family lineage than others.

Archeologists and scientists traveled the world trying to find the missing link in hope of proving Darwin's theory. Many specimens were found throughout the world such as the Neanderthal man. This excited the scientific community. In Sussex, England what was thought to be one of the greatest discoveries proving Darwin's Theory of Evolution, was Java Man in 1891 discovered by Eugene Dubois. During the early 1900's there were those who pushed the idea of teaching Darwin's Theory of Evolution as a fundamental teaching without evidence. During this time the naturalist movement and Darwin theorists would display without a conscience African people to prove how evolution had occurred. Ota Benga a member from the Pygmy tribe from Congo was displayed at the Bronx Zoo where his quarters were built at the monkey exhibit. The fact that Ota Benga as well as other Africans were used in zoos and other exhibits to prove how other races evolved was cruel and unjustified. Ota Benga had desires to go back to Congo, but unfortunately never had the opportunity and committed suicide. The thought that the naturalist and evolutionist movement would use a human being, while holding them captive to exhibit them in a zoo was a criminal act. This idea that one race evolved from another has created the ideology of a master race. Even a whole nation the Socialist Nazi Germany believed in this idea. The Germans believed they were the superior race because of this sickening ideology.

In 1912, scientists claimed another discovery of the missing link, the Piltdown Man. Many newspapers' headlines claimed excitingly that Darwin's Theory was finally proven. Darwin theorist started showing exhibits throughout the Western World, with fossil records proving men had evolved from apes. In 1922 there was another discovery made by Harold Cook, the Nebraska Man. What was found was a simple tooth that would fortify the belief of evolution for most of the scientific community. During the 1920's, many argued that they did not want their children to be taught the theory of evolution for it was against everything they believed in. In 1925, Mr. Butler passed a law in the state of Tennessee that prohibited the teachings of Darwin's Theory and many other states followed. John T. Scopes, a teacher, decided to challenge the Butler Law after he was encouraged by the American Civil Liberties Union. Mr. Scopes was later charged for teaching Darwin's Theory of Evolution. The trial found him guilty.

The Scopes Trial which is better known as the Monkey Trial was turned over for a technicality. John T. Scopes later announced he would continue to teach Darwin's Theory of Evolution. The guilty verdict being overturned, had added fuel to Darwin theorists to continue to spread their ideology. Their literature was spread throughout the world and even in museums where fossil records were displayed. Scientists that disputed Darwin's theory did not have the tools or the equipment to examine the fossil evidence that was found during this time. Eventually scientists would have the opportunity and technology to examine the evidence. A great proportion of the evidence that was presented by Darwin theorists was not allowed to be viewed by all of the scientific community. For 30 years, Eugene Dubois, did not allow scholars to view any fossils found of the Java Man. This was the evidence that evolutionist had claimed the Neanderthal and humans had evolved from. After severe scrutiny and pressure, Eugene Dubois finally allowed the scientific community to review the fossil records of Java man. This went down as the biggest hoax of the 20th century. What were found were a mixture of human and ape bones and teeth of different ages. After the truth came out the reputation of the scientific community was ridiculed for only a short time.

The Piltdown man, where British scientists had proclaimed that no other species were closer to humans was found to be a ridiculous hoax. The lower jaw bone teeth were filed down with a metal instrument to closer resemble human teeth. What shocked the scientists was that

Piltdown man had a human skull and orangutan jaw bone. The cranium was also stained to make it appear the same age as the orangutan jaw bone. We have to ask ourselves why scientists had to go to such lengths to deceive the people. In the end, the hoax was proved wrong by the authorities of the British Natural History Museum. The evolutionary chart illustrating how humankind had evolved from apes is ridiculous. This tool is used as a required teaching in our public schools and universities across our nation without a shred of evidence. The evolutionary chart supposedly indicates the process how humans evolved from apes, and yet, there is no genetic evidence to support this fabrication.

The Nebraska Man had been discovered from a single tooth that was found by a man named Harold Cook. For the life in me, I cannot understand how scientists could construct a whole life form from a single tooth as they did with the Nebraska man. Darwin Theorists drew pictures of this primate with fur that covered its body and somehow knew this creature was bipedal. How could they conclude so much evidence from a single tooth? Tell me where did they get the idea this creature had fur without DNA? Were Darwin theorists so desperate they had to fabricate their evidence to prove their theory of evolution? When Biochemist Duane Gish had the opportunity to examine the Nebraska man's tooth he quickly realized it had belonged to an extinct pig. He then claimed, "I believe this is a case in which a scientist made a man out of a pig, and the pig made a monkey out of the scientist." Mr. Gish has disputed and disproven Darwin's theory but few have listened. Those who opposed Darwin's theory had proven that all these primates that were considered evidence were hoaxes, but it had come far too late and the damage was done. Even today there are many scientists who have disputed or disproved Darwin's Theory in Evolution.

At one time, it was thought that the Neanderthal was part of the human Evolutionary Tree, until DNA experts proved this wrong. They have also analyzed the fossil records and they have never found a specimen with half ape and half human DNA. It was always 100% ape or

100% human. Even Lucy, according to evolutionary theorists, which they consider to be the beginning of human evolution, was found to be one hundred percent ape. We must ask ourselves if evolution is true then why are there no transitional life forms throughout all species? This within itself proves that the theory of evolution carries no credibility. Yet, the Department of Education has paid very little attention to this matter and still continues to teach this lesson to our children as a required teaching.

Archeologists are on the hunt for the missing link and every primate skeleton they find they are attempting to place them into the Evolutionary Tree to prove their theory. For scientist to indicate they are looking for the missing link would indicate they have a partial chain for the human lineage, but according to their own evolutionary chart there is no DNA evidence to connect our lineage with apes. The ignorance of the ideology of evolution is baffling, they are not looking for the missing link. These scientists who support these theories still need a whole chain to prove their theory on human evolution. According to Darwin, evolution is in constant motion so that should indicate that the fossil records should have adequate proof of complex life forms evolving from simple life forms, but there is not. There are also those who believe in spontaneous evolution. If this is true, why has there not been any adequate proof throughout the thousands of years of our recorded history? Those who believe in spontaneous evolution must realize, in order for that to happen, a male and female would have to have spontaneously change at the same time and then reproduce. If there was only one that had spontaneously evolved it would have gone extinct or the genetic code would have been so diluted into the population, it would have simply disappeared.

Scientists have even stated that they believe that life originated from meteors or comets. If they believe the earth was seeded in such a manner, then I want to see the rock that we all hatched from. You must realize that they are trillions upon trillions a different life forms on this earth, which include humans, birds, mammals, fish, reptilian, plants, and insects. This does not include the world of microscopic lifeforms such as microscopic bugs, viruses, etc. Evolutionist Dr. Knoll believes for life to have started it must have resulted from replicating molecules. This would have been impossible because before you had molecules replicating themselves, we must first have a combination of diverse chemicals for an extended time in a pacific order for evolution to have ever occurred. Darwin believed life originated from a homogeneous globule of protoplasm cell, how was it possible that this homogeneous globule of protoplasm cell formed and where did it form in the vastness of our oceans. Scientists claim that life began from a simple cell, but today scientists have disproven there is no such thing as a simple cell. In past years, many scientists have come forth with amazement of the complexity of single cell organisms. Even Dr. Knoll has admitted that he cannot prove how life began. I would like for you to use common sense, if life truly began from a simple cell organism and these cells came together to create complex organisms then why has this process stopped. Where did the molecules get the intelligent to communicate with each other to build a more complex life forms and how did they possibly write their own genetic code. Dr. Ranganathan indicated "the probability of life originating from accident is comparable to the unabridged dictionary resulting from an explosion in a printing shop." This idea of evolution must be ripped from the pages of science so these ridiculous theories may no longer deceive the people. The term evolution does not even stand up to the definition of science because it has never been observed.

The belief in simple cell organisms had somehow joined together to create multi-cell organisms is wrong. For this to have happened by accident would be impossible. There are so many building blocks to create life forms, such as amino acids and proteins it would be impossible to accidentally find a genetic sequence that would work. Plus, what organism having the correct code already would spend the time or have the intelligence to do this? We must realize in recorded human history we have never witnessed the creation of a new life form. If it was possible for spontaneous evolution to create a new life form, then how would we account for the simulation of the new genetic code. For this to have occurred by random or spontaneous evolution would mean we do not have a creator and our genetic sequence randomly changes with no guidance or direction at all. For life to have been created without an intelligent designer is impossible. The genetic code has to be assembled correctly in order for life to ever exist. Another fact that you cannot ignore is a tremendous amount of information in life's genetic code. These genetic codes are the blueprints on how to construct every life form on earth. There are trillions upon trillions of genetic strains that store information on the complexity of building lifeforms. This miracle of life was no miracle for if you simply look into this highway of information stored in our DNA you would come to the same conclusion it is impossible for this to have randomly happened. Theoretical physicist Paul Davis an Oxford professor said that the appearance of design is overwhelming. Even mathematicians such as Dr. Granville Sewell have proclaimed this is unviable. Dr. Granville has disputed and disproved Darwin's theory in his book "In the Beginning and Other Essays on Intelligent Design."

Many scientists also claim it is impossible for birds to have ever evolved from reptiles. First of all, for this to be believed is preposterous since it breaks the Law of Thermodynamics. It breaks the Law because it is impossible to go from cold blooded too warm blooded. The cardio system of a cold-blooded animal is entirely different than a warm-blooded animal. Another fact to consider is that even the respiratory system of a reptile is entirely different than that of a bird's. Paleontologist Barbara Stahl also indicates how reptiles have no genetic structure on how to construct a feather. She also states there is no evidence in fossil records of a transitional period of evolution. This also disproves that mammals have evolved from reptiles. The claim that reptiles have shed their scales and suddenly grew fur or went from cold blooded too warm blooded is misleading. The theory that animals suddenly went from egg laying to live birth leaves me with many questions. I find it unfeasible for this to have gradually happened. Do they truly expect us to believe that the eggshell got thinner and thinner till it was no more? This is the reason they had to conclude spontaneous evolution which still makes this theory ludicrous. For this miracle to have occurred the mother would have had to develop milk glands at the same time or her young would have starved. Evolutionists also expect people to believe that lifeforms crawled out of the ocean and suddenly had lungs and legs. For the multitudes of lifeforms that are on dry land today, you could easily conclude if this theory has any validity that an unbelievable number of lifeforms must have crawled out of the ocean. If this statement is true, then why are we not seeing the same massive migration crawling out of our oceans. I am not referring to the sea turtles or the variety of crabs that crawl out of our oceans onto the beach. I am referring to new species that suddenly has the ability to walk out of the oceans and suddenly breathe air. Another fact that I believe is impossible is how the plants from the sea suddenly realized they could grow on dry land as well. Seriously, how could this process begin; do they want you to believe the seed simply washed up on the beach and suddenly this seed evolved to grow on dryland. For plants to have evolved in this manner would have been met with great difficulties, such as how would the plant learn to breathe in air. The plant would have change its physical structure entirely because it would no longer have the buoyancy of water to aid in holding up the plant. The plant would not be accustomed to contend with climate changes.

It has been proven that there have been many cases of falsified evolutionary evidence that have corrupted our society through our education and faith. This has resulted in many Christians losing or questioning their faith by accepting evolution as God's divine plan. There has been an attack on Christian beliefs; these theories have not been proven, hold no merit and evidence has been falsified. An article was published by Der Spiegel, a German magazine that proved Professor Reiner Von Zieten was committing fraud. The professor was found falsifying the age of fossils found throughout Europe in order to meet the evolutionary timetable. Even though his works were disproven they are still being taught in universities around the world. The British Daily has reported that the professor has presented man made manufactured fossils and still these allegations are ignored. We must realize how detrimental these falsified convoluted theories have become. The seed of doubt is the seed of corruption and if you look around the world today you will see how corrupt we have become. I like to bring forth words of wisdom from Hebrews **"without faith it is impossible to please him; for he that comes to God must believe that he is…"**

Stanley Miller, a strong evolutionist, tried to prove Darwin's theory through The Origin of Life Experiment. His report in 1953, claimed he proved spontaneous evolution, but when other scientists tried to repeat his experiment, they failed repeatedly. This concluded that Stanley Miller's experiment was flawed and still this theory remains unproven. Stanley Miller later stated:

"The problem of the origin of life, has turned out to be much more difficult than I, and other people, envisioned."

- Stanley Miller Biochemist

"Scientists have never been able to prove that non-living chemicals could assemble themselves into a simple cell organism", **according to Klaus Dose "At present all discussions on principle theories and experiments in the field either end in stalemate or in a confession of ignorance."**

-Klaus Dose Biochemist

Archeologists also acknowledge they are looking for the first primate to have used tools. I think if they get their heads out of the dirt they may suddenly realize that there are many primates that use tools today. We have primates today that use rocks to crack open nuts and twigs to draw ants out of mounds. There are also groups of primates that build their own bedding and uses sticks and stones to defend their territory. There are even other groups of animals that show intelligent such as certain bird species that build complex structures for nesting and insect species such as wasp, honeybees, and even ants who also build complex homes. Tell me how did honeybees are even wasp learn to build the complexity of their homes and how did they learn to work together is a better question? The answer is not evolution; it was God's divine plan.

I find Darwin's Theory of Evolution impractical and the fact that the Department of Education continues to teach our children this theory is ridiculous. Many scientists have submitted their evidence that Darwin's Theory is incorrect and full of flaws. At the same time parents argue they don't want their children to be taught this theory. Does the Department of Education actually think they know more than scientists or the parents? Or are they just too hard headed to look at the facts? The Department of Education claim that there is evidence to support the teaching of evolution through the fossil record, and molecular biology. We must demand that the Department of Education submit their evidence because Dr. Derek Anger stated "it must be significant that nearly all the evolutionary stories I learned as a student have been debunked". There has been ancient artwork found around the world depicting early humanities encounter with dinosaurs. There has also been carvings or engravings illustrating dinosaurs found throughout our world. Stones were found with ancient artwork in Peru showing human interaction with dinosaurs. There is even a depiction of a warrior trying to defend himself against a T- Rex. There is even an ancient drawing of a dinosaur here in the United States in our Grand Canyon's. If this is even possible then how did ancient humankind learn to draw or carve with such precision the correct anatomical structure of a dinosaur. To prove evolution wrong we must first separate adaptability and survival of the fittest from this equation. Evolutionists like to keep these three together to prove their theory. First of all, we all have the natural defense for adaptability. They have even found fossilized footsteps in Dinosaur Park, Texas that depicts a human's footprint with a dinosaur's print overlapping the humans. These fossilized footprints called the Alvis Delk Print must have been applied within the same timeframe for this to have ever happened. This indicates that man once walked with dinosaurs and the evolutionary time line is wrong. Once again this is proof that our educational system is corrupted and will not allow our children to view any evidence that supports creation.

"If it could be demonstrated that any complex organ existed which could not possibly have been formed by numerous, successive, slight modifications, my theory would absolutely break down".

-Charles Darwin

"Behold now behemoth, which I made with thee, he eateth grass as an ox, lo now, his strength is in his loins, and his force is in the navel of his belly. He moveth his tail like a cedar, the sinews of his stones are wrapped together. His bones are as strong pieces of brass; his bones are like bars of iron."

Job 40:15-24King James

There are many tools used by the scientific community to measure time such as carbon dating, which I find full of flaws. The problem with carbon dating is the fact this practice is based on assumption. Carbon dating is the measurement of time, by the measure of C 14 in fossils. When cosmic rays enter the upper atmosphere, they convert into isotopes which later converts to carbon-14. This is supposed to give an accurate reading of time by the measurement of C 14 in fossils that are tested. Scientists claim's carbon dating become more difficult to detect C 14 in fossils that are older than 50,000 years, because through the year's carbon is released into the atmosphere from the fossil. This theory was disproven when scientists discovered C 14 in fossils that died before the Ice Age. According to scientists' own timetable the last ice age supposedly occurred 250,000 years ago. They have also found carbon 14 in coal, which is impossible because geologists claim it takes 250 million years for coal to form. Another fact our scientists failed to consider is how much our atmosphere has change throughout the thousands of years our planet has existed. For example, they could've been far less carbon-14 in our atmosphere 5,000 years ago then there is today. To measure time, you must first have a beginning and there is not a shred of evidence to establish an accurate recording of the time of creation of the universe or the beginning of life. Carbon dating has many more inaccuracies in dating fossils then scientists will omit and they have been known to manipulate their findings. It has been well documented that scientists have thrown out carbon dating results because it does not meet their evolutionary timetable. Scientists will test a fossilized plant or animal multiple times to get the carbon dating results they're looking for. They ignore or destroy any carbon dating results that contradicts the evolutionary time line. They claim results of carbon dating that defies evolution are contaminated, maybe the contamination is in their own personal ideology.

I would like for you to look into the matter where scientist's carbon dating a living snail to be 27,000 years old. There is only one timekeeper in our universe, the arrogance of humankind may pretend they know the age of the universe!!! Astronomers use tools such as the color spectrum to measure the light emitted from a distant galaxy to gather their distance from our own galaxy to measure time. The way astronomer's gauges the distance of a neighboring universe is through its light spectrum. The further away a galaxy from our own will supposedly determine what light colors will show up in the spectrum. They believe accurately recording the expansion of the universe would give them the accurate age of the universe. This is nothing more than speculation because it would indicate that the speed of the universe is constant, which contradict astronomers new finding that indicated the universe is speeding up. There have been several astronomers who has come forth with evidence that disproves the color spectrum as a tool for measuring time or distance, but their colleagues continue to ignore the evidence.

There is not a shred of evidence that backs up these theories on how you can measure time by measuring light through a spectrum or even carbon dating. In the early 1800s, scientists were primitive in their manner of research and had very little understanding of our planet. The early geologists had very little knowledge on the age of the earth or even how the Earth was formed. During this time, many geologists were traveling the world on expeditions that were sponsored or paid for by the elite. I find it very suspicious how the geologist's community had report findings that would contradict the Biblical age of the Earth, especially those geologists who had close ties with those who supported the naturalist movement. These geologists reported that the Earth was billions of years old, I believe their results were corrupted by the elite as well as the illuminati. There were many reports from geologists as well as astronomers on the age of the Earth that contradicted each other, there claims range from 3 billion years old to 20 billion years old. Today scientists are more uniform with their timetable, where most geologists claim the earth is 4.6 billion years old and astronomers proclaim the Earth is 4.5 billion years old. This gave adequate time for evolutionists to prove their theory through all stages of evolution, but what if the earth is not billions of years old! If man can produce enough energy and pressure to rapidly transform a lump of coal into a diamond, then I believe the Earth can replicate the same results. I would like to know how geologists derive the age of the earth in the early 1800s without advanced scientific equipment or computers that we have today. I understand the geologists were studying the rock formations and layers in the earth's crust, but how could this possibly indicate that the Earth was billions of years old. Geologists had divided the earth crust into layers to adequately age the fossil and to ensure the fossil records fits the timetable of evolution. These layers were divided into three groups the Cenozoic Era, Mesozoic Era, and the Paleozoic Era, which would age the earth according to evolutionary ideology. In the past decade's scientists has uncovered fossils in the wrong era. They've even found petrified trees that cross different boundaries or different eras. They have found fossils from the Paleozoic Era in the Cenozoic Era, which indicates a large flaw in the evolutionary timetable for the placement of different species. We must come to the realization that the earth age is numbered in the thousands of years not billions. A scientist from California State University, Mark Armitage discovered a Triceratops horn in Montana that still contained soft tissue inside the horn. This proves the Triceratops did not die 65 million years ago and when Mark Armitage attempted to report his findings he was met with resistance. Mark Armitage research was kept silence by the science community, and his archaeological funds were cut off. He was also terminated from his job because he was blurring the lines between creationists and evolutionists. How many scientists or professors have lost their jobs because they have become a creationist? A better question is, have we become a society that punishes people for their Christian beliefs?

The fact that the Department of Education has made it mandatory to teach our children the Big Bang Theory is ludicrous. First of all, where did matter or the energy come from that caused this "explosion?" Do you really believe all the matter in the universe came from one explosion? Even calculating the amount of matter that revolves around our sun, such as planets, moons and asteroids is mind blowing. Once again there is evidence to dispute this theory. If the universe originated from a massive explosion then the movement of the galaxies should be slowing down, but in fact they are speeding up. Astronomers and scientists were left confused when research indicated the expansion of universe was speeding up. This could disprove the Big Bang Theory. They then indicated the universe was speeding up due to dark matter which is unproven and has never been seen. Scientists also claim that the sound of cosmic radiation that we hear in space is the aftermath of the Big Bang. Could this sound not be from other stars that exploded from our past or even energy released from other stars?

Everyone understands that if there is an explosion, it blows matter from the inside out, leaving an empty space in the middle. Yet, there is no vast empty space in the center of our universe. If these scientists do not understand how nature or the universe works, then why can they not simply say they do not have an answer? We must realize theories are not facts but they continue to teach them as such. I compare these scientists to the ones long ago that thought the world was flat. Decades ago in America many Christian leaders and churches stood and fought to disprove Darwin's Theory but they would be overwhelmed with falsified evidence. I feel that many Christian leaders in the past have been overwhelmed with dishonorable research as they began to accept Darwinism as God's divine plan. Mankind did not evolve; we were created in God's image as it says in Genesis:

"So God created man in his own image, in the image of God he created him; male and female he created them."

"But at the beginning of creation God, made them male and female. For this reason, a man will leave his father and mother and be united to his wife, and the two will become one flesh. So, they are no longer two, but one flesh. Therefore, what God has joined together, let no one separate."

Mark 10:6

We must wake up as a society for I fear there is an attempt to remove God from the equation. If they continue to teach generation after generation that we evolved or that there would be no universe without the Big Bang, then where would that leave the belief in God? We must force the evolutionary theory to stand on its own without the theories of adaptability and survival of the fittest theory because these are God given abilities to help us survive on this planet. If this theory of evolution cannot stand alone then it has no validity.

We must demand more professionalism and honesty from the archaeologists' community. For well over a century they have found giant human skeletons through Asia, into Europe, and North America. They have placed these bones and other fossil records behind closed doors out of view of the public eye. Tell me why are these bones not on exhibit? Are they afraid this will confirm the story of David and Goliath? Scientists and archeologists are blatantly dismissing fossil evidence in fear it would prove the book of Genesis. Throughout my life I have met many atheists and many of them have indicated that it takes too much faith to believe in God. Sadly, what they do not realize if they have exchanged their faith in God for faith in science. If evolution is accepted without evidence, then it must be accepted on faith. The belief in evolution is the belief of many theories wrapped up as one, which neither has evidence to support its validity. Evolution is broken down into different stages such as Cosmic or Chemical Evolution to help prove their validity. I believe this is weekend their theory because if you destroy one part of the categorized stages of evolution then the whole theory of evolution will collapse.

For evolution to have occurred, we must first have had Cosmic Evolution. This is the Big Bang theory which contains no factual evidence. The belief that all matter in the universe came together in one single spec that was smaller than an atom is ridiculous. You must realize how ridiculous is theory is! I would like to know where the matter came from and where did the energy come from the causes this matter to spend. Scientists will attempt to explain this through mathematical equations and scientific terminology, but I will continue to remind you is still a theory. If all matter in the universe was compressed into a single spec, then I would like to know where the gravity came from that held this matter together? The next was Chemical Evolution which believes many elements especially the higher elements derived from hydrogen. This too is without merit because the only way hydrogen could have produced higher elements is through fusion but it is impossible to have fusion past the element of iron. The third is Stellar Evolution, which once again holds no merit. Stellar evolution is a study of stars and the planets and how they formed galaxies. This breaks another law in thermodynamics, you cannot have order out of chaos. The Big Bang was supposedly the largest explosion ever according to astronomers and if that fact is certain then how can we possibly have order from such a massive explosion. The universe has repeatedly disproven this theory because if all the matter in the universe derived from a single spec that was spinning then all matter would be traveling at the same speed and direction as the spin when the Big Bang occurred. Within our universe there are galaxies traveling at different speeds and directions which is impossible because if matter was blown outward in all the galaxies should be traveling in the same outward direction through the universe. Astronomers once believed the universe was slowing down but through advanced technology they realized the universe was speeding up. The fourth is Organic Evolution which is the creation of life. This theory has been repeatedly disproven over and over again. The fifth is Micro Evolution which believes that one life form can suddenly change into a nether life form. If this process is even possible then why in all recorded history no one has ever witnessed a species shape shifting into another species. To believe in these ridiculous theories that have never been proven take a tremendous amount of faith.

The definition of science is the intellectual and practical activity encompassing the systematic study of the structure and behavior of the physical and natural world through observation and experiment. Evolution has never been witnessed, neither has there been any samples of evolution to observe or experiment on that can prove this theory, we must reinsert the teachings of creation because evolution is the great lie that planted the seed of doubt. I ask everyone to do their own research into this matter so you too may see the great lie. To witness the lie, is to witness a great injustice, for we have allowed them to lie to our children.

I even question the teachings of sex education to our young children. Is this not perversion of our children's mind? When my grandmother was in school she said sex education was unheard of as well as teen pregnancies. Through my mother's generation sex education was taught to high school students in some states, and teen pregnancies rarely occurred. Through my generation sex education was taught in the seventh grade and through the late seventies and eighties, teen pregnancies exploded. Today they teach sex education to fifth graders and some school districts they even teach this course to kids at a younger age. My youngest daughter was taught at the age of four the correct terminology to the male and female anatomy through the head start program. Even though the Department of Education has significantly dropped the number of teen pregnancies, it is once again increased in this generation. They have also failed to admit their mistakes. What they did instead was introduce birth control and condoms to our young to correct their mistakes and yet America is still ranked very high in the world in teen pregnancies. You cannot teach a subject and not create an interest.

When I was taught sex education in the seventh grade, I have to admit it sparked a huge interest in sex. This not only sparked an interest in me but in the other kids around me as well. Today I hear stories about young boys daring one another to acquire condoms from their school or health department. Then they dare one another to find someone to use the condoms with. Is this not encouraging sexual behavior? Whatever happened to the lessons of abstinence? By giving condoms and birth control is it not giving our young permission to pursue sexual activity? Does this not put pressure on those who want refrain from having sex? What I find even more shocking is how our government is trying to impose unisex restrooms in our schools. Can you imagine the stress this will create for a 13-year-old girl to have to share a restroom with an 18-year-old boy? America our government has become immoral and the policies are unjustifiable.

Today it is estimated that one third of teenage girls will be pregnant before the age of twenty, while teen abortions continue to increase. Today abortions are being used as a form of birth control without realizing the physical and emotional damage that is caused. We must understand the severity of what is being taught to our children; over four thousand children will contract some form of Sexual Transmitted Disease every year. We must realize we are losing our moral standards and our Christian faith. I believe sex education is important but this lesson should be taught at home and not taught in school until the eighth grade in order to prepare children for high school. The primary goal for this course is to encourage children to discuss this matter with their parents and to encourage abstinence. If the teaching of sex education was not bad enough for our young minds, I find it disturbing that many schools are now teaching a course on gun control by installing fear in our children's minds. Are these not topics best taught at home? I find that public school policies are in disarray. Yet, they choose to take more responsibility from family while tightening their grip on our children. They continue to make more behavior policies changes, and increasing academic requirements with little regard to our children. Today we have become a society where many of our children are more apt to listen to school officials than they are their own parents? It is urgent for us to once again become part of our children's life and education. We need to go back to teaching our children responsibility, unconditional love, forgiveness, and self- control. These values seem to be consistently absent in our society. I believe this has led our society into a violent decline. In my opinion because of this many of our children and even adults have grown too comfortable and accustomed to violence. This is the reason we must reinstate prayer as well as the commandments into our school.

There is a tremendous amount of stress that has been placed on our children today. This is due to the demand of raising academic standards that Pres. Obama has placed on our school system. He has threatened to cut Federal funding for schools that fail to raise their standards. I have no doubt we will realize the damage Obama is creating. Half the states have already dropped the increased educational standards for a reasonable increase in their academic levels. I understand Pres. Obama is reaching for a better ranking amongst the nations in education. Today we are ranked 18th in education around the world and to tell you the truth, I would settle for that.

Many nations force their children to go to school for six days a week and they attend more hours per day then we do here in America. I am not willing to subject our children to spend most of their young life in school. What happened to family time? Another fact we must realize is how many children around the world never attend school. Their nations around the world of required parents to pay for their children's education and the poor children who do not have the funds will not attend school. Another policy many nations have accepted is only giving free education for the student to make good grades. Many of these children will only attend school up to the sixth grade because they will be discarded for poor grades or lack of effort. Unless their parents can pay for their child's education they will never get back in school. How they achieve educational ranking is through test scores, but how can these test scores be fair if all children are not being tested. This is the reason I do not care about the educational ranking; what does concern me is how many children around the world are denied an education. Many of these children have no alternative, but to either enroll in a trade school or be enslaved to some factory sweatshop for the rest of their lives.

Continuously pound knowledge into a child's mind and eventually something gives such as creativity or social skills. Do we truly want to make our children so unhappy? I want to see the smiles return to those children. I want to see them talk amongst themselves and see them laugh during lunch. America, we do not have to subject our children to such cruel, intensive learning. Pres. Obama blamed the educational system for our nation's lack of competitiveness in the world market. We must realize the problem does not lie within the education of our children, the true problem lies in our government's policies, such as the selling of technology, and jobs moving to other countries. America, we must realize we have wealth in resources. We are the most creative nation and we can control our own destiny.

America, we must wake up, our children are not receiving the appropriated funds that were set for them. We spend well over $10,000 per student, per year! I plead for you to do your own research then ask the questions that must be asked. Where are all these proceeds going? Do not accept their complex answers nor shall you allow them to confuse you with a massive amount of paperwork. This is an attempt that our Federal Government uses to confuse the people that look into this matter. We must demand transparency and common sense answers. We must not be detoured and we must take back control of this out-of-control spending.

It is urgent for us to wake up to ensure these proceeds are properly spent. You would think with all the proceeds going to public schools their education standards would be much higher. We are talking about thousands of dollars per child in public education spending. But according to the ACT and SAT, public school children score much lower than private or home school children. It is not just the inappropriate spending of our revenue that concerns me, it is how their agenda has destroyed faith, tarnish the moral fabric of our society, and the preparation for enslavement at our own financial costs.

The fact our government has allowed special interest groups to corrupt our educational system is disturbing. They have infected our children's education with their own ideology to serve their own agenda. They have destroyed what it is to be an American through corrupting our children's education. They have distorted the truth about our nation's history and villainize our forefathers. In many school districts, they have imposed socialist teaching and liberal points of view. America everything that made our country great is being destroyed by those with dark agendas. These evil deeds were orchestrated by those in the elite circles and other secret organizations such as the illuminati. They sought out a path of war against our Christian faith and has vanquished the Bible from our schools. They have ripped the Lord's Prayer from the pages of our schools and demolished God's commandments. We once taught our children to have faith in God and how they have a divine purpose. Today our educational system teaches her children how they are animals and how they derived from animals. Once they had weakened our children's faith through courses of evolution they then turn their assault on patriotism by removing the Pledge of Allegiance. They have imposed their educational standards with very little remorse for those who will be left behind. The fact they are making it mandatory for college courses to be taught in high school is ridiculous. What if someone only has the desire to be a farmer or some other trade that does not require such courses? The educational system pushes our children to choose a career path early in high school, which is ridiculous because many these children have no idea what career path they want to choose as their profession. Even college students take undecided courses in college until they can decide what career path they want to choose. We must give our children adequate time for them to choose their own career path.

Many school districts have electives such as Culinary Arts, Cosmetology, Mechanics, and other fields to help our children choose a career path. I strongly agree with such electives for it creates an opportunity for our young. We must broaden our children's opportunities for their futures. We must never forget the arts such as music or even woodshop. I do believe electronics is our future and I think it should be mandatory for all public schools to offer this course as an elective. Many school districts have also dropped the course in botany, which I strongly disagree with. We must broaden our children's minds through education, but a balance must remain for courses in theatrical arts or as a participant on a team. We must give our children the freedom to grow and with such electives would give our children the opportunity to broaden their own opportunities. It should not be mandatory for our children to take college courses in high school they should always remain as electives. We must realize that science and math is our future. I think it would be brilliant to have our high school students taking a course in everyday science. This would be a course not only based on a textbook but where you will be graded upon participation and imagination. The students would be taught on how to put solar panels together and other friendly environmental projects such as greenhouses. It will be a class where children are being taught to work together to work on new projects. They will study materials from great scientists such as Albert Einstein or Tesla.

To truly educate our children is it not to inspire their minds? We must allow our children the opportunity to think freely. The complexity of some subjects that are being taught in our schools creates tremendous amount of stress for our kids. A science class where kids can interact and create experimental projects will not only be fun but exhilarating. It is important for our students to take courses in English,

Math, as well as Biology. But to give our children the opportunity to think freely, to create a teamwork environment on science projects could not only prepare them for their future, it would also spark such an interest. I do agree that there should be discipline in our education but we must show that learning can be fun too. We must also show understanding and respect for our students. They are crushing our children's spirit with their behavior policies today. We must realize the more behavioral policies we burden our children with the more likely they are to rebel. I call out for the people to hear the children's cry for help. We must break the very back of this dark force that has imposed themselves upon our children. Through their twisted tongue we must unravel the truth of their agenda. We must make them know that no longer will we accept their policies. Today I call upon the parents, grandparents, aunts and uncles to not only know what is being taught to our children but to become part of their learning process. America, our children are our future. They must learn compassion and understanding. We must allow their spirits to be free. We cannot allow their minds to be filled with the ideology of evil and corrupt people. We must ensure that our children are proud to be American. We must allow their creativity to come out. We must reinstate the Lord's Prayer, so our children may walk in faith. We must reinstate God's commandments, so our children may once again live by divine morals. Let us cry out in one voice, "They are our children!"

Big Business (Killing Dreams)

Retail giants are destroying American dreams. This is a consequential fact. The very breed of retail giants and their desire to become a monopoly is a constant. It is not just enough for them to come to your town and take a large percentage of sales from small businesses, for their greed for money runs deep. Most retail giants have spies that work for them. They send these spies to small businesses to browse through stores comparing prices and merchandise. Then weeks later they have the same merchandise but with lower prices. They only carry one agenda and that is absolute power. It wasn't that long ago when I heard about a giant retail store planning to install their own banking systems in their stores. This giant retail company already cornered a huge market and if they are successful in establishing a banking system in their stores across our nation it would give them a tremendous amount of power. These giant retail stores have the benefits of receiving tax breaks or not even paying taxes at all while the government continues to lean on small businesses for more taxes. They also have the ability to lobby Washington for favors where as small businesses do not have the same opportunity.

The balance of trade is so unequal for small businesses. We must realize that most small businesses carry more goods that are made in America than big retail stores who buy their goods from overseas. In fact, some of these retail giants stock their shelves with up to 80% with foreign made goods. They buy their products from sweatshops where child labor is not only legal but is thriving. I cannot imagine the horrors of young children having to sew shoes or clothes when they should be in school or out playing. These premier elite bands of retail giants will pretend they are not aware of this practice yet they send representatives to inspect these factories and check the quality of goods they are producing on a regular basis. Many of these factories force their employees to work grueling twelve hour shifts in horrible conditions. For example, in the summer, some of these factories reach temperatures of well over a hundred degrees and in the winter their employees freeze. They also receive poor pay and have no employee rights, benefits or legal representation. The only standards these companies live by are wealth for they have neither compassion nor conscience.

With so many small businesses closing, where is this leaving U. S. factories? U.S. factories are struggling to compete with the abundance of foreign merchandise that is being brought in by these giant retail stores. There was once a balance in our country with the import tax which created a level playing field. But since Bill Clinton signed in the NAFTA Treaty American factories have lost their competitive edge. I will never forget how Bill Clinton paraded Al Gore around the country to promote this treaty, nor will I forget Al Gore's speech when he referred to one of his friends in the textile industry commenting that he would profit immensely from such a treaty. How were American factories capable of competing with foreign factories that pay very little wages and their employees have little or no rights and benefits? To make the same product the cost of materials is very similar between the two countries but when you have a factory that pays employees a little over a dollar an hour while we pay $14 to $20 an hour makes a huge difference. The quality of goods in America has significantly diminished.

When Bill Clinton was campaigning for President he often spoke of the benefits of the NAFTA Treaty. Ross Perot then warned our nation that if Clinton signed such a bill into action we would hear a giant sucking sound coming from south of our border. Ross Perot was dead on but not only did we hear a giant sucking sound to the south we also heard it from the east and north as well. What Ross Perot was referring to was if we were to sign in the NAFTA Treaty, in order to get free trade, American corporations would not only be unable to compete but they would have to go overseas as well. The crippling effect this has had on our country is as known as trickle economics.

For example, if you were to go to a small town and remove their economic cornerstone such as a small factory it would eventually create devastating effects. It would not only put the factory workers out of work but you would begin to see the breakdown of the entire economy of the whole town. It would start small with the mom and pop diners or the deli that served the factory workers and then the gas stations and other small businesses would close their doors. Larger businesses would then struggle and they would have to make cutbacks such as layoffs. Within a few years of the factory leaving the unemployment rate could easily triple and out of desperation people would flee the town.

The NAFTA Treaty did not just have an effect on small towns for even large towns would feel the impact of this treaty. Detroit and Buffalo were once proud industrial cities. These cities had many industries but they were more proud of their auto industries than anything. Today these cities have the highest poverty rate in the nation along with the highest unemployment rate which has left many on welfare. In fact, over 20% of Detroit's population has fled the city since the NAFTA Treaty was signed. The treaty was nothing more than the destruction of America's internal wealth while leaving millions of Americans in poverty.

What I find alarming is that we did not hear the outcry from big businesses before Bill Clinton signed the NAFTA Treaty. They had to have known this treaty would have a tremendous impact on America's economic structure. Today these large enterprises have not only transferred the production of goods overseas they are also selling the great machines that once put Americans to work to foreign nations. America, we must wake up, this is the process of worldwide redistribution for the New World order.

As I indicated before these corporations have no conscience. They care very little for their employees or their families. America, how many families have lost their homes because of Bill Clinton's ignorance or the endless greed of corporations? It is estimated that since the NAFTA Treaty we have lost well over 700,000 jobs to overseas competition and the trade deficit according to the Bureau of Labor Statistics has increased nearly 300%. America our nation will not last unless we become an industrial might once again.

I even find Clinton guilty of selling U.S. technology invented by NASA to countries such as China. This led to a crippling attack on technological goods created here in our own country. How can America compete when the people have been silenced and the line between big business and big government has become convoluted? I find that both of these entities are guilty of abusing their powers and lining their own pockets with wealth that belongs to Americans!

America, we have gone from an industrial society to one in ruin and poverty. We have gone from a technologically advanced society to a dependent society. Today we depend more on our government and giant retail stores than ever before. Due to the massive loss of industrial jobs we have seen a massive increase of Americans taking lower paid jobs which has left more Americans on welfare. What I find astonishing is the fact that some of the giant retail stores are not only encouraging they are assisting their low wage employees to apply for welfare benefits. Our government is expanding as it creates more governmental jobs in its thirst for power. Today, our government accounts for well over 40% of the jobs in America and I call out for you to take notice, for once it reaches 50%; we are no longer a free society. You must envision what it would be like to live in a nation where you have no voice, no representation, no privacy, and 50% of the workforce answers to the government. This grab for power has done nothing more than increase our deficit as our government borrows more money from foreign banks in order to sustain their massive growth.

We have gone from a people who had once governed themselves to a people who are governed by their leaders. The majority of most Americans once knew what prosperity was. Today too many Americans live in poverty and with our unemployment skyrocketing and more Americans than ever working for minimum wage our debt continues to climb. Our wallets are empty and so many babies are going to sleep hungry. It seems the task before us is impossible and in desperation I see so many people who have given up.

To know these facts and see what is going on with my eyes enrages me. America, you cannot run from this problem. The entity of big business and government will devour us for everything we are worth. America, we have allowed the elite to control our destiny, while stealing our wealth for far too long. It is ridiculous and criminal that these elites are worth trillions while so many people in the world are suffering. We must stand together and cry out "no more!" We must control our own destiny. Let us push back the powers of greed and let them know we will not be silently pushed away. They shall no longer keep us in the dark. Let us rip these chains of bondage which the government attempts to control us with. Let us step out of the misery that has muted us for so long and let them hear our voice. We must tell them their power is to come from the people. Let us support our small businesses because they are the backbone of our communities and we must make amendments to the NAFTA treaty so we may have a balance trade. Let us only buy American goods because that will multiply our work force. Let us boycott the American companies that have moved overseas. If you cannot find the will to stand up for these actions than I ask you to dig deep into your heart and pray to God for the strength to change yourself. This will surely show the government they are not in control. We must conquer this evil. We must do this for the love for our children and their children's' children!

Utilizing of Our Resources

Throughout the ages, civilizations have collapsed due to a lack of resources. In fact, mankind has gone to war when kingdoms invaded other kingdoms for precious metals or rich farmland. The victors would normally enslave the defeated and were forced to mine for precious metals or to farm the land. Through the years the faces of these wars have changed as kingdoms fell and nations rose from their ashes. This battle for resources has raged for ages but it exploded during World War II. This war would change the way wars were fought for no longer were precious metals or the conquest of land the only thing desired, for a new wealth had emerged, black gold. America was a proud and independent nation during the early 1900's because we had immense resources such as coal, steel, and even natural gases. We were also extremely rich in oil and were the largest exporters around the world. Through the years of over drilling we would deplete this valuable resource and become dependent on other nations for oil.

In the early 1950's, America was no longer self-dependent when it came to oil. We would import this precious resource from other nations. This would eventually lead to a secret war fought in the Middle East where nations would secretly plot against one another. America once proud, would begin to sacrifice their morals while making deals with rogue nations and dictators. For oil, we would attempt to bribe them by pouring foreign aid while promising security. This would eventually lead to wars fought in this region where American soldiers would give their lives. We have poured trillions of dollars into these nations for their oil, foreign aid and to secure their borders, and for what? To find our nation in the verge of bankruptcy?

America, we must remove our military from the Middle East and become less dependent on their oil. We must no longer promise security for these rogue nations nor shall we shower them with foreign aid or give them funds to build schools or mosques. With the problems of the Middle East and the fact that two super powers on the same continent are both grabbing for power and resources is bad enough. The United States has spent trillions of dollars trying to bring peace to this region. I find this to be wasteful spending. Most people like to indicate we are only there for the oil while our government indicates we are there fighting for Democracy and freedom. We must wake up because you cannot fight for democracy unless all the Middle Eastern people truly desire it. Due to these conflicts, America has lost its prestige for our enemies have labeled us as oppressors, occupiers and even colonialist. If the people of these nations truly desire democracy, then let them fight for it the same way we did for we can no longer afford to police the world.

For all the trillions of dollars we have spent we have gained very little. Much worse, how many soldiers have given their lives for people who do not care? Do you honestly think the people in the Middle East would ever pay their respect and honor our men and women who gave their lives for them? We give these countries foreign aid and we even help them build schools and for what? So, they can teach Jihad to their kids. This is an Islamic campaign to commit war against the non-believers. In other words, they plan to bathe the world in the blood of the infidels. This means they believe they must kill all people that are not Islam. How can we commit ourselves to such a cause? Not only are we paying for their oil with our dollars but we have paid with blood as well. We act as if though we have no choices but to buy oil from these countries when in fact we have other alternatives. Everyday America is growing weaker and weaker while our enemies wait for us to break.

We should have started looking for other solutions when we had the oil crises in the seventies. We can learn a lot from Brazil who is totally independent from foreign fuels today. During the oil crises, Brazilian scientists began researching for an alternative fuel. They created an ethanol made from sugarcane which releases zero harmful emissions into the atmosphere. In fact, Brazil leads the world in clean fuel research and exporting clean fuel as well. What I find shocking is how many Americans know very little about Brazil or their clean energy policy. If the EPA was truly concerned about clean air or creating a cleaner environment, then why have they not pushed or demanded America to follow suit with the same research? This is just another indication that shows how the EPA is corrupt but then again it is part of our federal government. The reason the EPA has not pushed for America to pursue a similar clean energy fuel is because they understood how much tax revenue our federal government receives from oil companies.

We must not dwell on the past; we must find solutions for us today and our children. We still have massive amounts of oil in this country while some claim it's a ten-year supply and others indicate it's a twenty-year supply. We have oil in the Gulf of Mexico, off the West Coast in the Pacific and a massive amount in Alaska. We must start drilling today. We must not allow foreign oil companies on our soil. This is our oil and we must ensure our profits stay in this country where it belongs. By using American oil companies, it would not only help us become more independent but would enable us to create thousands of jobs. This would increase the demand for special skills for tasks like exploration and finding better ways to retrieve oil from deep pockets within the earth. Before we can drill we need construction workers to build the platforms. This would aid in creating more jobs. We must refine the oil in this country as well. The trucking industry will also see a boom from transporting the oil and materials to drill the oil.

We must realize that we are running out of time so we have to act now. This would create more stability for America, and also create immense revenue for the government. We must not allow our government to wastefully spend the money they receive from the oil revenue. It is imperative that we invest this revenue towards research and alternative fuel sources. This is not the first time America has faced a deadline in 1963 John F. Kennedy challenged America and NASA to put a man on the moon. Six years later in 1969 John F. Kennedy's vision came true. He believed that if Americans could put their mind to this task, they could achieve it. We have to ask ourselves, where has our belief gone? It is imperative that we once again believe in this country. We must believe that we can find alternative fuel resources within ten years. The task will be difficult but we shall not allow it to detour us. We must fight for the future of America. We must fight for the future of our children.

We must not allow the EPA to restrain us any longer. They must understand we are doing research for a better America that cleaner and more independent. In the present time, we need oil to keep America moving. In the future, we need to make sure we use these funds wisely. The decision of President Obama to spend taxpayers' dollars on his project cash for clunkers, I feel was a waste. It would have been much wiser to have given Americans a five-thousand-dollar rebate on an alternative fuel car, such as hydrogen or electric. Before we ever see service stations pop up for hydrogen or electric cars, a demand must be created.

By giving people the alternative to buy these vehicles would have created this demand. The rebate should have also included corporations with company vehicles to purchase electric or hydrogen cars. Within ten years, if American auto industries could change from gasoline engines to clean energy engines then other auto industries around the world would follow suit. This would dramatically decrease the world's dependency on oil. By decreasing the worlds dependency on oil would help resolve many of the conflicts in the Middle East. I truly believe hydrogen is the fuel of the future because it produces zero harmful emissions. This fuel could also be used in planes and boats and many other forms of transportation.

Investing in cleaner energy would assure America's independence for many generations. America is still one of the richest nations in resources around the world. We have an abundant amount of natural resources and natural gases. We are the Saudi Arabia of coal and we are rich in raw and precious metals. We still lead the world in the production of food and our exports help feed over half the countries around the world. I truly believe if America commits itself we can create a clean and reliable energy that would change the world. We need to increase our research into Tesla's ideas for free energy around the world. Nikola Tesla's theories on obtaining free energy from within the earth or atmosphere has been proven repeatedly. Tesla worked as a scientist under Thomas Edison for years and made many improvements to Edison's DC Generator. Eventually Tesla had branched out on his own and created many inventions that were utilized by a Westinghouse Electric Company, as well as Edison Electric Company. For years Tesla, had envisioned free energy for the world through alternating current that was proving to be more reliable and safer. His discovery of a rotating magnetic field has led to many patents that are still being used today. Nikola Tesla's creation of the AC Generator was more cost-efficient and had proven that you could transport alternating current on vast distances more reliable than direct current. Thomas Edison became threatened by Nikola Tesla's new inventions and his theory for free power. Edison began a smear campaign against Tesla in trying to convince the public how dangerous alternating current was. Edison resulted to stunts like electrocuting animals such as elephants to install fear in the public. J.P. Morgan strongly supported Thomas Edison which led to the end of the war of the currents. The reason why Nikola Tesla's ideas for free energy was not accepted by the financial community was because it was not profitable. J.P. Morgan refuses support Nikola Tesla's ideas and even stated that it would be a bad investment because it would be impossible to measure the amount of energy used. America, I urge you to wake up, free energy would have changed our world dramatically. I truly believe our world would be safer and many the wars of our past would've never occurred. Free energy would've taken a huge financial burden off the shoulders for people around the world and could have brought many out of poverty. Even the original idea for the Internet was to be free for the people around the world, which could have been a great step for humankind. America this goes to show the power of the elite and how far they will go to control every aspect of your life. Nikola Tesla's idea for free energy was a clean energy but unfortunately we would adopt the pollutant energy of the elite. Let us shatter this control of the grand puppet master and bring the elite to their knees for the crimes against humanity. The only way for humankind to be free is by removing their controls and influence they have over us all. I am calling for legal actions in the World Court' against the elite for their control and manipulation of governments around the world.

Another valuable resource is America's infrastructure. The quality of a nation's infrastructure such as interstates, bridges, and ports determine how fast products can move across the nation or export goods to other nations. We were once great builders of our nation but if you look around our infrastructure are in disarray. By committing to prepare our infrastructure would not only help America deliver goods faster but it would multiply our work force dramatically. There is a quote that I live by, "Failure to prepare, is preparing to fail." - John Wooden. Today we spent a tremendous amount of revenue on welfare and other corrupt programs that is leading to America's downfall. We can better utilize this money by creating jobs in repairing America's infrastructure, which would help stimulate our economy.

Our natural gas is another resource that we have an abundance of. By utilizing our technology along with our mechanical advancements, we can find a better, safer and quicker ways to ship this natural resource around the world. We could also alleviate Europe's dependency on Russia's natural gases. America today we have the technology to ship large quantities of natural gas safely across oceans. This project could create thousands of new jobs in our nation, which would strengthen our economy. We must create a fleet of ships that can transport natural gas to nations around the world, especially nations in Europe who are dependent on Russia. There is no denying the truth about Russia attempt to insert their control and influence over the world. America if we can produce an efficient way of transporting affordable natural gas, it would alleviate the control or influence Russia has over the world today. I do not believe oil, coal, or natural gas is the future energy for the world but we must utilize this resource until we can produce a safe and clean energy for the whole world. America, this is our opportunity! One of the greatest opportunities we have ever had but it is extremely important we act now. With the advanced technology, we have today we can drastically change our nation. We must not allow distractions to sway us. Many people in America are without jobs and so many do not have the means to feed their families. The situation can no longer be ignored.

The Eastern section of the United States has an abundance amount of water but the Midwest to West Coast is certainly derived of this life-giving substance. What if I told you of a project that could create thousands of jobs and bring fresh water all the way to the West Coast? It would generate enough farmland to harvest a tremendous amount of produce. Livestock ranches could settle in places where few animals could live before. Most people do not realize that meat and produce are bid on by supermarkets and retail stores. The less meat and produce that are available will increase the demand, which would increase the prices of goods that are essential in our everyday lives. This project of true water management would create such a vast amount of meat and produce that the price in our market would dramatically drop. America, we spent trillions in research for fossil fuels and the cost was astronomical in building the large pipelines for oil in Alaska as well as other places in the world. We seem to ignore our most valuable resource of water, without this precious resource there is no life.

There are many states in our nation running out of fresh water such as California, Oregon, Utah, and even states on the East Coast such as South Carolina or Georgia is being depleted of this valuable resource. It has also been reported by Water Management Authorities that the High Plains Aquifer is being depleted, which would have a severe impact on several Midwestern states. America, we have neglected our responsibility in assuring freshwater is preserved for the future generations. It is time for true water management that produces clean and affordable water for everybody. I truly believe that we can transform our nation by creating manmade lakes and large reservoirs in places that very rarely see rain. With true water management, we could replenish water levels in the natural aquifers across the southwestern states and would also greatly benefit states that suffer from droughts. We could then stock the lakes with fish and develop bird sanctuaries. This would result to an explosion of production of new homes and new communities. Towns would form overnight and anywhere you have lakes tourist locations spring up. This could create an abundance of jobs and revenue for our nation. Can you imagine having your home near one these prestigious lakes where the sky is always blue?

Presently today the Western section of the United States is extremely dry. You will find most of the land parched and barren. There are very few animals that can survive this climate. There is a way to fix this problem; there are fifty billion gallons of fresh water that spill from the Mississippi River into the Gulf of Mexico every day. With our ingenuity, we could develop a water pipe line to pull this life-giving source to the West Coast. We must not allow anyone to tell us it cannot be done. We could dig tunnels through mountains to lay track for the railroad. We have completed a massive pipeline once before. We built the Alaskan pipeline to deliver oil to seaports. If we could harvest at least fifty percent of the fresh water that spills into the Gulf of Mexico from the Mississippi River before it drains it would create twenty-five billion gallons of fresh water daily for the South West. I believe the water pipe lines should be developed in three phases. This could also be a great opportunity to help correct a great injustice. Many of the Native American reservations were pushed onto dry and arid land. By bringing the American Indians this valuable resource of water would create the opportunity to grow crops or the ability to own livestock ranches.

The first phase should be developed for the South West. We could take this water pipe line all the way from the mouth of Mississippi and Louisiana to Arizona. This pipe line could bring fresh water to drought stricken states like Texas, New Mexico, Arizona and even Southern California. This pipe line could also pull water from other rivers along its path such as the Red River and many other rivers. This will also take the burden off to Colorado River that has been the primary water source for several southwestern cities. The second phase could bring water from the Midwest to Nevada. This pipe line would start from the Ohio River in Ohio and only pull a minimum amount of water from each river along its path to Nevada. These are rivers like the Wabash, Illinois, Missouri and many others. This pipe line would help bring an abundance amount of fresh water to the Mid-Western states but it could also aid in flood control. The third phase of this plan would be to utilize other rivers that drain into the Gulf of Mexico, Atlantic or Pacific Oceans. For example, we could install a pipe line from the Alabama River to the Chattahoochee River to bring fresh water to drought stricken Florida and Georgia. Even the Columbia River that drains into the Pacific could be utilized for Southern California or Oregon. I also believe that we should develop reservoirs along many of the mighty rivers across America to utilize this precious resource.

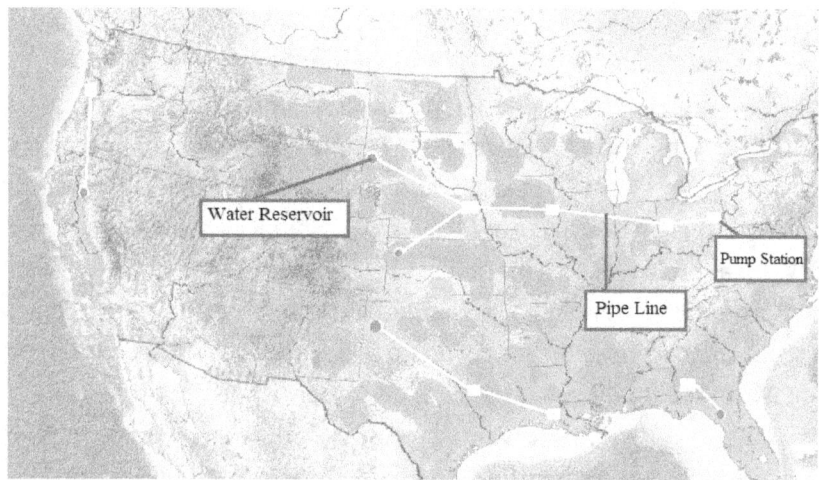

This project can be done. If the Romans could move water over two thousand years ago then why can we not do the same? America has already accomplished this great task of redirecting water from the Colorado River to Nevada which helped create Las Vegas. America, we have the technology and we need to dream big in order achieve big results! We must once again dream big not just for yourselves but for the future of our country.

I know many states like to argue over water rights but this project can help every American. This could create so many jobs. It would put engineers to work and we must build the pipes here in America to multiply our own workforce. You would then have to have pipe installers as well. A large work force would be required to tunnel through mountains and clear pathways for the water pipelines. There would also be a huge boom in the trucking industry because they would transport the pipe as well as other materials. This would also create an abundance of electricity through the Hoover Dam because it has only been running at sixty percent due to massive water shortages. If we put forth the effort and truly believe we could turn the barren lands in the southwestern states into an oasis. We could give thousands the opportunity to farm which would help feed millions. I can hear the argument now. How can we pay for such a task? The answer to this problem is simple. Since the federal government has put us in the situation we are in today we must come together and demand the Federal Government to sell the 650 million acres they own. We have to realize that the government owns one third of the real a state in our country. States receiving the fresh water should also share the expense of this project. We must realize we are all going to benefit from this project through the creation of jobs and lowering of food costs in our markets.

This would also help prevent massive flooding throughout the Midwestern States such as Illinois, Louisiana, Arkansas, Western Kentucky and many other states by simply moving water. When these rivers start to rise we simply pump more water out west and that is flood control. Imagine the billions we would save from flooding. Let's engineer America. Right now, we have more capability than we have ever before. We must realize we are facing a crisis but we can divert this and make a brighter future for our children.

Another problem we are facing in America is the massive strain we are putting on corn crops. Because of the fact we use 10% ethanol as an additive to gasoline it has caused the price of cereal and corn made products to increase. There is a solution: we could start growing Agave in the southwestern states. This is a plant that grows mostly in Mexico and needs very little water. They harvest this plant to make Tequila. This is a great opportunity to take the strain off our corn crops by farming

Agave in massive quantity. If you can make alcohol from this plant, then you can make a fuel additive. If it burns it is a fuel. This plant grows very slowly and needs very little care but we can utilize our vast lands to farm this crop. Agave is just an idea but we must do research for other alternative crops for a reliable clean fuel source.

Another crop we can start growing is cannabis. When growing cannabis, the farmer attempts to only grow the male plant which yields no fruit containing the THC molecule. The cannabis plant can be very important to our society. Just one of its attributes is that it is four times stronger than cotton. This could help us create a line of products that would be more durable and desirable due to its high quality. Canvas can also be used for the production of paper goods which would result in less deforestation.

We have to understand how our world works before we can reap the rewards, not the path of control the world governments seek out. We have to become creative. Our population is not getting any smaller. It is going to continually increase and with all this vast land out west we must utilize it. We have cities on the East Coast that are so overpopulated that this not only creates a burden on their school systems but they have major traffic congestion. In California, they are facing the same problem with overpopulation in cities like Los Angeles. By opening up the Midwest and giving people the chance for a new life, we will help these cities with the problem of overpopulation. We must also realize that the Mid Western states have an abundant amount of sunlight and wind which could be utilized for solar panel installations and wind turbine farms.

Investing in solar research to obtain optimal solar energy from the sun would also create many jobs. In the future, more corporations can break off the power grid by creating their own solar power. By giving the corporations the opportunity to break free from the energy grid would save billions of dollars. As companies save money we will all benefit because it would lower the prices of their goods.

There are other things we can do as individuals. We can start installing solar panels around our homes. There are solar panels today that are easily installed to your power grid. With the rising cost of utilities, can we afford not to do this? You may not be able to get off the power grid entirely but any amount of electricity created can lower your power bill significantly which would offset the cost of the installation of the solar panels. If you create an excess amount of electricity by federal law the power company has to purchase the extra power. That gives you the opportunity to take money from the big corporations and put it in your pocket where it belongs. Some who live in rural areas and can install a well on their property. Today the technology of pump houses that draw water from the well as well as coming equipped with water filtration systems can turn hard water into soft water. Imagine breaking totally free from the power grid as well as the water company. Now that is total independence.

We can also become totally self-sufficient by installing a greenhouse in our backyard. Today greenhouses come with solar panels and heaters. They even have the ability to collect and save rain water through a gutter system that stores it in containers. They are sufficient. Today you can grow food such as strawberries, cantaloupes, watermelons, bell peppers and tomatoes year around. It is not necessary to grow multitudes of one particular plant because with a greenhouse you can harvest year around. Which gives you the opportunity to grow a variety of different plants that produces different fruits or vegetables. Most families would consider two or three tomato plants sufficient. We also need to learn how to can our bountiful harvests. This is almost a forgotten trade. This can save you up to fifty percent on your grocery bills. For example, my family usually spends around $250 a week so that would be a savings of $125 each week. This would result to a savings for my family of $6500 a year. We can also grow root vegetables in our own backyard such as potatoes, sweet potatoes and carrots. We could even grow garlic and our own herbs and it just doesn't stop there the sky is the limit! We can also plant pecan trees or even grow our own apples and plums. Let's face it; you will never taste fresher fruits or vegetables than fresh picked. We can bring back the barter system, which is an old system of trade. Imagine yourself growing pecans and your neighbor growing apples. You would trade a portion of your harvest for theirs. The benefits of harvesting your own food is not just the money you save but the satisfaction of growing your own food and the quality time you could spend with your family. You could teach your children a valuable lesson. You can also turn a profit. I have a good friend and every year he plants a small pumpkin patch. He normally only grows maybe fifty or sixty large pumpkins. He sells his pumpkins for twenty dollars and profit's a little over a thousand dollars. I know this is not much but he uses his profit for the holidays shopping. We all know the chaos and stress that come with the expenses for the holidays. The fact that he plans ahead and supplements his income is inspiring.

While I owned my own business and even after it closed I met many successful people in my life. I admire their independence and ingenuity. I admire their courage to go out on a limb and take a chance. Every time I have the chance to go to my local flea market I meet someone new that strives for independence. I have been doing business with an elderly couple for several years. They grow their own peppers which they use to make their own hot sauce and to be honest it is some of the best I have tasted. They have one particular sauce that I love; it is their homemade chili lime hot sauce. There is also a mother and daughter that I met at the flea market who they make their own custom jewelry. They have a small drill where they drill holes through small precious stones so they can string them onto necklaces. I think their business will continue to do extremely well. Due to the high price of gold and other precious metals more people are going to start wearing custom jewelry. I have also met people who can their homemade jelly and make homemade candles. There are so many opportunities to start your own business or supplement your income. All you have to do is research and find something that appeals to you. There is this particular story that has inspired me greatly. I unfortunately did not know this woman personally but I have heard her success story. Before her husband died they had owned a very large farm and due to his death and high medical bills she had no choice but to allow the banks to repossess her farm. She was left with her house and a little over an acre of land. She had farmed all her life and she was now uncertain about her future. What I admired about this lady is she did not give up. She dug in and started doing research for the most profitable crops she could grow. She decided to grow this flower called lilac and as she grew this flower she started producing her own soaps, lotions and oils. Today she is a successful small business owner.

We have to realize that there is a potential for another crisis such as a recession or depression. I have heard so many horror stories about the last depression in this country that I don't want to go into them because I believe we have a chance to change our course. There are three plans I wrote in this chapter that I believe can change the course of this country for many years to come. Developing a water pipeline would not only bring water to the Midwest but it would help create opportunities for millions of Americans. The revenue created by selling the 650 million acres of government owned land would help pay for the project. The second phase is drilling our own oil would not only give us our independence back, it would also create the revenue needed for research in alternative fuels. We could also increase the revenue needed for research on an alternative fuel source by selling natural gas to overseas nations. The third phase is repairing our infrastructure, which would create jobs and give our nation longevity. If people were to do their own part and become more independent, it would give us an opportunity to save money and even help supplement our income.

We must realize how dependent we have become on our government as well as retail stores. If a depression was to hit and our government ceases to be able to give aid to those who are in need or the retail stores were to go out of business how would anyone survive? We must realize our dependency on big government and business is not a safe route for us to take. Our very lives may depend on us being independent. We need to learn to work together and even support one another. If we see our local farmer selling vegetables or fruits, we need to support them. We even need to support our local businesses. When I speak of local businesses I'm not talking about a fast food or restaurant chains I'm talking about the mom and pop restaurants and locally owned gas stations. I'm also talking about your specialty shops. These are people who work with leather or do wood carvings. It is very rare today to see furniture made out of real wood.

I remember when I was a kid my grandmother would take me to a furniture store. The man who owned the business actually made his own furniture from solid wood. I will never forget how beautiful his furniture was. It was not just the design but the fact he would spend so much time carving the pieces by hand. There are very few people in this country with such talent. We must support these dying trades and bring them back. This is not the same furniture you buy from stores that is made from particle board and held together by glue. This was made out of real wood and would last a lifetime. My grandmother today has a lot of the same furniture she bought from his store so many years ago. She even told me she was going to put her furniture in her will. You have to ask yourself how long particle board held together by glue will last. How many bedroom suits could you purchase in a twenty-year period and where does it end up? All this furniture made from particle board ends up in landfills. Are the glue and all the chemicals safe for our environment?

I ask you whose pockets do you want to line with money? Your local business or the farmer down the street or would you rather line the pockets of big businesses? America it's time to wake up! Stand shoulder to shoulder and get to work! The path for true freedom is independence and the path for enslavement is dependence.

"All labor that uplifts humanity has dignity and importance and should be undertaken with painstaking excellence."

-Martin Luther King, Jr.

Our Precious Earth

The shocking truth I have come to realize is very few people care about our planet. Every day poisons are being pumped into our atmosphere, and trash is being dumped into our oceans. Around the world, unregulated chemical and coal burning plants are spreading their toxins like a dark cloak over the Earth. Can we not see how we are suffocating all life forms on Earth? The answer is no; we have become a selfish self-centered society. Today most people are so wrapped up in their personal lives, they no longer see the beauty of being human. Today most governments around the world have become more global but humankind as individuals have become more isolated. Most of us see the world through cell phones or laptops and never look up to see the beauty of the world. Mankind has neglected a great responsibility in being a good steward to the earth. Today people care little about their environment in fact very few will ever explore the forest, hike into the mountains, or sail the oceans.

Today, we as a society, we have lost touch with our planet, and we neglect or bring suffering to all the species on earth. "GOD" gave all mankind the responsibility of being good stewards! You cannot neglect your responsibility by passing it off in to your government's hands, in which have failed miserably at every task or responsibility given to them. Today we must wake up, for not only have we lost control to what happens to our planet we were also losing control of ourselves. Today our government leads us like sheep while keeping us blinded by their evil intent. Our government continuously reassures the people that they are doing all they can to clean up our world and have even created programs like the EPA. The reality is our government have created a tremendous wealth in fossil fuel regulations and fuel tax. This has placed a tremendous burden on every American's budget. Do you honestly think these giant corporate fossil fuel companies are going to be responsible with this tremendous burden of lessening fees, over regulation and high taxes? The answer is no!!!! This burden has been placed on our shoulders from the increased in costs for utilities and gas.

We are also burdened with the increasing costs in products that we purchase in our everyday lives, due to the increased cost for manufacturing or shipping goods. The truth is America we could have been off fossil fuels decades ago! The tremendous revenue our government receives from fossil fuel companies, along with the lobbying in Washington has stifled any opportunity for clean energy.

If we kill off the micro-organisms and plankton in the ocean, it would result to too many species going extinct. If several fish species in our oceans were to die off, this could decimate several different types of sea mammals, birds and even sea turtles. We must realize our actions on Earth create a chain of events that can be detrimental. It will not only affect the animals in the water but the animals on land as well. The removal of the forested lands and the destruction of rain forests is destroying many habitats. This is the reason why we constantly hear reports of animals; such as bears or deer moving into the neighborhoods that we live in. Is it not us who are invading their habitats? Even our lakes and rivers have been polluted with so much trash that many no longer meet requirements that allow us to safely swim in them. How many times have you been on the shores of a river or lake and seen trash wash up along the shoreline?

I find myself digging deep to find hope in order to find a solution to overcome these problems. I try to encourage people not to litter or throw trash out but many times I find my words to be spoken in vein. I have even heard people try to rationalize what little trash they throw out by saying it's so minimal it does not matter on a large scale. I use reason to explain to them there are over six billion people on this Earth; 330 million of which live in this country today and that if everyone felt the same way how terrible our daily lives would be. The sight would be horrendous. We must realize that every American produces several pounds of trash per day. It is unimaginable the tons of waste that accumulate in American landfills every day. We must find solutions to minimize our waste. We could also cut back on plastic bottles use by purchasing concentrated detergents and soaps.

I was extremely disappointed when I took my daughters on an exploration hike in the woods behind our house. I wanted to show my daughters how wild animals live so close to where we live. I had seen bears, dears, and even heard coyotes at night. What my daughters and I found in the woods was horrible. We found a car battery lying on its side next to a tree. This was not just simply thrown into the woods from someone's backyard; someone took the time to carry it down into the woods to discard it. I find such a careless act extremely idiotic. Did they not know of the harmful wastes that leak from this battery? The acid that can leak from this battery could have severe consequences on the plants and animals living near it. Do they not realize how long it will take for this battery to decompose? We also found a container where someone had changed their oil and discarded into the woods as well. This too is extremely hazardous to our environment. We also found empty plastic bottles, cans and discarded tires. This creates the perfect breeding ground for mosquitoes which could spread diseases through our communities.

Come on America we must wake up! Let's show the world we can clean up our act. We can become the model country for others to follow. The consequences are too severe. I have met people comment on this crisis, "It will not happen in my life time." Do they not think about their children or grandchildren that will be affected in the future? I have also heard people claim that the Earth will not be here in another hundred years. (Gee, thanks for dooming us.) No one can be certain about humanity's destiny. But one thing is for certain, if we do not change today we will be putting our future generations through hardships that are unimaginable.

There are hardships that are starting to fall upon us today. There are islands fading away because of the rise of oceans. In Indonesia, they are starting to find salt water has gotten into their freshwater and is destroying their rice crops. There are lakes and rivers in America that we cannot eat fish from while some are so polluted that we cannot even swim in. There are cities across our nation that have smog alerts. This has been a brutal assault in our Earth that has lasted well over a century. Can you imagine this continuing for another hundred years? Come on America stand to your feet and let us take control over Washington from this billionaire club called the elite. By ending lobbying in Washington will stop the influence and control the elite has over our politicians. We need to become a more modern open society that is willing to listen to new ideas for clean energy. For years, our government has secretly purchase patents for clean energy formulas or alternative fuel engines that could have drastically changed our whole world. We must realize as long as we allow the elite to control Washington we will never see change.

What stories will we have to tell our grandchildren? Would it be the stories of how Earth once was? Will they ask us questions like, "What is a blue sky, and what did it look like?" For me the horror that our future generations will only know of a gray sky is unimaginable. We will have to explain to them what it was like to see the sun rise or a starlit night. What it was like to walk into the grass with bare feet or dive into a lake. Will we have to describe the beauty as well as the animals that once lived? Are we prepared to deal with the shame when they ask us, "Why did you let this happen?"

All that I have written in this book will be for nothing if we do not come together and save our world. It is time for a call to action. There can be no more waiting. The destruction is happening right before our eyes. The consequences if we do not save our world are incomprehensible. We must realize that there are four things that are so important that we cannot exist without.

The first is our sun that warms our planet and gives nutrients or vitamin to almost all life forms on earth. If we continue to pollute the sky in the manner we have done in the past century, then within our next century the plants will not be able to photosynthesis, and we will starve. A more horrific scenario is if we do not stop the depletion of the Ozone Layer from pollutants the Earth will be left to bake and nothing will survive.

The second is the very air we breathe. Without clean, oxygen rich air, the mammals of the Earth, the birds in the sky, and even the insects will cease to exist. Today we have already seen the side effects of polluted air through acid rain, diseases and the increase of cancer in ourselves and other life forms. Do we not realize if we continue on this path the problems will intensify? The first step to cleaner air is to stop pumping pollutants into our atmosphere. This is no easy task, for our own government has kept us in the dark for far too long. America if Brazil can create a clean energy fuel for cars then we can do it to. We have allowed oil companies to dictate their policies in Washington and even commit us to war for their profits. The reality is the fact we must get off fossil fuels but reasonably we must commit ourselves to common sense. Most of a nation's electricity comes from burning coal, and America's transportation still depends on petroleum. You cannot force a nation to convert at will, we the people must all come together to transform our nation to clean energy. We must organize ourselves and establish a deadline that is fair and reasonable to establish a clean energy that we can depend on.

The third is the importance of clean fresh water. We must realize how many toxins we consume while drinking water. In most countries around the world it is not safe to drink their water. We must realize that water is the cradle of life. Even our oceans have become polluted, which causes toxins to build up in salt water and fresh water fish.

The fourth is the soil of the Earth. If the meats and vegetables we eat today are poisoned by toxins, then are we not poisoning ourselves? We must realize this is a priority but this problem cannot be fixed overnight. We must push our government to find alternative fuel resources but we too must do our part. There are many things we can do. I think one of the most important things is to get off the energy grid. Most of the energy plants burn coals and we do not want to talk about the horrors of nuclear power. One word: Fukushima.

There are those in our government and the elite society who want to push us towards nuclear power. I find many flaws with this but will only name one in this chapter. What are we going to do with all the spent radioactive nuclear reactor rods? This is unimaginable for me. There are many ways to create a cheaper and more affordable clean energy through solar, wind, and even wave power from our oceans. I do believe solar power will play a big part in our future, when it comes to clean and affordable energy. Solar energy is free and abundant, the only tremendous cost is a panel's, the insulation, and maintenance. I truly believe we should utilize solar panel farms in our southwestern states, where there is an abundant amount of sunlight year-round. Wind turbines can also produce a great amount of electricity, but we can also utilize them to help clean the air by installing a cellulose filtration system within the blade. By creating a turbine blade that would produce energy while cleaning the air would be brilliant. Wave power or tidal power can produce a clean energy from the power of ocean currents. We ourselves can produce a clean energy by installing solar panels in our roofs. I have read reports where you can get up to 95% of your energy from solar panels. This will lower your power bill significantly to offset the cost of the panels. If you continue to use the panels or even install extra panels you can then sell any extra power, you create back to the power company. Will that not be a massive change to receive a check instead of a bill?

I truly believe that there are some in our government that are fearful that people will start utilizing free power because this is a huge tax revenue for our government. Nikola Tesla attempted to give the world a great gift in free power. His idea of creating a clean energy that would have been free and abundant from our own Earth. Tesla understood that the earth had a strong energy field that could be utilized for free energy for everyone around the world. There were those in Tesla's time that use false propaganda to smear his name and ideas. Giving away a free product was unheard of them as it is today, but we must realize how different our world could have been if his idea for free clean energy was accomplished. His idea was never accepted by the elite for free energy because there was no profit.

When it comes to energy efficient vehicles we must not move quickly. We must create the revenue for more alternative fuel research for a vehicle that is environmental, safe, and affordable. We must drill our own oil to create the extra revenue to engineer a reliable clean energy vehicle. By drilling our own oil would create a tremendous amount of revenue for research and create multitudes of jobs in the oilfield as well as the auto research industry. We must push our auto companies and universities to produce an affordable clean energy vehicle through competition for grants. When we start to see the increase in sales of clean energy vehicles we will see service stations popping up offering alternative fuels or the ability to recharge your vehicle.

By better insulating our homes and using more energy efficient appliances will lower our power usage significantly. There are also small ways we can help save our world that will have a big impact. Today you will find recycling bins at shopping centers and even at public schools. We can even encourage our children to become more involved by taking recyclable materials such as plastic, aluminum and paper to their school to place into the proper bins. If we could only learn to recycle all the paper products we use in this country, it would preserve more forest lands. Motor and cooking oil can also be recycled. There are so many other great ideas out there.

America companies burns fossil fuels cleaner and more efficiently than any other country. Yet, our government and the EPA continuously create restrictions or even laws that make it difficult for these industries to create energy. We can no longer allow our government to perform this cloak and dagger war against fossil fuel companies and the fact that we've had two presidents commit themselves to this war is ridiculous. Let us not forget how Pres. Obama pledged to shut down all coal burning Plants. We must realize that America's foundation has been built on burning fossil fuels for well over a century. Because of this war on our own fossil fuel companies has allowed other rogue nations to become wealthy. America, we must use common sense for this has put a burden upon our collective shoulders. Today we are more dependent on other nations to develop our fuel at her own expense. It is urgent for America to become energy independent once again so we may have a brighter future. It is critical that we utilize the extra revenue for research and development. If we all do our research and work together we can save our world for many future generations to come. This is not just a fight to save our species; it is a fight to save all life forms on Earth. It is our responsibility to right the wrongs from our past. I would like to close this with an American Indian saying: *"We do not inherit the earth from our ancestors; we borrow it from our children."*

Martin Luther King, Jr.

I Have a Dream

"I have a dream that one day, down in Alabama, with its vicious racists, with its governor having his lips dripping with the words of "interposition" and "nullification" -- one day right there in Alabama little black boys and black girls will be able to join hands with little white boys and white girls as sisters and brothers."

Racism

Racism. I find myself searching for one powerful word to bring light into this darkness that seems to envelop us all. The word love seems to come to mind but I find so many have turned away from their own hearts. In the last days of Jesus, did he not leave us another commandment which was to love one another as he had loved us. I believe that love is the most powerful emotion that we have. Some believe love comes straight from the heart but I believe the cradle of love is deep within our soul. Throughout my life I have felt pain within my own heart from the loss of a loved one and I have even been heartbroken with pain felt deep within my soul. I have also felt true love and I have felt the most powerful and instantaneous love when I held my first-born child.

When my first baby girl was born, I already had so much love for her. But it was when I first saw her and held her in my arms; I felt a love that I had never felt before in my life an instantaneous love. My eyes filled with tears as I held this tender little girl in my arms. Do we not all feel this much love for our children no matter the "race?" What about a mother just returning from the doctor with her latest picture of an ultrasound of a little baby within her womb? She is so excited she wants to show the world her picture. It does not matter the "race," hair or eye color. Everyone wants to see the picture of the unborn child. Does it not bring a smile across their face as they see the picture of the child? Does it not lift our hearts when we see a newborn child no matter the color of the child's skin? Love is the most powerful word in our vocabulary; no matter what language it is spoken in. To me love is the meaning of everything. If you truly love someone you do not wish them harm.

What happened to the meaning of hope for humankind? I find this to be another powerful word. I wonder if we still carry hope in our hearts today. I hear people say the hope for unity of humankind is dead. Others proclaim the end of the world is upon us. As long as there is a will there is hope. As long as people stand shoulder to shoulder willing to fix our problems and find solutions there will be hope. What about the word faith? How many of us actually put our faith in God? Many people go through life with hate in their hearts and desiring vengeance on others while spreading their words of hate. Does it not say in the Bible that God loves all his children and we can bare our problems upon his shoulders? I find the meaning of God's word has such a purpose if we would only listen. Whatever happened to faith in humanity? Do we not believe in ourselves anymore? Do we not believe that we can overcome the tasks before us? I have heard great men shout out that we shall overcome. We must bring faith back into our lives and dig deep to find hope. We must open our hearts and allow love to shine.

Before we can conquer racism or make it a faded memory we must understand why there is so much hate and division in our country. I think the root of hatred runs so deep it affects our very way of life. It seems the people are so divided and have their own argument. It is hard to find where racism started in human history. I find that racism has been around for thousands of years. This hatred for people of different colors or nationalities could have rooted itself in slavery. Slavery has a deep dark past that goes back thousands of years. You can even find the stories in our Bible of Israel being conquered by Babylon and later Egypt. Many European nations were enslaved by the Romans as well as invaded by a Western African tribe called the Moors who also enslaved the people. Through time when a kingdom would invade another kingdom they would either enslave their people or worse, commit genocide. I find the evils of slavery and racism has rooted hate deep in human society around the world. During the 1940's the Germans slaughtered seven million Jews. Even in recent years there have been acts of genocide in Africa and even the Middle East. These horrors of human history are unthinkable and I find it shameful that America is also guilty of the horrors of slavery.

I remember as a young child seeing the movie "Roots." The horror and brutality I witnessed in this movie was horrifying. It gave me an understanding and opportunity to see what was right and what was wrong. It made me conscious that we are all human and we all have the right to be free. In my past I studied slavery and other acts of horrors throughout human history. I have read books on how African people were ripped from their families and homes while others were sold into slavery by other tribal leaders. You can read hundreds of books on slavery and watch countless documentaries but you will never understand slavery until you have lived the life of a slave.

Imagine someone coming into your life, stripping your freedom away and telling you that you cannot speak unless spoken to and then proceeds to put you in shackles. The abuse you will receive from your captors will be gruesome and the work will be endless. (Yet what you imagine is a hundred times worse in reality. The isolation and hopelessness that a slave must have felt seeing their family being sold for monetary gain is heartbreaking. In my heart, I believe this atrocity will never recur in America because I believe we are a better people.

"I have always thought that all men should be free; but if any should be slaves, it should first be those who desire it for themselves, and secondly those who desire it for others. Whenever I hear anyone arguing for slavery, I feel a strong impulse to see it tried on them personally."

-Abraham Lincoln

Today there are organizations and even historical groups that continue to pour salt into these wounds by honoring or flying the rebel flag or having reenactments of the Civil War. I firmly disagree with these actions for three reasons: First, it is a reminder of how so many people were oppressed by slavery. Would you personally want to see a reenactment of the horrors and brutality that slaves had to endure? Could you bear to see a reenactment of a family being ripped apart just so their loved ones could be sold? It is horrible that America had to go to such an extreme to stop such a wrong. Secondly we must remember that over 600,000 soldiers died in this war. It is tragic knowing Americans were killing Americans in such a manner and the third reason for me is that it represents a divided nation. I feel that this is something that we should not reenact especially when there is so much talk about dividing our nation today.

America is guilty of the horrific crimes of slavery and racism, but we must shed the layers of hate and seek out forgiveness for one another. When I was a young boy I was taught by my grandmother that you could not get into heaven's gates with hate in your heart. For me this means that you cannot allow hate to reside in your heart. America, we must put ourselves on the pathway to find forgiveness because for far too long this bitter arguing has poisoned our society. The great divide is spurring civil unrest that is leading to governmental corruption that will eventually lead to the collapse of our nation. It is urgent for us to become the beacon of hope for not only for ourselves but the world as well. These horrors of slavery are still alive and you will find that human trafficking is still a big business today. Across the world people are still being sold into slavery and even across America's border there are those who are sold into sex slavery. I encourage my readers to watch the movie I am Slave. You will see these horrible deeds are not just from humanity's past but are still alive today. America let us shed our differences and hate for one another and lets us come together as brothers and sisters. Together let us light this beacon of hope and let the light guide us. For the path to equality will be rough and less traveled.

Today we are facing too many problems to allow racism to be an issue. Racism divides us all even those who are not affected by this disease. There are so many hate groups in this country that spread their venom and who wish to deceive us. We must come together as a people and realize that there is no difference between us. Are we so shallow we cannot see through the skin color of others? Are we so heartless that we cannot see the pain in a child's heart? Imagine a world without racism. I believe in my heart that it is possible but so many times I have met opposition. I have been told that we are all racist and when I try to dispute this they try to convince me I'm lying or denying my own feelings. Why have so many taken to the idea we are all racist? Have so many given up?

Today I look unto the playground and see kids of all colors playing together. I know we are not born racist. To understand the direction, we must go we must understand the true meaning of the word racism. To me the meaning is not just in the dictionary, but it has a personal meaning for so many. The rift it causes and carnage that it leaves in its wake only leads to heartache. It is to judge someone by the color of their skin and to deny them equal opportunity or justice based in this judgment. I wish this horrific word could be stricken from our vocabulary. Due to this terrible word, untold millions have died. Is this the mentality we are leaving for all our children?

What is the meaning of race? We are often asked through the government as well as other programs what our racial identity is. For me this is a way of dividing the people. Why do so many desire to know our racial identification? Is it so important for government and business to know the racial makeup of our community? What is the definition of humanity? To me humanity is color blind. Humanity is the opening of the heart and assisting those in need and not judging others by categorizing them into groups. It is the acceptance of all and being human. To me the word human means to be one. Are we not all human? We must not allow hate groups to spread their cloak of darkness on our fabric of life. How long are we going to allow this to continue? Nor shall we allow the government to divide the people any longer. This has weakened our nation so severely we cannot resolve other important issues.

I spent most of my life living in the city and this was a great experience to have the opportunity to see so many different cultures. It was a true melting pot. I was fascinated with the different cultures as well as the people I had the chance to meet. Growing up I became friends with a group of boys that always seemed to hang out together. The group of boys I grew up with was made up of different races and we seemed to be untouched by racism. I did encounter racism in the city though. I remember a boy that went to our school his skin was reddish brown and his hair was auburn. So many kids made fun of him by calling him red bone. At times this would anger me because I could see in his eyes it hurt him. There was another girl that kids made fun of as well. Her skin was white as snow and her hair was so blonde it was almost white. They called her Q-tip and you could tell it bothered her as well. Even in high school I remember a boy called piggy because he was overweight and his skin was a little pinkish. In my life, I have heard on many comments that someone was either too white or too black. Is this not racism? Where does it stop?

I wonder how many kids look in the mirror and wonder what is wrong with their skin color. Can you imagine the heartbreak they feel because they are not accepted? How many people rub oil on their skin and bake themselves in the sun to have color while others use bleaching creams to lighten their skin? We must see the physiological damage that people endure because people judge them by their skin color. Through the years I do believe racism has improved dramatically.

As I sit back in my chair and reflect I recall a sweet lady from my childhood who had marched with Dr. Martin Luther King Jr. during the Civil Rights Movement. I remember how much she praised him for how much he had accomplished through his short life. She told me how the black and whites came together and marched for equality for all. The one thing that seemed to bother her though was the fact that through the year's people of different races had not seemed to truly come together yet.

Today I look around and see that we are closer than ever before to crossing that threshold. I see the number of people of different races that have come out in support of the candidacy for Pres. Obama. I myself, do not support Pres. Barack Obama because I did not believe in his policies; this is my divine right. What I find disturbing is how many people claimed if someone opposed or did not support Obama he or she was a racist. During this time, even the Black Panthers began protesting or intimidating white voters. They chanted let's kill all the cracker babies. I remember not even a week later hearing on the news that gun sales were at an all-time high. You have to wonder if people so frightened that they felt the need to prepare to defend their homes.

I had an encounter with a man at a park once. We began to talk about politics. He asked me if I had seen on the news how the Black Panthers were intimidating white voters. I replied I had and he made the comment there was going to be a race war very soon. I told him that I believed this action would never occur in this nation as he attempted to confirm it would. As the debate continued I finally asked the man if this action was what he truly desired. With a firm voice I told him that this would be no war on some far-off battlefield. It would be a war in his neighborhood, on his street and even in his home. This would be no war between just men, for even women and children would be victims of this horrible conflict. I can tell I shook this man up as I looked into his eyes and walked away. I reconfirmed this horrible deed would never happen. I understood this man was shook up from what he saw in the media but even his comments or his belief that a race war would be the only way to resolve this matter was foolish. Come on America! This kind of mentality stains our very fabric. Comments like these will only deepen the rift between all races in America.

I believe America has crossed a huge hurdle by electing our first black Pres. Obama. It was not just one race that came and voted for Pres. Obama it was all races. People saw an opportunity for change in

America and this confirmed my beliefs that there are more people that are not racist than people who are. Years ago, I talked about writing a book on the issues of racism, but after reviewing these topics I became discouraged. There are so many hate groups on the internet today. I even found one on the internet that desires the North-Western section of the United States to succeed from the Union. They want to create an Aryan nation. This worries me so greatly because if we allow our nation to separate we may see the death of democracy. It seems like people are open to discussion while most have given up or pretend what they are seeing on the news is not happening. I know so many people in this country know what they are seeing before their eyes is wrong yet they still hold their tongues. Is it not right to correct this wrong for our children? If people don't listen, then how can they hear? If they block out what they see, then how can they understand? I even began to think my fight was hopeless. I started to instill hope in my girls. I would tell them there are no differences among all the races. I have taught them that everyone deserves to be treated equally in hope that one or all my girls can help change the world one day.

I remember when the Census Bureau report came to my house. I methodically filled out the whole report except for the racial makeup of my family. I felt that it was irrelevant and after teaching all my girls we were all human I was not going to contradict myself so I left that section blank. A few months later a Census Bureau agent came to my house and informed me that I did not completely fill out my form. I invited her to my home so we could discuss the matter inside. She sat down on the chair and pulled out the form and informed me I did not fill out the racial makeup of my family. I asked her what the relevance of that section was. We must have gone back and forth for a while with this debate because I could not get an adequate answer. She became frustrated and said she was just going to put me down as white. I then told her it was not completely true because I was also part American Indian. She then wanted to know the racial makeup of my wife. Once again, I did not think it was relevant but after seeing my wife she indicated she was going to put her down as Latino. I told her that was not entirely true as well. I told her that my wife's grandparents were from Europe. I am not entirely sure what she put down for my kids but I guess she put them down as white, Hispanic and American Indian. I do not understand why it is so important for the government to know the racial makeup of our family. What is the importance of knowing how many of each race live in this country? How can I teach my children about equality if our government divides us and categorizes us? Can I cry out in one loud voice, I do not want to be labeled! I know one thing for sure, I am tired of being contradicted.

My oldest daughter came home from high school one day. She informed me how upset she was when she tried to attend a Hispanic heritage party at her school and was denied entrance. The teacher had stopped her and said it was only for Hispanic people and club members. The teacher did not believe she was Hispanic and would not allow her to go in. One of her friends corrected the teacher and reassured her my daughter was Hispanic and was allowed to attend the party. This upset me for two reasons. The first reason was my daughter's skin not dark enough to attend this party? The second reason is how can they alienate so many other groups of people? If you are truly looking for unity, then why do we build so many walls between us? The very next year my oldest daughter comes home from school. She tells me about a form she had to fill out before she took a state test. After she reviewed the form she realized she had to fill out her racial makeup and religion. It was not only my daughter but there were other kids asking the importance of answering the form. The teacher informed the students by filling out the racial makeup as well as religion they would receive forms to what scholarships they could apply for and what colleges they would receive mail from. In more ways than one this has thrust me back into the fight. I am very proud of those kids who asked the importance of answering those questions. This has enraged me to no end. How is it possibly legal to judge our children or even ask what race they are? How can a society be equal if they choose who gets scholarships based on the color of their skin? I did not wish to write about all this negativity I see today but if we do not see the whole picture then how can this matter be resolved? If we continue to leave people out because of the color of their skin, they will eventually rise up. Are we truly going to leave this matter for our children to deal with?

I find that even politics are attempting to divide us. We often hear the Democratic Party cry out racism every time they meet opposition. Does this not stir more racism? This tactic the Democratic Party is using is intended to intimidate others so they can silence their opposition. What made America great was opposition. The freedom to express your opinion without criticism is crucial to the American spirit. If the Democratic Party is going to use tactics such as fear to quiet their opposition, then what will happen to democracy? What will happen to the freedom of expressing new ideas?

I even find the media guilty. Do they not see how divided we are today? They give the opportunity for these hate groups to spread their venom. These are groups like the KKK, Skinheads, and many others who chant out hurtful slurs. Tell me America, what gives anyone the right to offend another because the color of their skin? What bothers me far worse is seeing these racial groups marching with their children on national TV. This is teaching hate to our future generations. I have often heard the news media proclaim that the Democratic Party will receive all the black votes. Is this not a racist comment? I know it is a lie because I know many black people have voted Republican. To assume one group of people, think alike is to assume they function as a hive mind. I know that black people do not think as one but think independently. I have talked to numerous black people and found many of them supported Romney or McCain. One of them in particular, was a Vietnam veteran who supported McCain. He did not see the color of skin as an important issue but what he saw was another veteran who had spent his life serving his country. I have heard the issue of racism from many different angles. It seems whites, blacks and even Hispanics all have an argument on how they are being discriminated against.

One thing that shocks me is how other races has to use the term reverse discrimination. This too is dividing our society because discrimination is discrimination. We must become a society where everyone is treated equally and protected under one law. For us to get over the issue of racism we must create laws that protect everyone equally. I believe the first step is we should no longer allow a public platform for racial motivated groups to spread their hate. We must realize that people have the right to be who they are and no one has the right to offend them because of their race. We can never become an equal society as long as hate groups yell out slurs and spread their venom across our nation. We must keep in mind that we are a free society and hate groups have the right to organize but we must not allow them to speak out on public platforms where they can directly offend others. What I am indicating is if these racially motivated groups want to spread their hateful propaganda then they must do it in private. The first amendment gives us the right to peacefully assemble and these racial groups may argue that they are peacefully assembling but how many deaths have result from such hateful rhetoric?

The second thing we must do is to not allow organizations to represent one race while denying the representation of all other races. This too is discrimination. How can we become an equal society if such actions are allowed to occur? These are groups like the NAACP (National Association for the Advancement of Colored People) which is an organization that was the voice of the black people when our government did not stand up for them, but today this is no longer the problem. There are other groups such as the WBA (White Brothers of America) and the National Association for the Advancement of White People. If these organizations want to continue to exist in our society, then they must open their doors to all races and represent them equally. Many of these groups have no desire to bring forth peace, instead they install fear and hate that brings forth more racial division. For America to become an equal society we must all be represented equally. Thirdly we must eliminate the need for affirmative action.

I have heard the problems for equal opportunity for employment in America. I hear the black community cry out that they still do not have the equal opportunities that white people have for employment. At the same time, I hear people cry out they don't have the equal opportunities and that affirmative action is not fair. I have heard people claim that they were turned down a job or passed over for a promotion because of affirmative action. We have heard the argument about those who have been skipped over in law enforcement and even the fire department just because they have to fill a quota. America there is a right way and a wrong way and we are definitely on the wrong path. America, it is time for a leap of faith for humanity. I do agree that we must have stiffer laws for those who violate human rights and make it mandatory for those who violate human rights to be subjected to severe consequences.

Did Martin Luther King Jr. not say "...let my people be judged by their merit not by the color of their skin?" You cannot disagree with this fact. Affirmative action is being used as a tool to judge a person by the color of their skin. We can no longer allow this practice to carry on in America. We shall become a society where all are judged by their merit! We must become a society that no longer supports or tolerates racial division. No longer shall we allow organizations or clubs to deny membership because of race. Nor shall we allow contests or pageants to be represented by one race. Having pageants such as Miss Black America or Miss Latino American is discrimination and could eventually lead to a Miss White America. I have heard the argument that black women were not allowed to participate in Miss America pageants in the past and I do agree this was an injustice. However, we must realize two wrongs don't make a right and or children should not have to pay for this. There are even scholarships being passed out based on the color of skin and there is even a scholarship for being white. America let's take this leap and judge people by their merit.

Even today you will find channels or programs that primarily represent one race, which should not be allowed. I have expressed my concerns and debated these issues on many occasions and I find that most people agree with me until I begin to talk about how we could create a truly equal society. What has shocked me is how many have told me this would be a loss to their culture and heritage. This upset me for two reasons. The first reason being the thought that you have to hold on to your culture or heritage by creating racial division. The second reason is the fact that all races have a culture and heritage. For America to become a true and equal society we must all be governed under the same law.

This is not something I want for my kids or any other child. I do not wish for them to live in a society that is divided. This leads me to responsibility. We are responsible to ensure our children have a fair and equal society for all races. I know there are some people out there that believe in segregation but I believe that there are more of us who don't. We can see the trouble that can be stirred from such a division. Do we really want our children to have to grow up in such an environment? Do we want them to have to fix all the problems that we left for them? We must create one law that is fair and equal to all. It must protect people of all color. No longer can people be discriminated against because of the color of their skin. No longer shall we allow people to be discriminated against because of their gender. The very same law should protect the rights of the elderly as well as our children. The disabled must be included as well. A person's religious preference should be protected in this bill also. This should be one law for all of humanity. We can call it the Human Act.

If we cannot come together today and resolve these issues, we will go down in history as a foolish society that allowed themselves to be divided by the color of our skin. They will talk about our ignorance and how unmotivated we were to stand up for what was right. Is this the legacy we all desire? Not for me. I want to be known as the society that shattered the walls which divided us and that found forgiveness in one another. Does it not say in the Lord's Prayer, "Forgive me for my trespasses as I forgive those who trespass against me". To me this means I am asking God to forgive me as I forgive those who have wronged me. We have to ask ourselves today if we put our faith in God how many of these problems we are facing today would even exist? I have an entirely different view then most people for our future. I believe we will see the ignorance one day and we will become one people.

This is the dream I have for my children. Is this not the same you have for your own? Let us not pass this burden to our children. No longer shall we be divided. No longer shall we allow the government or media to divide us. Let me ask: what is the difference between us other than the color of our skin? Can a black person not receive a blood transfusion from a white person? Can a white person not receive an organ transplant from a black person? Besides the color of our skin we are genetically the same. You will find my heart within my chest beats the same as yours. Do we not all have a common bond? We all want to worship and live free. We all have such a great love for our children and want the best for them. For this very reason, we must come together. Let us go down in history as the generation that lit the beacon of hope. There are hate groups among us that want to divide us. They want to intimidate us and make us live in fear. Even our own government creates fear in our own society. Let us not allow the lies to divide us any longer for our children are counting on us. To all good people across America who do not believe in racism and truly believe it is a disease that only leads to evil. Let us come together.

We will outnumber all these hate groups by the millions. Let us meet them in their path of war. Not with fight in our hearts but with an iron will. While they spill out their hate and deceit let us extract their venom with prayer. You cannot meet aggression with aggression. This only increases their numbers. If you throw stones will they not pick them up and throw them back? Instead let's show them that we are one people. Do we not believe that love will conquer evil and break the shackles that bind their heart? Let us not be labeled any longer. If someone is to ask you your race declare you are human. If someone asks your nationality declare you are an American. We must all start teaching our children to love one another. Preachers need to start teaching the congregation the very words Jesus spoke in his last days; we need to love one another as he loved us. Does it not say in the book of John, "A new command I give you: Love one another? As I have loved you, so you must love one another. By this everyone will know that you are my disciples, if you love one another." Have you ever pondered the idea that God's greatest challenge for humanity is for us to come together and realize we are all brothers and sisters? He also desires for us to not to be a judgmental society and to have love for one another. We must realize we are all God's children.

Freedom of Speech

Today we are overcome by those who declare their rights for freedom of speech while spreading their madness and polluting the minds of our young. They spill their words of hate and even desire to hurt those who are different. They are asking for the horrific crime to prevent racial equality. How many more times should we repeat our past before we learn? We must never forget how Hitler came to power in Germany by spreading deceitful racial hatred. When Hitler finally gained power in Germany, he had only won the election by a few points but this terrible man had deceived and manipulated the whole nation. The consequences of Hitler gaining power gave him the platform to spread his hate which resulted in the horrific genocide of the Jewish people.

Before Hitler gained power, there were many that thought it was impossible and even laughed at the idea of Hitler winning an election. The horrible truth of genocide has continuously reoccurred throughout our history. Today there are those who speak out their desire for hate and even a racial war. Do they not realize millions will die? Without constraint, they pound at the podium and scream out their words of hate. This is not just for those who are a different race but those of different faith. How many times have we seen racially motivated graffiti on walls or public restrooms?

Not long ago I heard about a racially motivated hate group who had severely beaten a Jewish man to the brink of death. Was this not enough to wake the people? When spreading their hate, do they not realize they will excite the masses? Have they not in the past provoked those to action? Yet they stand and deny the guilt does not lie upon them. They declare they do not want such action while they declare they are exercising their right for freedom of speech. Will we allow them to deceit us in this manner? We must see the evil that lies within their heart.

I think it is pathetic how such hate groups hide behind our freedom. How many more must die before we become wise? There are those who even protest funerals with picket signs that bring dishonor and disgrace to those soldiers that have served our country so bravely. It is their right to protest against our government to declare an end to war, and bring our soldiers back home. However, to protest against our soldiers whose desire was to only serve our country is shameful. So many have given their lives to protect our freedom and protect those abroad. They truly believe they are bringing freedom and democracy to faraway lands. Protesting against our fallen soldiers is not only despicable but I find it cowardly as well. These brave men and women cannot speak out from their graves and defend their honor. Do their families not deserve to mourn in peace? Has America truly lost their heart? My heart cries out to you. We must think of the mothers and fathers who have lost their children. We must think of the children who have lost a mother or father. For these children see the signs of hate that read "You should have died," "You murder!" Or "God will judge you now." Is that not heartbreaking?

We have all seen the result of a hate rally on the news or in cities where we live. They bring so much hate to so many people across our country, as they install anger into the crowd with their lies and deceit. Then violence falls upon our streets. We have all seen the aftermath of destruction and even death from racially motivated riots. So many people proclaim this rhetoric is not dangerous but how many must die before we see the truth? For me one is too many! You can never bring unity or equality for the people by spreading hate, only the power of love can bring us together. For over a century many have argued for limitations on freedom of speech. Cases have gone before the Supreme Court on this matter. America, I am not the type of person that believes in placing limitations on our rights but you cannot constitute one freedom that will conflict with the freedom to be who you are without harassment. We must realize that everyone has the right to live free and to be free. People have the right to exist, and not bounded or judged by the color of their skin or their beliefs. God has given all mankind free will and only evil would attempt to remove our cherished gift.

There have already been laws established that limits freedom of speech. For example, it is against the law to yell fire in a theater or bomb on an airplane. The consequences of such an act would create a panic which could result in deaths. How many deaths have resulted from the hateful rhetoric that has been spread across the nation like a disease? Recently I heard the story of a man that was dragged to death by another man driving a truck because of the color of his skin. Can we not agree that the ones that were guilty of these horrible crimes could have been influenced by such hate groups? What about those who were brutally beaten through the horrific riots from our past?

There is a consequence to such actions that hide behind our first amendment. To me our first amendment gives us the right to protest against wrongs or injustices. It gives us the right to argue for better living standards or to protect our very freedom. It gives us the right to argue for better wages and I can think of many more reasons why we have the First Amendment. I do not believe that our forefathers intended for us to abuse the First Amendment the way we do today. If we continue to allow this privilege to be abused, then can we not lose the right to freedom of speech? With the first amendment comes responsibility.

Today we must set the standards to ensure our future generations can cherish the freedoms that we are blessed with today. We cannot allow those to spread their hate or desires to hurt someone else because the color of their skin. Nor can we allow those to slander others because of their race or their faith on public property. There must be consequences for those who talk about killing or committing genocide. These hate groups have pushed their way into our living rooms today. We see them on TV marching down the street with their children chanting hurtful slurs that cause hurt to others. They scream out they must fight. What lesson is this teaching our children? Our first amendment gives us the right to assemble peacefully but racial slurs or to bash someone because of their religion is not peaceful. These racially motivated groups only have one agenda, to plant the seed of hate. We must speak out in one loud voice and push their evil boundaries back to prevent them from poison the minds of our children. We must push our government to set the rules or regulations in order to protect all of those within our society. Our first amendment must be protected but we have to be responsible with such a cherished freedom. We need to become a moral society that realizes that people have a right to be who they are without harassment. By allowing hate groups to have a public platform is in direct violation of personal freedoms. All people have the right to be on public property without harassment and by allowing hate groups to slander people of different races or religion is a violation against their personal freedom. Our freedom of speech is a cherished right that needs to be protected but we cannot allow our freedom to conflict with the freedom to be who you are without harassment. We must establish a law that prohibits racial slurs, religious bashing, or any other hatred rhetoric that is offensive in speeches on public property. We must learn to debate in an intelligent manner with good reasoning and our faith in God to reestablish good morals. America if we could only purge the hate from our society, maybe then we'll see ourselves as part of the human family.

Immigration Reform

I can understand the concerns many Americans have today regarding the uncertainty of our future especially with the escalating unemployment rate. The complexity of immigration reform along with the breakdown in our government has compounded this problem. What alarms me is the hateful rhetoric I hear spilling out from racially motivated hate groups. I find myself disgusted for I have heard the hurtful racial insults. I have seen the graffiti that calls out for the death of Hispanics. I hear people shouting out "They are stealing our jobs and taking over our communities!" I find such great concern for such behavior. Imagine what a child thinks when they read the graffiti "Die Mexicans," or for them to hear the chants "Go home Mexicans!" Have we become a society that allows such torment? We must remember we are not just dealing with adults here. It wasn't that long ago when I heard the chants from racially motivated groups calling out to send the mud people back home. A group of people that was motivated by a racial group hurled rocks through the windows of Hispanic homes. There is no honor in a despicable action such as this. How can you take pride in such scare tactics when children are involved? Is it so easy for us not to think of their children? I would like to ask where our compassion is.

Throughout human history we have heard the same propaganda and the racial smears against the people that were different. It was a little more than seven decades ago when the world heard similar propaganda. During the 1930's Germany faced many problems. Many Germans were out of work and did not have ability to feed their children. The citizens of Germany were very angry at the government for not solving their economic problems. This is when the Nazi Party realized they could gain power by manipulating the Germans by projecting the hate towards the Jews. This evil manifested itself to commit the slaughter of nearly 7,000,000 Jews. The Jewish people were blamed for their countries' economic problems. The hate seemed to intensify as the people were led to believe the Jews were taking their jobs and taking over their communities. There was graffiti over Jewish businesses and homes which read "Get out or die Jews." In fact, the Jewish people were not the problem. The intense pressure placed on the country to make reparations for World War I caused many of these problems.

I do not believe this horrific crime will ever happen in the United States because there are too many people that lead with their hearts and would never allow this to happen. Regrettably there are those in our country who truly desire such appalling action. We have to remember one of the causes of us going to war with Iraq was the vile genocide that Saddam Hussein committed against the Kurds. We all saw the pictures of the aftermath of the chemical weapons that were dropped on the Kurdish villages. In vain, parents used their garments to cover their children's mouths in an attempt to shield them from harm. Do you honestly believe the Kurdish people ever thought these actions would happen to them? There were pictures of mothers and children lying dead in the streets. There were lifeless bodies of parents clinging to their babies. How can people have such hate in their hearts? Do they not feel sadness? Does our heart not cry out to despise such crimes against humanity? I know in many ways this is not a fair comparison but I feel like I have to bring light to the horrors and consequences when people are hated or unwelcome. I truly believe that there are people filled with evil through every culture and civilization past or present. Their only desire is to create turmoil and pain for those who are different races or different faiths. Tell me, who has the authority to judge God's creation!!!

I do agree that immigration needs to be solved but we must not allow those to twist the truth. The massive job loss we are seeing in the country today is the result of the NAFTA treaty that our government signed in. The restrictions and the over taxations of so many businesses are being felt today. The selling of technology and jobs to countries overseas is killing us. Let the truth not be distorted. Let us place the blame where it truly lies— with our government. Another fact that truly seems to bother me about our government is the fight for credit on who creates immigration reform. When George Bush Junior was in office he wanted to create a bill that gave the immigrants a pathway for citizenship. The Republican and Democrats both opposed this bill but as soon as Barack Obama took office the Democrats were suddenly for immigration reform. If President Obama was so much for immigration reform, then why did he vote against it as a Democratic Senator? This is another attempt for the Democrat party to divide the people. I believe their ideology was if the Democratic Party could pass the immigration reform bill they would receive the credit and the support of the Latino community. This is not a game. There are many people suffering because of this foolishness. Our society is led to believe all immigrants are Hispanic when, in reality, 70% are Hispanic. The other thirty percent are from Europe, Russia and other countries. Why is the government and media fixated on the Hispanic portion of the immigrants? Whatever happened to the meaning of the statue of liberty? Have we allowed such negativity and disparity to dim her light? Have we lost our spirit and the true meaning of what made our country great? Has her message been silenced and lost in the darkness?

"Give me your tired, your poor,
Your huddled masses yearning to breathe free,
The wretched refuse of your teeming shore. Send these,
the homeless, tempest-tossed to me.
I lift my lamp beside the golden door."

America was once viewed as a great country and a land of golden opportunity. We must bring greatness and prosperity back to our country. We must not allow Lady Liberty's torch to fade away nor can we allow her message to be lost. This is not the first-time America has had a huge problem with immigration. You can go back a hundred years and see how poorly the Irish and Chinese were treated. They were treated like second class citizens and even the Italians, Jews and other people were treated poorly.

I believe we have many problems in our country. We must stiffen our border's security and halt the action of those who want to find refuge within our borders. We have a massive overflow of immigrants which is creating many problems for our government. Our judicial system is bogged down from this problem. We have states making their own immigration laws while our Federal government argues amongst themselves on how to resolve this issue. When you have a massive overflow, you must cut off its source to allow our government to resolve the matter. We must find solutions to our immigration problems. We cannot simply send these people back home. The cost would be unimaginable. This would not just be a huge financial burden on our country; it would be a crime against humanity to send them back because it would destroy so many families. Each year we spend well over $5 billion in deportation, which is a huge waste of tax payer expense and has left broken families and its aftermath. This revenue should have been used for education or for other governmental departments.

Throughout my life I have had the opportunity to meet several families from different parts of the world and I have become really good friends with them. For me to see how happy and prideful they are to live in such a country made me realize that America is still a great country. I have talked to several families about immigration reform and some have told me if they were to be sent back to their country they would leave their kids here. I even had a lady from Russian tell me the same thing, she then went on to tell me that it would be selfish of her to deny her child a brighter future. I was shocked to hear such a comment but as I looked into her eyes I could see tears had started to well up. This woman shared with me that she would leave her children in America if she were to be deported back to Russia. That truly touched me because that is true love from a mother's heart. Most people have given up everything just to come here to this land of opportunity. They believed in the spirit of America, while so many Americans has lost their spirit. We must allow their hopes and dreams to inspire us all. We cannot allow immigration to be a rift in our country any longer. Many of these immigrants have lived in our nation for well over a decade and have become integrated into our society. By denying citizenship would truly be a crime that would shatter so many people's hopes and dreams of becoming an American. By creating a pathway for citizenship for immigrants would increase our tax revenue and shatter the walls that has divided us. Immigration reform would create well over 2 billion per year in tax revenue and add an additional 1.5 trillion to our GDP within the next decade. This is not including the 5 billion we would save each year by ending deportation.

America is facing many problems. Our infrastructure is falling apart. We must find a way to bury our differences and become one people. It is imperative that we rebuild our great nation. The task before us is tremendous but with all hands in our hearts can be filled with spirit. America was once a nation that dreamed big and achieved those dreams. Today we have dreamt little and we have fallen into disarray. We must solve this immigration issue and remove this hurdle that has been blocking our prosperity. I do believe in immigration reform. I think it would take everyone to take our great nation from the abyss. We act as if though there are no solutions and we argue amongst each other yet we find no results. With the problems in our country today we must limit our military support for countries abroad. The army of engineers that has been assigned to build buildings and schools in countries such as Afghanistan and Iraq should be called back; their help is mostly needed here within our borders to help build a great wall.

I have an idea for a three-step plan to solve our immigration issue in our country. I believe we must secure our borders before we can have immigration reform. I find our borders are a great security risk for us all. If people can simply cross our borders what will stop a terrorist from invading our country? We do not need a flimsy fence that can be easily climbed or easily cut through. The other problem with our fence is too easy to tunnel under. There is also a huge problem with drug trafficking and illegal weapons being smuggled into and out of our country. I believe we must build a wall equipped with observation towers. The wall must be at least ten feet high and with towers every mile or half a mile apart depending on viewing area. Twelve feet behind the wall we need to install a fence at least eight feet high. This will give enough distance for patrol vehicles to patrol within this enclosure. The ten-foot wall will create such an obstacle that anyone trying to climb it will need a ladder. It must be required for one arm guard for each tower, along with a border agents patrolling the perimeter. We can also utilize technology by using drones or field sound devices to alert us when someone is attempting to cross the border. The wall must also be equipped with motion detection lights and speaker system to deter anyone from attempting to cross our borders illegally. There is around two thousand miles of border that divides the United States and Mexico and there is a little over 17,000 border patrol agents patrolling this border. That is equivalent to 8.5 border agents patrolling every mile of our border. That would be the same equivalence as three patrol agents per shift per mile. You can get the same results by placing one agent per tower while having two on patrol. There also needs to be sound detection equipment to alert if there is an intruder. Each tower must be equipped with the latest technology and seismographic meters to detect if someone is digging under the wall. This will help secure the safety of our border patrol agents and help protect American citizens from another terrorist attack.

We also need to limit the number port of entries in the United States and build humanitarian accommodation facilities while we run extensive background checks. This will drastically limit the number of illegal aliens entering the United States and have a huge impact on drug trafficking. With such an impact on the drug trafficking our streets will become safer and the cartel wars that we are seeing south of our border will fade away. Having such an imposing wall could save thousands of lives. It has been reported that thousands have died attempting to cross the desert terrain. There will be those that will tell us that it is impossible to build such a wall. Have we forgotten that the Chinese built their walls to protect their border over two thousand years ago? What about the Romans, they built their massive streets along with aqueducts that stretched across their lands? This massive task can be done if we truly believe. It would create thousands of jobs and most of the resources that we need are in the southwestern states.

There will be those who will claim that it will be idiotic to spend so much money. Statistics show that we spend over three hundred billion dollars yearly on immigrants and protecting our border. I cannot tell you how much money it will take to build a wall but what I can tell you is that three hundred billion dollars is a massive amount of tax payer's money. If our government had utilized tax revenue responsibly, then this project could have been done years ago. We must realize that hundreds of billions of dollars are spent yearly on the War against Terrorism in faraway lands. If we pull our military from the Middle East and allow United Nations to deal with these problems in the Islamic nations. Imagine what we can do with the tax revenue that has been so foolishly wasted in the past years. If you simply took just one hundred billion and divided it by the two thousand miles of border you will find that this will generate fifty million dollars per mile. How can anyone claim we do not have the revenue to take on such a massive task?

I do agree with presidential nominee Donald Trump on several issues such as the wall to better protect our borders. I do not agree with his idea that Mexico should be required to pay for this wall. America if Mexico builds the wall, then Mexico owns the wall!!! This wall is our responsibility and is about our security. We will build a great wall with pride, and it will be our men and women that will be assigned to the guard towers, and to patrol the border to ensure every American is safe. I know everyone will not agree with the concept of building a wall to secure our borders and I have seen the protests against this idea. At one protest rally I witnessed a protester screaming "a free society does not build walls." They will, if the society wants to remain safe!!! America, you must wake up, if drugs or guns are smuggled across our border is an indication that our borders are not secure. Today the number of immigrants crossing the border has dropped significantly but thousands every year are still getting into our country illegally. America, you must realize if people are crossing our borders then what stops a terrorist from falling suit. There's also the multitudes of cases of human trafficking – across our border in many the victims were kidnapped from their homes. America, the term human trafficking does not apply here, this is slave smuggling and it has to stop.

Building this wall would not only create thousands of jobs and stimulate our economy but it would help remove the criminals from our streets. I ask you what our priority is today. Secure our nation or the ones abroad? We must push our federal government to take actions to secure all borders. We must motivate our southwestern states to take action and put pressure on the Federal Government. It is our government's job to secure the safety of those who live within our border. It is not just the guns or drugs that are being smuggled into our country but there are children who are being kidnapped off our streets and smuggled out of our country to be sold into slavery. The dangers that we could be facing from the terrorists that have already snuck into this country could have massive consequences. Let us remind the government that they serve us and they must resolve this problem. We must not allow the naysayers to deter us. This one massive project could not only save taxpayers billions of dollars but could help save thousands of lives on both sides of the border.

My second plan would be to temporarily suspend work and student visas until the unemployment rate drops below 4%. However, excluding professional visas which include fields such as scientists, doctors and engineers so they may remain in our country to further our scientific pursuits. We receive over 300,000 of illegal and legal immigrants per year. They achieve entry into our country through programs such as work and student visas. By following steps one and two this will bring the over flow of immigrants to a trickle. It would give our government the opportunity to catch up with the process of immigration reform and the people an opportunity to adjust as well.

My third and final phase would be to initiate a process for immigration reform. I do not believe we need to pass an unconditional immigration bill. The idea of amnesty would not be fair for those who have gone through the long process of becoming a citizen. It is imperative that we have knowledge of who is living within our borders. The idea of terrorists or groups of terrorists living among us is frightening. We must mobilize our military to assist law enforcement to screen and run thoroughly background checks on illegal immigrants. Those who are partaking in criminal activity, such as drug trafficking or have had a violent history must be deported immediately. If we find that they have had a criminal past from the country, they have arrived from or have warrants outside of our country they must be deported. We must realize that America is in a rebuilding stage and we do not need any criminal activity detouring us from our goals.

Once again we can utilize our military to transport the unlawful immigrants back to their countries which would lower the cost of transporting them dramatically. There are those that claim this will be too costly yet we spend billions of dollars in Afghanistan and Iraq. Would you not agree the billions that we are spending on other countries could be better utilized in our country? Also, there are those who claim it will be impossible. I declare that no task is impossible when the people stand together and declare in one loud voice: *"We Will Not Falter!"* There will be those sympathizers that will state that this is unfair and inhumane and will attempt to overload our courts. For those unlawful immigrants, we must bypass the court process; we must not allow our judicial system to become bogged down. We must not be detoured. I find that it will be reckless to allow the unlawful immigrants to remain on our streets. We must remove the bad apples for ourselves and our children.

Since immigration reform will create such an immense task, we need to make it clear this is going to be a onetime process. We cannot continue to repeat this process through the years, especially at such a massive scale. We must set up a time line and give those who are seeking citizenship adequate time to gather up their papers, this will not be a process that will be done overnight. I do think the pathway to citizenship needs to be simplified regarding the test. Most Americans would find difficulties in passing the test. I believe they should be required to speak our language as well as know and understand the Pledge of Allegiance. They must have respect for our great nation and feel honored to know they are on the pathway to citizenship.

If we are truly a compassionate society then we must have compassion for the immigrants, because many of them have struggled immensely through their life. Many of the immigrants fled to America to avoid the ruthlessness of the cartel. I have heard many stories about how their streets and even cities are controlled by the cartel. Even young teenagers are forced into prostitution or into smuggling drugs. There are so many other reasons why so many people fled to our country, such as the lack of employment or the inability to feed their children. These people came to America for refuge and to escape the horrible conditions that have been suppressing them for so long. These people are human and have the same heartfelt desire for their children to be cared for as all of us. Let me ask you America how far would you go to ensure your children were safe and cared for? They came to our country to seek out employment to provide for their family. They came to America for freedom and prosperity and the hope they could become citizen one day in our great nation.

Our government has made it very difficult for the immigrants to find a pathway for citizenship and even more difficult to live or work in our country. The majority of the states prohibits illegal immigrants from obtaining a driver's license, which creates a tremendous amount of hardship for them to find work and many of them settle for low paying jobs. The fact that they cannot obtain a state issued ID or driver's license brings forth multitudes of problems. Our government has made it illegal for them to drive themselves back and forth to work or to pick their children up from school. It is difficult to see a doctor without a state issued ID and it is impossible to open up checking accounts without proper ID. All these issues have made it difficult for so many of them to find suitable housing for their family. They also find complications when trying to have their utilities turned on. Why must our government make their lives so complicated? We are denying them the opportunity of prosperity. Many of the immigrants live in poverty and live in fear of even reporting a crime because their status. Do we not realize this has a dramatic impact on their children? This is the very reason so much protest has spilled throughout the immigrant communities. They are asking for the opportunity to create a better life for themselves and their children.

I do not believe we are a heartless society. So how can we deny immigrants the opportunity to put clothes on their children's backs or put food in their mouths? Instead of the government resolving this problem they continue to argue which has resulted in communities dividing. Today I hear many Americans claiming that the Latinos have created their own communities and refuse to learn our language. We must realize throughout our history many cultures and many people with different ethnical backgrounds have done the same thing. The Chinese, Jewish, Irish and German have all created their own communities in the past. Today if you look at their descendants you will see that they speak perfect English. Even today you will find that the immigrant's children speak English very well. I do agree that the immigrants need to embrace America's customs and language. They also need to share their customs with us. This is one thing that has made America great and the melting pot we are today.

My wife has shared such customs with me and the one that has really touched me; we still follow to this day. Years ago, my wife had purchased a beautiful nativity scene of Jesus' birth. The characters as well as the animals were all created from beautiful porcelain. Every year after thanksgiving my family and I put up the Christmas tree as well as all the other decorations throughout our home. I noticed that when my wife was first setting up the nativity scene she did not place baby Jesus in the Meijer. I asked my wife where the figure of baby Jesus was at and she informed me that in Mexico they had a tradition. They did not place baby Jesus in his crib till the night of Christmas Eve. Not only did I honor such a custom but I respected it as well. It does not mean we all have to honor all customs that are brought to our country but we should respect them. I would hate to live in a country where everyone acted the same or we could only obey certain customs. This is the very freedom that makes our country shine like a torch in the night. We must solve the problems and difficulties we are facing today. We must humble ourselves and learn to be tolerant of those who are different. We must understand the true meaning of freedom: it is the ability to be true to yourself. It gives us the very right to follow our own customs and beliefs. In our hearts, do we not all desire to be free? Does it not make us one people? Today, I am proud president Obama has created a path for citizenship for the lawful immigrants but it has taken far too long. The dream act that was signed in by Pres. Obama has helped immigrant children in our nation to go to college and seek out a pathway for citizenship. This program does not help the parents who have labored for many years under grueling conditions. Are we to deny their dream of becoming lawful citizens and productive members of our society. This reminds me of a great Civil Rights leader quote:

"A RIGHT DELAYED IS A RIGHT DENIED"

-MARTIN LUTHER KING JR.

So, let us come together and be great citizens of our wonderful nation. Together we can rebuild America but we must first break the chains of despair. We must break through the walls that has divided the people and together we can accomplish anything. Today most immigrants live in fear not knowing when they will be ripped from their family. This fear has intensified with the pledge of a presidential nominee Donald Trump to send all immigrants back to their country. The deportation of immigrants would lead to the destruction of many families across our nation. We must realize how many immigrants have become Americanized over the years, especially their children. This is a serious matter on how so many children that have only known what it is like to live in America would adjust to being relocated to another country. This can create massive problems in their education as well as communicational skills. I call out for the people in America to have heart because this horrendous action will tear apart thousands of families. Many the immigrants have married Americans, as well as married other immigrants from other nations. Tell me if you have a mother from Mexico and a father from Russia, then where would you send the children if their parents are sent back to the country they fled? America, I call out for you to open your hearts and hear the cries of the children because horrible deeds have gone unnoticed for far too long. Children are being torn from the parents in this horrible action of deportation. Today we have young adults raising their siblings because their parents were deported and far worse many of the children were turned over to foster care. How can we possibly call ourselves a civilized society, if we are so willing to tear children from the parents! I hear those who cry out is the law, well my question is where was the law that allowed millions who cross our borders. I tell you I want no part of the law the steps on love or family values. They are not just immigrants they are people with families, with friends, and let us not forget America is a nation of immigrants. We must realize that millions of the immigrants are part of American families. Tell me are you prepared to witness children's eyes filled with tears as the arms are reaching out screaming for the mother or father as their parents are being hauled off in handcuffs to be deported. Let us not be a nation that shatters families, let us not be a nation that shatters hope. Let us rise from disparity and shattered the evil that dwells within our own nation. Let us come together as brothers and sisters, for we are all God's children.

The Irreplaceable Bond

To me there is nothing more important than family. It is the unconditional love you receive from your family and the security of knowing someone will always be there. Everyone has the desire to love, or to be loved, and in my opinion love is what makes a family. The understanding that you will be accepted as you are guided through life. Family is the warm embrace you receive when heartbroken or the care you will receive when ill. Family provides the courage to handle life's challenges, and to stand for what you believe. Family is lifting, especially when your confidence is down, or under tremendous pressure. Family is love that blossoms from the heart, which commits us all to care for one another. This is our irreplaceable family bond.

Sadly, I look around and see so many broken families or families that are barely holding on. You can see the loneliness in a person's eyes when they tell you that they do not have a family. Could have the destruction of these families been avoided? I think this is such an unnecessary walk for so many. Living in uncertainty and having no one to fall back on is a terrible position to be in. Others carry foolish pride like a shield to hide the hole that has been left in their heart. Through their journey in life they try to fill this emptiness in their heart. Some turn to drugs or alcohol while some cling to people that are abusive to them. Today there are more people taking antidepressants or seeking therapy than ever before. So many people are angry, defensive and live reclusive lives. Even the horrors of suicide have steadily increased in our nation, it truly saddens my heart to know that over 42,000 people will take their own life this year. Suicide has become the 10th leading cause of death in our nation and will cost taxpayers well over 40 billion yearly. What evil has gripped our land so viciously to afflict such disparity and hopelessness in our society. In a little over a half a century we have become a society filled with anger, addiction, and immoral behavior.

As I sit here today I wonder what happened to the family values. There are very few people left that have the family unity that was so common many years ago. I found myself digging deep to understand what happened to family unity. What I found was shocking. In recent years, the government has added many more welfare programs to the already extensive list. The original purpose was to help families and single parents that were in need. There were other programs created to help assist those who were seeking a higher education. The original plan was well thought out and it helped so many families create a better life. Today I call it a monster. Its appetite of power thrives on control. At its will it was signing bills that at first seemed harmless but as time went on gained power. You could see destruction through broken families and even broken hearts. Through the years it moved slowly at a snail's pace. While we slept there have been laws that divided the families and have stolen our rights. There was once a time when families stood together. If there was a loved one who felt ill or was in despair their family would rush to their aid. Today it seems as if though no one cares about family unity or values. It seems as if though this irreplaceable bond has been forgotten. I blame several issues such as governmental control and the fact that they have weakened our economy through over taxation and overregulated to support our over bloated government has put a tremendous hardship on families across our nation. The welfare system has put more middle class families in poverty, which results to more broken families. The welfare system destroys dreams, by devouring ambition to enslave you to a life of poverty. Their control smothers motivation by exerting limitations on the wealth a person could achieve, under the threat of losing their welfare.

In recent decades, we have become a society that is far more divided. For ages, we have been foolishly divided by race but today we are more divided by wealth, age and gender. So, it is not just our family unit that has been divided but our whole society. There are even books that claim women and men are from different planets. Race is limited to physical features alone. For those who claim women and men are totally different are foolish. Men and women are very similar but our culture has dictated that we play specific roles, take certain interests and act in certain ways. Does it not say in the Bible that God created Eve by removing a rib from Adam? This indicates that men and women complete one another and we are all family. We are children in God's family.

What happened to the days when harmony fell upon this land? I am only forty-four years today but I still remember the days of my childhood as if it were yesterday. It was such a thrill to know when the whole family was planning a special event. The opportunity to see my grandparents, aunts, uncles and cousins was exciting. I can still remember the sweet smell of barbeque and running free with my cousins while the adults talked. I enjoyed the long walks with my grandparents as they passed down the lessons they had learned throughout their lives. During those days' children were taught to carry honor and if you were to do something wrong in school it seemed as if your whole family knew about it. With a sad heart, I have to admit that I come from a family that has been torn apart. We do not have any more gatherings and it seems like everyone just scattered to the wind.

To understand how to fix the problems in our society today we must understand our past. Today I hear that the complexity of life has become too much and limits family communication. I repeatedly hear people say that the holidays are too stressful and their daily lives are compounded with stress as well. Why has it become such a burden for us to simply see our families or even friends? Throughout the generations when a new product was introduced, we heard the same sales pitch "This going to simplify your life!" Yet our lives have become more complicated and what has compounded this issue is the fact that it takes two incomes today to support a family. My grandmother had told me stories of how excited she was to see the washer and dryer come on to the market. As a child, I remember the microwave as well as the remote-control TV. Today we have better electronics and our vehicles need less maintenance. You would think with all these new inventions would have made our lives simpler. WRONG! Life has become more complicated than it has ever been before. With all the great inventions, along with all the great advances in technology will never compensate for the loss of the family bond. Are we living the lives our parents and grandparents intended for us? How many of us truly believe we are living the American dream?

Through the decades there have been those in our government that have divided our families. Several of them think that a socialist country would be better for all of us. They believe they can raise our children better than we can. We must have been asleep to allow so much control to slip from our hands. Our politicians pass laws that have had severe consequences in our family's lives. They pass laws without our consent or knowledge by hiding them in lengthy bills. Whatever happened for the people, by the people? Have they truly forgotten their place? There are even organizations out there such as ACORN that has in the past encourage single parents to stay single so they can reap the benefits from social services. They have even taught people how to manipulate or falsify their tax forms to receive a larger return. What morals are we teaching people by encouraging them to lie? These organizations have not only been sponsored by our government but they have been praised by our politicians. In our past our government has established tax laws and has given more benefits to single parents.

Does this not encourage people to remain single? You must also realize what this has done to the children. Today well over 40% of all children will live without their father within their young life. In this wicked society, have we truly created a false reality that fathers are no longer needed as a productive member of the family. How have we become a society filled with deadbeat fathers, today well over 15 million children are being raised without their father. In our nation, today well over 50% of all children are raised in single parent homes, and this number has doubled in the past 50 years. The most massive flaws in the welfare system is it gives permission for people to be irresponsible. Another major issue with the social welfare system is the fact that so many families are left in poverty. It is a system that ensures poverty as those who gets entangled into its web of deceit will become prisoners of disparity. The social welfare system has also put a tremendous amount of stress on middle class families through over taxation or redistribution of wealth. This is one of the reasons why the average American works more hours per week than any other nation in the world. Many of these issues has contributed to the destruction of the family and has left so many in poverty. In desperation, many have turned to a life of crime to support their family because they are limited by the welfare system on how much they can earn. They live with the threat of losing their benefits so many will refuse a job with higher pay or even a promotion, just to remain shackled to a life of poverty.

If our government continues this path of destruction the family bond will cease to exist. Where shall the people go for support and guidance? They will have no choice but to turn to our bloated government who has spent us into oblivion. While we foolishly seek them out for guidance they are taking our place as teaches to our children. America, wake up! This atrocity is happening right before your eyes. Kids today are being taught the liberal and socialist points of view. They are being taught how greedy and irresponsible America is. They are taught to be ashamed of American history. Was it not America that truly started the industrial revolution? Was it not America that has come up with so many antibiotics and procedures that have saved so many lives? Was it not America that prevented the Nazis and communists from taking over the world? Was it not America that invented the airplane? What about our great inventors such as Benjamin Franklin, Thomas Edison, Alexander Bell, George Washington Carver and Albert Einstein? This list can go on and on. What about Martin Luther King Jr, who was a great Civil rights leader or Helen Keller who helped the blind to read?

We have made horrendous mistakes in our past but the important part is that we have learned from our mistakes. We must teach our children to be proud of our history and be proud to be an American. We must not allow this propaganda to spill over into our schools any longer.

If we continue to make the same mistakes over and over again and expect different results, then we have truly gone insane.

Our government has taken the responsibility to teach our kids sex education and many other subjects best fitted for family teaching. This program started decades ago in high school. Today they teach it to children in middle school and even younger in some states. They claim it's to prevent teen pregnancies and STD's. The horrible truth, since the introduction of sex education into our school system had created a large increase in teen pregnancy. Shamefully they attempted to cover up this huge mistake by issuing condoms or encouraging parents to put their daughters on birth control. They have taken the responsibility of properly teaching our children away from the parents. Can our government not admit they have made a mistake? Instead they blame the parents and continue to teach our children inappropriate subjects at a younger age. A few years ago, my daughter was enrolled in a program at head start. They took it upon themselves to teach my daughter the correct terms of the female and male anatomy. At this age my daughter didn't even know there was a difference between boys and girls and of course this made her curious. She came to me and asked me a question that I have never been asked by my eight-year-old daughter, she wanted to know why boys had penises. I was not prepared to answer this question and especially for my four-year-old daughter. Children of this age do not need to know about anatomy. Is this not perversion of a child's mind? I have heard stories of fourth graders who were given condoms. As the principal was questioned on the news he indicated due to children having more sexual intercourse he felt that it was a proper procedure. He then indicated that they were encouraging abstinence while they were passing out the condoms. I sarcastically made the comment "I guess the next thing they are going to be giving kids is hypodermic needles while telling them not to do drugs. They will probably justify it by saying it will prevent the spread of aids."

We must realize that kids are curious by nature. You cannot give children condoms and expect them not to use them. Does anyone out there think the government can do a better job than us parents? Our government has failed miserably in every place they have intervened in our lives and has created tremendous problems for the people.

There was a girl that was attending a neighboring high school and the mother of this teenage girl was a friend of my wife's. At the young age of thirteen this young girl became pregnant. She was quite distraught so she sought advice from her guidance counselor. This young girl expressed her concerns about telling her mother. The guidance counselor told her not to worry and if she had any problems with her mother or if she threatened to put her out of the house they would put her in a home for teenage girls. When the teenage girl gathered her confidence, she told her mother she was pregnant. She then told her mother what the counselor had informed her. Her mother was furious when she came to my wife. She informed my wife she felt she could not even discipline her own daughter. Today this teenager is pregnant once again at the age of sixteen.

Another situation at the head start program involved the teachers notifying the parents if they saw any signs of abuse on the children they would notify the police. Right after making that statement they informed us they did not believe children should be whipped. I do agree they should report abuse to the authorities and I think everyone should. Because they compounded those two statements they struck fear into the parents. I remember speaking to some the parents after the conference outside. They expressed their concerns about how they could discipline their children. One gentleman spoke up and claimed that the speaker had conjoined those two statements on purpose. I am not sure if that was their attempt to get their point across but I do know it is wrong for them to put their nose into family affairs concerning discipline. They are even teaching children in kindergarten about gun control, I do not believe that children at the age of five has the mental capacity to understand the dangers of guns. We must realize that a five-year-old child doesn't always have the ability to separate reality from fantasy. The danger of teaching a five-year-old child a course on gun safety would conflict with the violence many children see in cartoons our video games they play. I do believe that children should learn a course on gun safety, but it is the manner our educators are using that I find disturbing. They are installing fear in our children through their course in guns' safety.

By manipulating our children's mind in such a manner could one day bring forth a generation that disproves of firearms and would allow the government to remove all guns from the private sector. I am not indicating that this lesson is used for propaganda by our government, but you cannot exclude the fact that there are many politicians that would go to great links to destroy the Constitution. America our government is bent on control and they have taken in the responsibility of nurturing our children away from us the parents. Many schools across America has in doctrine a behavior policy, which one of the policies makes it mandatory for quiet time in the lunch room is ludicrous. This is about control over our own children and are we to stand back and allow this atrocity to happen. There have been accounts of teachers telling their students not to listen to their parents. The one thing that disturbs me greatly is how teachers push their students to memorize chants, speeches, or songs for visiting politicians, is this not brain washing? Today more children are more likely to follow the instructions of their teachers then their own parents.

The way you judge if a system is working is by reviewing the success of the program or lessons. I think if we truly looked into all these matters, I think we would all see that the government has failed miserably. Today more and more families are homeschooling their children while politicians speak out against this form of education. What are they afraid of? Children learning the truth? Or are they afraid they won't have the opportunity to brainwash our children? America don't take my word for it. Look this matter up for yourself. I challenge you to do your own homework. You will realize I barely touched on this subject. Is it not your right to know what your child is being taught at school? We must preserve our rights to just disagree but to argue our opinions as well. It is time for us to take control of our family's destiny and tell the government to get out of our family affairs!

The government is not the only intrusion in our family affairs. I find that big businesses have caused a considerable amount of damage. Big businesses care very little about the family and intrude on family time. I have heard many stories from our elders about how families used to spend their Sundays together. They told me how life was so different many years ago when businesses were not allowed to be open on Sundays. Due to corporate greed, many businesses challenges law by making it mandatory for their stores or restaurants to be open on Sunday. Other businesses feared they would lose sales so they too started opening their doors. I truly believe this has wrecked the quality time that families once spent together. Due to this greed, parents have to work odd shifts and even on the weekends. Do we not see the damage that this has done to our families? Parents on average spend a little over an hour of quality time with their children per day. Can you imagine if big businesses, retail stores and all other businesses were closed on Sunday? Already government employees and majority of business offices are closed on the weekend. I do realize that the police, fire departments and other emergency services must remain in operation on Sundays but even they deserve a rotating schedule where they are off every other Sunday.

You will hear big businesses argue they will lose sales or have to cut their staff if they were closed one day a week; this is a ridiculous argument. Are we not smart enough to do our shopping the day before or the day after? Are we really going to go without the items because the store is closed on Sunday? Due to the store being closed on Sunday would increase sales for Saturday or Monday. This would increase the number of employees that would need to handle the extra sales. Can you imagine how much more money businesses could save by shutting their doors one day a week on utilities? This would also lower the demand we have on our utility companies as well as cut back in the pollution we put in our atmosphere. Let's start boycotting the businesses that are open on Sundays and do more business with those who are closed such as Chick-fil-a. Not only do I love their sandwiches but I also respect the standards they set. They actually put family first. I am not proposing to re-enact the Blue Laws; that would only result in churches over stepping their boundaries with state which would be unconstitutional. We can call this day whatever we want. This day can be for family and friends or worship or a day to simply rest. Can you imagine having a whole day that you can spend with your family? Churches will be filled to capacity once again. Neighbors will have the opportunity to get to know each other. This is another value that we have all lost touch with. How many of us actually know our neighbors? Many years ago, when a new family moved into a neighborhood the community would come to their house and welcome them or even bring them foods they had cooked. Do we not all miss that community bond? Yet today we live in a community of strangers and since we do not know our neighbors we seem to fear them. We must tell businesses they have intruded long enough and take our Sunday back.

It is so important for us to do this because our family has been splintered long enough. Too often I hear parents claim or cry out they cannot wait for their children to turn eighteen so they can put them out of the house or how parents love the TV as they call it their babysitter. Whatever happened to the joy of raising children? Did so many of these parents feel the same way when their children were born? I have seen parents push their children away because they were watching a television program. What message are you sending to your child? Are we telling our children the TV is more important than them? The next time you push your child away, look back at your child and see how your child walks away from you. Their head will hang low and their shoulders will sag. Imagine what must be going through their mind. The average adult watches around four hours of television a day while at the same time many claim they don't have time to spend with their children. Where are these children left to learn their morals from? The streets?

Another issue that seems to worry me lately is how little tolerance parents have for their children today. I have seen so many parents strike at their children out of anger in public. Recently I saw a mother slap her daughter on the mouth. Are these parents today so stressed out that they don't have patience for their kids? What lesson is this teaching our children? We are teaching them that it is okay to strike out in anger. Do we not realize that this is teaching our young to become more violent? We should never strike our children in anger. We need to show compassion and understanding. I believe this is one of the reasons so many children act up or commit the crimes they do today. How many children today feel lonely and feel that life is without direction or purpose? Do we not realize that maybe the reason that our children are acting up is because they are looking for attention? This is the reason; I truly believe we must correct the wrongs that we have allowed to happen from our past. It is urgent for us to once again make family a priority.

Tell me America what is more important than family, for life is not about what you built here on earth with your hands. Life is about what character you build within yourself, the irreplaceable family bond and the relationship you have with God. Life is about the loving embrace you receive from a loved one. Life is about the instantaneous love that overwhelms you when holding your child for the first time. Life is about the joy you feel when witnessing your child's first step or hearing their first spoken word. Today too many children grow up without a family and never understand the true meaning of love. When do so many children quit telling their parents I love you, maybe when they fail to get a response. We must reassert our rights as loving parents and be the role models our children are looking for. By setting the example, let us come together to teach our children the true power of love, the value of honesty, and the importance for integrity.

Life is not about being enslaved to a timeclock, the meaning of life is to live. Our children depend on us for more than a roof over their head or food on the table. Children desire nothing more than the loving embrace of the parents and the security to know that they are truly loved. It is also our responsibility to guide our children through their young life and to prepare them for their future. America, we must face the reality on how immoral our society has become since the removal of prayer as well as the commandments from our society. America this evil assault has attacked every aspect of our lives! First those in the elite circles attacked religion through falsified materials in evolution to destroy faith or to install doubt in our society. This evil beast then lashed out against Democratic values, attempting to replace them with communism or socialism, where humankind has no rights or freedom. The elite controls the economy and inflation around the world putting tremendous amount of stress on the people. They have corrupted our government through socialism ideology, and today this beast glares down upon us as it tightens its grip. Today our government controls nearly every business in America and the grand puppet master is the elite. This has led to the destruction of small family businesses across our nation, and has left our society depended upon large retail companies or welfare to survive. There are those in our society will tell you that the elite is not evil, but I will tell you those who plot by lying or to manipulate governments through bribery to assert their control for dominance has no mercy for humankind.

America, it is time to wake up, for their grab for power is almost complete. Their trail of destruction is evident today, through the elite greed and grasp for power has left one third of the world's population in poverty. The fact that less than 10% of the world's wealthiest owns and controls 80% of the world's wealth is ridiculous. This leaves 90% of the rest of the population of the world to fight over 20% of the world's wealth has left all people in despair. All these issues have led to the breakdown of the family, and has left us with a corrupt society were evil has no restraints. It is time for us to rise to control our destiny, for we are the parents of tomorrow's generation. We must reinstate prayer in school and once again teach our children the value of God's commandments.

The first amendment clearly states we had the freedom to exercise religion and what book could teach better morals for our children than the Bible. Commandments such as honor thy father and mother will set in stone good behavior for our children to follow and would strengthen the family bond. We the people need to be bold if we truly want to bring our great nation back to her glory and strength. America, it is time for a Christian awakening to bring forth truth so we may stomp out the lies and plots with evil intent. It is our responsibility as parents to ensure our children has a strong spiritual faith and are on the right path for salvation. We must declare Sunday as our day, so we can once again know our children. It is very important for us to reunite the family through faith and love. Grandparents we owe you a debt of gratitude. You come from a generation that helped build America and today I ask you to become more involved with your grandchildren. Help us to right the wrongs that have been committed from our past decades. Parents, look into your children's eyes and remember that special bond and the very love that you felt when your child was born. Let us all cry out in one loud voice, "No more." Let us tell the government no more intrusions and let us force big business to close their doors once and for all on Sundays and holidays.

I am calling for families to unify and forgive the wrongs of the past. Our government claims that parents are no longer teaching their kids good morals or values, but they are the ones who have taken this role away from us. Parents I am calling out for you to reinstate your role for our government is only an entity that knows no love and views your child as a number. We must teach our children good principles and morals and more important love. I truly do believe in the saying, "the family that prays together stays together."

"Love is patient, love is kind. It does not envy, it does not boast, it is not proud. It is not rude, it is not self-seeking, it is not easily angered, it keeps no record of wrongs. Love does not delight in evil but rejoices with the truth. It always protects, always trusts, always hopes, always perseveres. Love never fails. But where there are prophecies, they will cease; where there are tongues, they will be stilled; where there is knowledge, it will pass away. For we know in part and we prophesy in part, but when perfection comes, the imperfect disappears. When I was a child, I talked like a child, I thought like a child, I reasoned like a child. When I became a man, I put childish ways behind me. Now we see but a poor reflection as in a mirror; then we shall see face to face. Now I know in part; then I shall know fully, even as I am fully known. And now these three remain: faith, hope and love. But the greatest of these is love.

I Corinthians 13: 4-8

Foundation on Christian Principles

Today our society is crumbling under the wickedness of sin. Darkness has blanketed our land, feeling the people's hearts with greed and hate for their fellow man. I look through the masses and so many people seem lost and confused. The cruel and unjust life that has been molded by the wickedness of the elite and our corrupted politicians carries no compassion for the people. The aftershock of evil is hopelessness that leaves so many in despair as they go through life without purpose. In life, many are left in despair as they turn to drugs or alcohol to fill the void in their hearts. How has disparity gripped our land so viciously? It is time for a March of the saints, it is time for a march for faith to undo the madness that has enveloped the people. It is time for a union of the people so we may shatter the untruths and vanquish this darkness from our land. Let us come together and be deceived no more by hate or greed. Let us light the torch of hope and be directed by our faith in God to spread the true word.

Our Christian beliefs helped inspire the foundation of America which inspired communities with strong Christian morals and family unity. There has been a savage war on the Christian faith by non-Christian radical groups that have left many communities abandoned to the darkest desires of hate, lust, and greed. This brutal attack has been going on for centuries from atheism, communism and many other groups such as the illuminati. They spread their cloak of lies over our young and their deceitfulness weakens the faith for so many. The primary goal for the illuminati was to abolish religion and replace it with reasoning or humanism. The illuminati were established in 1776 by Adam Weishaupt and many of the organization members were also members of the Freemasons.

In 1786, the illuminati's evil intent was exposed, which caused the organization to go underground. The Illuminati also had close ties and supported the naturalist movement. The Freemasons as well as illuminati are both known for using ancient Egyptian hieroglyphics symbols that has rooted itself deep in our society. The influence these organizations have had over our government is horrendous. Washington has been laid out in a pattern where you can see symbols from the air such as the inverted pentagram or the Masonic symbol. The fact that they would take the time to position the streets as well as the capital buildings, and the Washington Monument is extremely suspicious. Even our own currency cannot escape the wicked symbols with the All-Seeing Eye on the back of the dollar, which is an ancient Egyptian symbol. Even the unfinished pyramid symbol can be seen from the air over Washington.

There are multitudes of hieroglyphics symbols throughout Washington DC, and the most disturbing symbols is the inverted pentagram or the unfinished pyramid that can be easily seen from the sky over Washington. Even our currency cannot escape their symbols with the unfinished pyramid on the back of the dollar with the Latin phrase that translates to "One World Order". This Latin phrase is found at the bottom of the unfinished pyramid, along with the Roman

Numerals that translates to 1776. I would like to believe that this year represents the birth of our nation but when you conclude the facts, and the issue that the year the illuminati was established in 1776 brings forth tremendous doubt. The All-Seeing Eye represents the ancient Egyptian god Horus and the unfinished pyramid is a symbol used by the illuminati as well as the Freemasons. There also statues of ancient gods in Washington and New York City. You will find a statue of the Greek God Atlas in the front entrance of the United Nations building in New York City or a gold statue of the illuminated one in front of the Rockefeller Plaza. There also multitudes of statues in New York of Lucifer, I ask you America how could this abomination ever occur in our nation.

The illuminati's evil intent was to create a one world order without a religion. Another attack on Christian beliefs was directed by communism and even socialist ideology. These ideologies support atheism, where in a Democratic style government believes the people are free to make their own decisions on faith. Karl Marx had stated that "religious beliefs must be destroyed for the advancement of communism." Vladimir Lenin of the old USSR stated "there is nothing more abominable than religion." Communist and socialist's leaders has made it a priority to publish all articles on evolutionist theories that supported atheism, even if they were not backed by scientific evidence.

Prayer has been abolished from our public schools across our nation. Would you say our school systems are better without prayer? Since these radical changes crime has intensified in our schools and the dropout rate continues to increase. Our children seem lost and confused as so many of them go through life without direction or purpose. The perversion teachings of sex education and the lustful sickness that has enveloped our society has destroyed the belief in abstinence. Honor thy father and mother has no meaning for so many children as they come from broken homes with broken hearts. I think many people realize the mistake of removing prayer from our schools and God from our society. What greater book could teach values and morals than the Bible? Shall we continue to deny our children the understanding and value of God's words? What lesson have we taught our children by removing the Bible from our schools?

Today less people know about the Bible than ever before. I believe removing religion from our schools has created a rift in our nation. I remember how a gentleman tried to convince me the reason the Bible was removed was because it was full of lies and contradictions. The horrendous assault on Christian beliefs has been devastating and has weakened the faith in the Christian community. With the teachings of Evolution and the Big Bang theory has conflicted with the teachings of creation in Genesis. Scientists as well as historians proclaim that the Bible is not based in historical fact and stories such as Sodom and Gomorrah or the great flood have never occurred. Even though Sodom, Gomorrah, and even Jericho has been found, the archaeologist community pays very little attention to these findings. Pottery has been found in an ancient Philistine community with the name Goliath which gives validity to the story of David and Goliath, but once again this finding was barely noticed by the world. There has even been evidence of the great flood throughout the world, but geologists as well as other scientists continue deny or ignore the evidence.

America this is madness for a society to ignore evidence of creation and to continue to poison the minds of our young by teaching subjects that has no factual basis. This is proof within itself that there is a conspiracy to destroy religion in the world. This monster has spread its tentacles across our nation to fund or operate these organizations to continue to spill out false propaganda or to block the truth from ever getting out. These organizations have secretly plotted to not only remove The Ten Commandments from our schools but our courthouses. What lesson is this teaching us? It is showing that these very commandments are irrelevant or are not politically correct. What was wrong with, "Thou shall not kill" or "Thou shall not steal?" Yet today there are many more murders and thieves and our prisons are overloaded. There are those who want to remove "In God we trust." Or want to remove from our very lips "One nation under God." These groups have assaulted the Pledge of Allegiance to a point where many schools don't even give pledge to the American flag. There are even those who desire to destroy our flag by fire. Did our sons and daughters of our great nation shed their blood for the American flag? Our great flag symbolizes freedom, liberty, and justice. The greatest is the freedom that we all have been blessed with. Our forefathers fought for the very freedom that we cherish today, but this was no gift by a man for God gave all free will. If we allow these villainous groups to destroy our pledge or the American flag will eventually destroy patriotism. If we continue to allow evil to root itself so deep into our society by false teachings, foolish propaganda and manipulation of laws will lead to the destruction of our nation. If we allow our great nation to crumble under those filled with wickedness or evil intent will lead to the destruction of all our indelible rights as we will be enslaved to those who plotted our own destruction.

There is a true evil. This evil does not just live abroad but resides within our own borders. It disguises itself with many faces as it manipulates the laws. Are we to stand silent while it sends our great nation into the abyss? Was this great nation not founded on Christianity? The foundation that was laid by our forefathers truly understood the importance of Christian values. The separation of church and state gave back what God intended for humankind to have, free will. The Constitution extended the freedoms for every American, with the freedom of speech act, and many other great rights that protects our freedom. I truly believe we were blessed by the very framework our forefathers laid before us. How can we possibly allow those who want to destroy our country to tear down this frame? Our great American builders of our nation truly believed in the right of freedom of religion. They did not force their religion on the people like so many other nations. They did not declare one religion for the people. So many other governments or kingdoms have forced people to only worship under one religion. Our forefathers understood that God had given mankind free will. They knew it would be wrong to tell the people how to worship. Since this evil has begun attacking our foundation we have witnessed one disaster after another. We must realize what made our nation so great was the very freedom we all shared; the belief we were one nation under God and the right for people to worship as they wish. There are many nations in the world today that will not allow Christian religions to practice their faith. There are even governments around the world that are tearing down churches to prohibit people from worshiping God! In nations throughout Asia Christians are being assaulted and even beheaded for their faith.

I call out for all Christians to take notice for our Christian principles are being attacked by those who have no faith and their thirst is for power to dominate the world into enslavement. There are also private organizations which are funded by atheists, communist, and those who support the new world order are working together to erase Christian faith from the world. These organizations have even taken action against those who like to display the nativity scene of Christ during the holidays. Do they not understand this is the Christian principle that founded our nation? In the past I have even worked for a company who mandated employees to hide any symbol of Christianity including jewelry in fear it would offend others. We must never forget how Christians had to meet in secret in fear of persecution from the Roman Empire or other Islamic nations. The slaughter of Christians had become so severe during the Roman era had left them no alternative, but to go underground and they adopted the symbol of the fish to keep their faith hidden. I have even heard politicians attack Christian principles and even the Judicial Branch has declared that prayer day is unconstitutional.

The battle that rages here is not just for different religious beliefs but it is also for the freedom of personal beliefs and personal expressions. Atheism has attacked our Christian teachings with unproven theories such as Darwinism and even the Big Bang Theory. These both discredit the book of Genesis. They silenced Christian voices through the judicial system by declaring the separation of church and state. America was founded on Christian principles and what our forefathers intended in the terminology of separation of church and state was to not allow one religion to control the state or the state to control religion.

What our forefathers were referring to was not allowing Presbyterian, Catholics or other Christian faiths to have dominance over another through a national religion. I have heard the argument that our forefathers were not Christian but I will tell you our first elected president George Washington prayed quite often according to the history books and his personal notes. We must not allow those whose intent is to change our history. If we continue to allow this attack on our Christian principles or faith, then where would that leave free will? I will let the words from our past speak the truth:

"It is impossible to rightly govern a nation without God and the Bible."
-George Washington

"It is when people forget God that tyrants forge their chains."
-Patrick Henry

"God who gave us life gave us liberty..."

-Thomas Jefferson

"Those people who will not be governed by God will be ruled by tyrants."
-William Penn

Since this assault on our Christian principles, has our nation not fallen under governmental control? I call out for those with Christian faith to take a stand today. For far too long we have been divided. Nearly seventy percent of America is of Christian faith, yet we cannot work together because we are divided by different Christian beliefs. What we do not realize is we share more beliefs than what we disagree on. Most Christians do not believe in abortion, pornography or even the radical teachings of Darwinism. We believe our nation is one nation under God, and yet we have been weakened to the point our voices are no more than a whisper. I am not asking Christians to give up their personal beliefs but I am asking all who have Christian faith to take a stand together on these issues of corruption. Imagine how powerful we can become if Baptist, Catholic, Presbyterian, Church of Latter Day Saints and all other Christian faiths stood together and said, "No more! This will be a nation under God." Together we must rise and rise we must for we are a sleeping giant. God did not intend for people to be divided by his word. We must put these differences aside and once again honor God and country. Let's show that we are not going to allow them to tear down our foundation.

Our forefathers fought tyranny. They fought for a better nation, a nation under God. They fought not just for themselves but for the future generations. Will we be the generation to let it all go? If we allow our great nation to collapse under the weight of communism or socialism, then where would that leave us with our faith in Christian beliefs? In the old Soviet Union and even communist China today have destroyed churches by tearing them down. Even the socialist Nazi's burn Bibles and distributed propaganda to support evolution. If our Christian faith is destroyed, then where does that leave freewill. We must realize that a communist or socialist regime has only one desire absolute power, which leaves no room for free will as mankind destiny is enslaved. Let us come together and cry out in one loud voice our Christian faith shall not be weakened. Nor shall we allow our great nation to tremble at your wake of deception. We must shatter the walls of deception and bring forth illumination so we may better see the lies that has poisoned our children's minds. These theories of evolution or even the Big Bang theory hold no merit and even contradict the meaning of science. There is been a tremendous amount of evidence that has been brought forth to disprove these theories but those fascist groups with dark agendas will do anything to block the truth. Scientists have come forth with evidence that disproves these theories of evolution but they are ignored or ridiculed by their own pears. Many of the scientists have been shunned by the scientific community and has even lost their jobs. These are scientists who have turned from the falsified teachings of evolution and has become believers of creation.

Where was the outcry from the Christian community to support the scientists when they were in need, these innocent victims of truth not only lost their jobs, their credibility was destroyed. It is time for the churches to unify the people to stand against this evil. We can no longer procrastinate or pretend these evil deeds are not occurring.

Today our society has become a sinful society full of greed, and lustful desires. Our society has become diseased by drugs, alcoholism, and even violence. I call out for you America to strengthen your conviction for the path we will take will be met with tremendous difficulties. We shall carry faith in our heart like a shield and allow the words of God to cut the chains that has enslaved the people. We cannot allow despair to weaken our cause because the fate of humankind depends on what we do today. Let us all come together as brothers and sisters, no longer divided by race or different nominations, for we are all God's children. Let us carry in our heart Jesus last words to love one another as he had loved us. I call out for you to no longer allow the weight of sin to bind you to wicked ways, for the word of God will set you free. God has given us the freedom to choose our path in life through free will and the path we choose is our greatest challenge. We can choose the wrong path to deny God existence and be filled with greed and lustful desires that only leads to emptiness in our heart or we can choose the right path and be filled with God's love. What good will it be for a man if he gains the whole world, yet forfeits his soul? Or what can a man give in exchange for his soul?" Matthew 16:26

America there are moral absolutes they cannot be denied. The perils of the evil have practically erased or destroyed faith in the commandments in our society. Wickedness is devouring our nation; its aftermath is the banishment of hope for humanity and stomping out dreams of our children. There is no denying the importance of the commandments as it is the cornerstone of civilization. The virtues that was anointed by the hand of God is the only passage written by God's hand in the Bible. Even Jesus commanded his followers and disciples to follow the commandments. There are those in our society whose evil intent is to destroy faith in God and replace it with faith in man. There are those with evil intent or those who have been led astray proclaim the commandments are no longer relevant because they were from the Old Testament. This is the evil tactic used by those with evil agendas, they spread their lies like poison over humanity to deceive or to weaken the faith for so many of our brothers and sisters. Let us shatter this unholy bond that has bounded our hands and has led so many astray like sheep to the wolf's lair. This dark path has led humankind to an entangled labyrinth field with malevolence that has led us all to a path that is destitute for enslavement.

There evil propaganda proclaim that God is not real as they destroy the moralities and Christian principles that created our great nation. Even Christian leaders have been winded as they began to surrender their own faith in the acceptance of the banishment of the commandments from our society. Since the banishment of God's Commandments, written by his own hand our society has become corrupted to its core and immoral behavior has become unrestrained. This life that has been molded before us has a grand architect filled with evil intent. The grand puppet master's ranks are filled with those born under the wicked seed of greed and their thirst for power can never be quenched. The evil that has spawned from the elite is grasping for the rings of power and world dominance. There evil intent runs unchecked as they sneak through shadows in our government. I plead with you not to underestimate their power, for their dominance has grown immensely. They have assembled an army of bought politicians that are passing unfavorable laws for us all, as the check and balance has been dismantled by corrupt judges. There evil intent has filled their ranks of scholars and educators with falsified teachings that has polluted their own minds and has denied their tongues to teach the truth to our children. They have corrupted our military through corruption and government and have even inserted their control over our law department officials in preparation when society revolts against their quest for dominance. The grand puppet master optimal goals are to install the New World Order through a One World Government that would lead to the destruction of our religion and freedom as we will be enslaved. This horrific action would lead to the completion of the unfinished pyramid and the eye represented at the top of the pyramid represents how the superiors will watch over us all to ensure our obedience and submission. The elite has deceived the world in order to rob us all of our wealth through deception and division.

There evil intent has divided our hearts through religion, age, gender, politics, and they have spurred racial division that has created a tremendous rift in our nation. Their evil intent was to weaken the people through division so they may assert their dominance over the world. God did not intend for humankind to be divided and there's only one truth, for we are all the children of God!!! Let us come together to shatter this evil plot, let us rise as brothers and sisters to vanquish the darkness that has enveloped our nation. Let our hearts be filled with love and let our children once again believe that they have a divine purpose. Let us reassert God's teachings and the Commandments to reestablish the morals and Christian principles that founded our nation. The Commandments was God's divine plan to establish true civilization, and a path for humankind to find happiness. The righteous path of salvation is obeying God's laws and our faith in Jesus. These evil forces do not want humankind to obey or even to acknowledge the commandments because through acknowledgment of God's laws brings forth the reality that we are all with sin and in need for a Savior. "For the wages of sin is death." Romans 6:23. Let the hearts of humankind unite in faith and together let us bring forth the age of truth and love for one another.

- "Therefore by the deeds of the law there shall no flesh be justified in his sight, for by the law is the knowledge of sin." Roman 3:20

- "He that saith I know him, and keepeth not his commandments is a liar, and the truth is not in him." I John 2:4

- "Wherefore the law was our schoolmaster to bring us unto Christ, that he might be justified by faith." Galatians 3:24

- "What shall we say then? Is the law sin? God forbid, nay, I had not known sin, but by the law: for had not known lust, except the law had said thou shalt not covet." Romans 7:7

- "Here is the patients of the saints: here are they that keep the commandments of God, and the faith of Jesus." Revelations 14:12

- "Put on the full armor of God, so that you will be able to stand firm against the schemes of the devil. For our struggle is not against flesh and blood, but against the rulers, against the powers, against the world forces of this darkness, against the spiritual forces of wickedness in the heavenly places. Therefore, take up the full armor of God, so that you will be able to resist in the evil day, and having done everything, to stand firm...." Ephesians 6:12

Closing

America, I lay before you the truth and I fear if we do not act now, the America we know now will cease to exist. Many claim Democracy is dead, but I tell you it is not. She has been bounded and pushed into a dark corner. Today the fight is within us, the people. We must reach into the abyss and pull our nation back to prosperity. We must re-establish "In God We Trust" and not only carry God in our hearts but have faith that God will be with us. We can no longer be divided as a people; we must put aside our differences, for the future generations depend on what we do today. Do not surrender the fight, put your trust in God and know that our faith conjoined can move mountains.

Our leaders are weak for they have already bowed to our enemies. I tell you, we bow to no one but the supreme ruler. For those who feel weak, I plead for you to dig deep and find the energy. For those who have thrown their hands up in frustration, how dare you? For our future generation is at your feet. Let our children be our courage, let God give us wisdom and fill us with knowledge. Let us strengthen our morals by re-establishing God's Ten Commandments.

We must not fear those with wicked agendas as we walk through the dark chambers of congress. We must expose those who have concealed their evil intent from the people. We must illuminate the truth and bring light to the darkness, where secrets once reigned. We must not fear the senate for they have been blind and deaf for too long. We must hold accountability for those who have falsely represented the people, who have silenced our voices or ignored the cries of the people. Our politicians have lined their pockets with wealth while so many were left in disparity. Let there be no doubt America the principalities that we are facing is evil. The elite is the grand puppet master that controls governments around the world and many of our own politicians has bowed to their allegiance. Their beastly tentacles have manipulated their way through all branches of government. Their influence is far reaching as they also have massive control over the world economy and even our media. The elite have bribed or bought their way to power as they manipulate the system and the world governments for their own wealth. Their evil plot is unfolding before your eyes and they have masterfully positioned themselves to be our masters in the New World order. They are a breath away from establishing a complete world central bank and the fact that less than 1% of the world population controls over 50% of the world's wealth is truly disturbing. Those who are called the elite have no bond with humanity and have stolen the wealth from every citizen in the world. We must rebalance the scales of justice, so they may have the true justice they have denied so many. The true spirit of freedom and liberty cries out for us to rise and rise, we must! We must preserve our nation for the future generations and bring prosperity back. We must rekindle the passion for freedom and restore the very foundation of our country. One nation under God.

I tell you, we must become the very patriots that established our great nation, and believe in the very freedom our forefathers believed in. Many across the world did not believe in their cause, nor believed they could stand up to the mightiest army in the world but they did. Now take your place among the watchtower, exercise your right to assemble and be bold and demand for the truth so help us God.

www.ingramcontent.com/pod-product-compliance
Lightning Source LLC
Chambersburg PA
CBHW060233290526
45789CB00001B/29